WINDSOR GREAT PARK

A Visitor's Guide

Andrew Fielder

FOREWORD

There has been much written over the years on the splendours of Windsor Great Park; its rich history and heritage, its links with the Royal Family and its natural diversity. This new Visitor's Guide, researched and written with great care and attention to detail by Andrew Fielder, who resided within the Great Park for many years, is a welcome addition to the bookshelf. It provides the reader with information both historical and practical on many of the key features of the Great Park.

The Crown Estate Commissioners, who manage the Crown Estate, are required under the Crown Estate Act 1961 to retain the Royal Park and Forest at Windsor. There is no doubt to those of us who are fortunate enough to be entrusted with its management that Windsor Great Park is unique. From oak trees that pre-date the Norman conquest, right up to the 21st Century addition of the magnificent Savill Building, the Great Park has continued to evolve and develop over the years.

I hope that this book will encourage you to visit if you have not done so before, and that it will become your companion if you are already a regular visitor to Windsor Great Park.

Philip Everett. LVO, FRICS.
Deputy Ranger.

CONTENTS

Part One (p9-17)   - An overview of Windsor Great Park

Part Two (p18-22)   - 'The Royal Landscape'

Part Three (p23-30)   - Savill Garden and Obelisk Pond

Part Four (p31-54)   - Virginia Water

Part Five (p55-66)   - Smiths Lawn and Valley Gardens

Part Six (p67-82)   - The Deer Park and Long Walk

Part Seven (p83-114) - The Village and Mezel Hill

Part Eight (p115-130) - Cranbourne Chase & the 'Picnic Area'

Index (p132-138)

Selected Bibliography (p139)

Photographic Acknowledgements (p142-144)

MAPS

Front inner cover - An overview of Windsor Great Park
p16 - Cranbourne Rails; Norden's Survey 1607
p19 - The Royal Landscape
p24 - The Savill Garden and Obelisk Pond
p34 - Virginia Water
p56 - Smith's Lawn and the Valley Gardens
p68 - The Deer Park and the Long Walk
p84 - The Village and Mezel Hill
p109 - The Village (detail)
p116 - Cranbourne Chase and the Picnic Area
p123 - Plan of Cranbourne Chase, c1752
Rear inner cover - Norden's 'Survey of the Honor of Windsor' 1607

ILLUSTRATIONS

Front cover – Red Deer in Windsor Great Park
p7   –   Savill Garden - the Upper Pond in May
p9   –   View from the Long Walk to Windsor Castle
p11 –   Sunrise at Holly Bush, Dukes Lane
p12 –   Stag hunting (a mediaeval scene)
p13 –   Old Windsor Wood
p14 –   Queen Elizabeth I at a stag hunt, c1575
p20 –   HRH William Augustus, Duke of Cumberland
p21 –   Obelisk Ride
p22 –   Thomas Sandby
p22 –   Paul Sandby
p23 –   The Savill Building
p23 –   Interior of The Savill Building
p26 –   Magnolia in Valley Gardens
p27 –   The Obelisk monument
p28 –   Obelisk Pond, from the pondhead
p29 –   Obelisk Bridge
p31 –   'Virginia Water, from Shrubs Hill' c1753
p32 –   Detail from 'Virginia Water, from Shrubs Hill'
p33 –   The Wheatsheaf Hotel, Virginia Water
p35 –   Virginia Water, looking northwest
p36 –   The Cascade, Virginia Water
p37 –   Virginia Water Lodge
p37 –   The Northeastern Arm, or Wick Branch, Virginia Water
p38 –   The 'Ruins', Virginia Water
p39 –   'The New Building on Shrubbs Hill' c1754
p40 –   A view across to Botany Bay Point, Virginia Water
p41 –   'Virginia Water from the Manor Lodge' c1754
p42 –   HM King George IV
p43 –   'The Boathouse, Fishing Temple and Tents' c1829
p44 –   'The Great Bridge over the Virginia River' c1754
p45 –   The Five Arch Bridge, Virginia Water
p46 –   Blacknest Gate Lodge
p47 –   Approach to Five Arch Bridge, Virginia Water

p48   – 'The Building on China Island, 1829-36'
p49   - Dockyard Cottages, Virginia Water
p50   – Breakheart Hill
p51   – The Boathouse, Virginia Water
p52   – Virginia Water Cottage
p53   – The Totem Pole, Virginia Water
p54   – Wick Pond, Virginia Water
p57   – 'The Moveable (or Flying) Barn' c1794
p58   – Flying Barn Cottage, Smith's Lawn
p59   – Guards Polo Club and the Royal Box, Smith's Lawn
p60   – The Prince Consort's Statue, Smith's Lawn
p61   – 'Planes of the US Air Force on Smith's Lawn, 1944'
p61   – Cumberland Gate, Smith's Lawn
p63   – The Punchbowl, Valley Gardens
p64   – The Plunket Pavilion, Valley Gardens
p65   – Canadian Avenue, Valley Gardens
p66   – Autumn colour in the Valley Gardens
p69   – The Long Walk, from Snow Hill
p70   – Queen Anne's Gate – shortcut to Long Walk
p71   – Double Gates
p72   – View to the Copper Horse, from the Review Ground
p73   – Red Deer
p74   – Red Deer
p75   – Red Deer
p75   – Stags Horns
p76   – Prince of Wales Pond, Deer Park
p77   – Bears Rails, Old Windsor
p78   – Exit from the Deer Park, Cookes Hill
p79   – A view to Windsor from Spring Hill
p80   – The Copper Horse, Snow Hill
p82   - Deepstrood
p85   – Ranger's Gate
p86   – Cranbourne Gate
p87   – Forest Lodge
p88   – Isle of Wight Pond
p88   – The York Club
p89   – Sandpit Gate Lodge
p90   – The HM Queen Elizabeth II Statue
p91   – Queen Anne's Ride

p92   – The 'Change', Dukes Lane
p93   – Prince Consort's Gate
p94   – Mezel Hill Cottages
p95   – The Royal School, Mezel Hill
p96   – Part of the Kitchen Gardens, Cumberland Lodge
p97   – Chaplain's Lodge
p98   – 'Great Meadow Pond' c1752
p99   – Great Meadow Pond
p100 – Limetree Avenue, Cumberland Lodge
p102 – 'The Great Lodge, east front' c1754
p103 - Cumberland Lodge
p104 – Groom's House, Cumberland Lodge
p104 – The Mews, Cumberland Lodge
p105 – Cow Pond
p106 – Bishopsgate Lodge
p107 – Royal Lodge Gates
p110 – Windsor Castle and the Deer Park from The Gallop
p111 – The Village Post Office and General Store
p112 – Richardson's Lawn
p113 – 'Wheeler's Yard' c1858
p114 – Russell's Field Farm
p117 – Queen Anne's Gate
p117 – Forest Gate
p118 – 'Moat Island Cottage' c1754
p119 – Swan Pond
p120 – 'Ranger's Lodge' c1839
p120 – Ranger's Lodge
p121 – The line of the old road (Sheet Street Road, now A332)
p122 – Longhorn cattle
p124 – 'Cranbourne Lodge' c1765
p125 – New Rise, Cranbourne Chase
p126 – 'Eclipse, at New Market with a Groom' c1770
p127 – Eclipse's celebratory plate, Cranbourne Tower
p128 – 'Cranbourne Lodge' c1820
p129 – Cranbourne Tower
p130 – Cranbourne Tower, west front
p140 – Savill Garden – a Winter Sunset

SAVILL GARDEN: the Upper Pond in May, a time of year when the Garden is bursting into life, with vibrant displays of Spring flowering colour, and the majestic oak and beech trees drape themselves once again in the freshest of green verdure.

ACKNOWLEDGEMENTS

I would just like to take a moment to put on record my most grateful acknowledgement to The Crown Estate Commissioners and the Windsor Great Park Estate Office, especially to Mr Philip Everett (Deputy Ranger), Mr Nicholas Day (Operations Manager), Mr Graham Sanderson (Keeper of the Valley Gardens), and to Mr Gino Caiafa (Media Archivist, The Royal Landscape) for their co-operation and assistance with this project.

My warmest thanks must also be given to the following persons, all of whom have been more than generous with their co-operation, support, advice and encouragement in helping me throughout the long days of preparation and production of this guidebook.

Dr Alastair Niven OBE (Principal, Cumberland Lodge)

Mr John J.Taylor (Forest Ranger, Windsor Great Park)

Mr Graham Dennis (Blacklock's Bookshop)

Mrs Claire McGuinness (Windsor Digital Print)

Ms Louise Oliver (The Royal Collection)

Ms Diane Naylor (Chatsworth Collection)

Ms Nikita Hooper (The National Trust)

Ms Auste Mickunaite (British Library)

Ms Gudrun Muller (Tate Gallery)

Mr Matthew Bailey (National Portrait Gallery)

Ms Victoria Hogarth (Bridgeman Art Library, London)

Mr Andrew O'Connell

Mr Anthony Bish

Last but most definitely not least, my biggest thanks are saved for my wife, Dawn and my two children, Deborah and Mark; not forgetting my dear parents, Jean and Peter, and my sister, Eve, all of whom have had to endure the trials and tribulations of long days and late nights reading, checking and commenting on the constantly-changing stream of information which I intended to include in my publication. I certainly could not have done this without your unending supply of patience, help, support and love.

My most heartfelt and warmest thanks to each and every one of you.

An Overview of Windsor Great Park

Set in the Berkshire and Surrey countryside, some 20 miles to the southwest of Central London, Windsor Great Park, and the Forests which lie adjacent, is rapidly becoming one of our last green 'sanctuaries' and that rarest of commodities, a peaceful oasis amidst a turbulent environment. The constantly changing and busy South East of England makes the continued existence of our green spaces very desirable indeed, and here, in Windsor Great Park, it is still possible to discover a sense of peace and solitude. You can spend an entire day just walking in clear, clean open spaces and never set foot on the same spot twice.

A VIEW OF WINDSOR CASTLE: as seen from the intersection of the A308 Albert Road with the Long Walk, close by the entrance to Windsor Great Park at Shaw Farm and the Double Gates. For the visitor to Windsor, the Town Centre is but a short stroll away from this point, making for pleasant and easy access on foot to the wide expanses of the Great Park.

There are stunning views to be seen over the Thames Valley, and many an author has commented on the delights to be found within its extensive boundaries. For the more athletic, what could be better than a run or a brisk walk in such invigorating surroundings? The bike riders are not forgotten either, with specially prepared cycle paths and routes provided. For the slightly less physically active amongst us, and particularly for the disabled, there are many places of interest and beauty available to see, with facilities catered to your needs.

Location: Berkshire and Surrey, bounded, in general terms, by the A30, A329, A332 and A308 trunk roads, with small B-roads connecting to the main thoroughfares. Easily accessible from the M3, M4 and M25 motorways.

Size: The Great Park covers an area of approximately 5000 acres. The local forest areas, also managed as part of the Windsor Estate, total a further 7900 acres. The four largest ones are Swinley Forest, Lower Forest, Cranbourne Forest and South Forest. Access to the Forest areas is available under certain circumstances, but it will be necessary to check with the Windsor Estate Office for full details.

Transportation: Good public transport links using First Great Western (FGW) train services via Slough to Windsor Central, or South West Trains (SWT) to Windsor Riverside, Datchet, Staines, Egham, and Virginia Water stations. Onward bus and/or taxi services are available from all of these points, and if you are visiting Windsor, you can conveniently access the Great Park on foot at the Double Gates (see p70-71) via the Long Walk adjacent to the Castle. It is also possible to walk to the Great Park from Virginia Water station – a brisk 20 minute walk (about 1 mile) will see you there.

Car Parking: There are six main Car Parks provided, five of which require the purchase of a parking ticket. The area on the NW side of the Great Park, adjacent to Cranbourne, has free parking within a designated 'Picnic Area', and is within walking distance of the castle town of Windsor itself.

Byelaws: The Crown Estate byelaws relating to Windsor Great Park are prominently displayed at every main entrance. On arrival, please take a few moments to read the notices – they are there for your personal benefit, as well as for the wellbeing of the Estate itself.

Access: Although large parts of the Great Park are open to the public, areas where access is restricted (eg: private residences, game coverts) are either clearly marked or fenced off. Wardens are on-hand to keep a discreet but watchful eye on things, and to assist the public. There are flat areas, gentle gradients, steep hills and valleys, and to help you make your way across this landscape there are a combination of tarmac roads, gravel tracks, grass rides and paths to traverse, dependent on the location you choose to visit, and the weather conditions. Paths can sometimes be rather muddy - suitable footwear is, therefore, a must.

Mobile phone reception is wholly dependent on your network and your whereabouts within the Great Park – some networks and areas are better than others! It would be advisable to take along a small bottle of water and a snack, just as a 'top-up' if your walk takes you longer than anticipated. The map printed on the inside of the front book cover illustrates the geographical location of the main features and points of interest within the Great Park. Details of 'how to get there' plus information for the relevant Car Parks and on-site facilities are at the start of each Part of the book.

SUNRISE AT HOLLY BUSH, DUKES LANE

So what are the origins and history of the Great Park?

It was never my intention to put pen to paper and create yet another 'History', – there have been many more accomplished authors than myself who have already chronicled the story of the Great Park. The standard reference work on the complete history of the Great Park is undoubtedly Jane Roberts' 'Royal Landscape – the Gardens and Parks of Windsor' published in 1997. There are also some very comprehensive books available which more than adequately cover individual aspects of the subject, and for those who wish to take their interests further, I have endeavoured to list a selection of these titles in the Bibliography at the back of this book.

The concept of this book is to provide a simple Guide to what you will see and experience when walking within the ancient boundaries of today's Windsor Great Park. However, in order to achieve my aim, I do feel it will be necessary to briefly touch on aspects of each area's historical past.

'STAG HUNTING'

In this illustration, we can see the principal elements of the Mediaeval Hunt. The nobleman, with possibly his own small castle shown in the background, pursues two deer through open woodland, aided by a huntsman (the yeoman pricker) with his three dogs. Note the use of the nets (toils) strung tightly between the trees. From the Book of Hours, Use of Worms (Hours of the Death) with elements of a Breviary; (Germany 14th Century) © The British Library Board. Egerton 1146

So, its back to the beginning – around about the time of the Norman Conquest of 1066 AD. What became known as the Forest of Windsor was already anciently established, (if not in name), by the time that William the Conqueror first set foot in the Manor of Clewer, where in 1070 AD he established a motte and bailey fortress which would evolve to become Windsor Castle. Over 120 miles around its perimeter, the Forest covered nearly all of the County of Surrey and a small part of the County of Middlesex. It extended westwards out towards Hungerford, thereby covering the vast majority of Southeast Berkshire as well.

OLD WINDSOR WOOD: woodland similar to this would have formed the core of the original Forest, plus areas of barren heathland, referred to as 'waste'. The waste was an important part of the Mediaeval economy, as it was the only source of the most basic of foods, free fuel, and scant building materials for the destitute and poor of the local area. Any restrictions or enclosures imposed on an area of waste was a disaster for these people, as they could then be effectively banned from either accessing or utilising, what was to them, their most valuable resource.

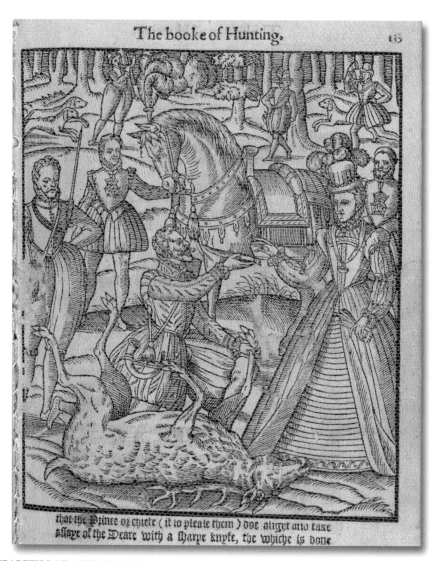

that the Prince or chiefe (it is pleate them) doe alight and take
affaye of the Deare with a sharpe knyfe, the whiche is done

'ELIZABETH I AT A STAG HUNT': Queen Elizabeth I is depicted being offered a knife with which to 'take assaye', or evaluate, the condition of the flesh of the Stag, preceded by the ceremonial cutting off of the front foot, and prior to the butchering of the carcass. From 'the Booke of Hunting', Turberville 1576. © The British Library Board. C.31.g.1.(2), liii r

William of Normandy, along with the vast majority of the European Royal Families and nobles of the time, had a favourite pastime – they liked to hunt. So, where better for the King to indulge in this pastime to his heart's content than in the very Forest over which he now found himself the new Ruler? The means by which William kept the locals out, and the Forest for himself and his retainers, was by the implementation and strict enforcement of Forest Law.

Forest Law was extremely unpopular with those who now found themselves securely tethered to the yoke of Norman rule. Forest Law took away certain rights and customs. For example, you could no longer freely walk into the Forest and collect fallen wood for fuel; nor could you freely use the beech seeds and acorns on the Forest floor to feed your pigs in the Autumn – in fact, Forest Law essentially denied the common man the right to even be in there at all! All these rules were created for one main purpose – to create deerparks and preserve the game within, which the King and his retinue would then come to hunt.

The actual definition of the area which eventually became the Great Park did not take place until around the middle of the 13th Century, when specific reference was first made to ditches and fences (known as pales, or Rails) being erected around a smaller, more defined area within the Forest itself. There were other 'Rails' close to the Great Park, and which worked in the same way. Examples of this can be found at Cranbourne (p16), Swinley (to the SW of Cranbourne) and Bagshot. Within this area, if the space allowed, the land was divided into separate game parks, known as 'Walks'. Each Walk had a Keeper, and the King and his Court would come into these Walks in order to hunt.

This arrangement continued right up to the start of the English Civil War in 1642, after which time the Great Park, along with many others, was systematically ransacked for whatever it could provide. There followed, after the execution of Charles I in 1649, the period of the 'Commonwealth', when parcels of land within the Park were given to various Parliamentarian soldiers in lieu of pay, and were exchanged and sold between many of them in the form of debentures. One such man to benefit from this was Captain John Byfield, who purchased the debentures of many other soldiers and became the occupier of a large tract of land upon which he built a house. This building, known as Byfield House, would evolve and enlarge, finally to become known as Cumberland Lodge (see p101).

All of this changed, however, upon the Restoration of the Monarchy in 1660, when all the lands and holdings seized by Parliament after the Civil War were successively taken or handed back to the new King, Charles II. The full restoration of the Great Park back to a private Royal Park was achieved within a few years thereafter. In the 80 years that followed, various styles and themes of landscaping and estate management of the Park took place, but it wasn't until 1746 that we encounter for the first time a man whose vision and ideas shaped and moulded Windsor Great Park essentially into its present form – William Augustus, 1st Duke of Cumberland.

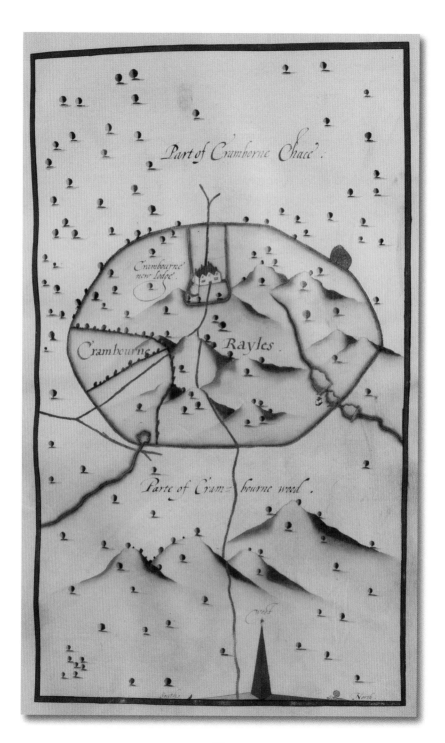

William's vision for the Park was to use wide-scale, highly ambitious landscaping, and the construction of many and varied buildings, bridges and waterways. These would all serve to embellish the project he had undertaken, and on sheer scale alone, the project was nothing short of remarkable. He took wild, uncultivated land and turned it into a vivid landscape, rich in views and contrasts. The many landscape creations thus begun under his direction have now evolved with the fullness of time allowing us the benefit of seeing his plans, ideas and visions reaching maturity. It has been well worth the wait!

As with all the other ancient Forests in England, Windsor Forest slowly decreased in size, partly due to clearances, illegal encroachments and the expansion of local villages and towns into the surrounding countryside as their populations gradually increased. George III and Parliament's Enclosure Act, which first looked at Windsor Forest in 1806, and which was eventually completed in 1817, finally established the boundaries with which we are familiar today. The death of George IV in 1830 brought about one of the most significant changes that the Great Park had seen to date. His successor, William IV, opened up the Great Park to the general public for the first time. Thus began the closer relationship between Windsor Great Park and the people.

Time to take a look inside....

OPPOSITE: **CRANBOURNE RAILS:** (RCIN 1142252 Table X)
The map shows the fenced enclosure, denoting the deerpark boundary, and the hunting lodge within. The protected status of all deer throughout the ages was a constant source of problems for those who lived in areas where deer were either stocked or lived in the wild. A serious upsurge in organised poaching, deerpark vandalism and violence towards the Keepers both at Cranbourne, New Lodge and at many other Deer Parks across the country by groups of men known as the 'Blacks' (due to the blacking of their faces to help avoid visual detection) would eventually lead to Parliament's creation of the notorious Black Act in 1723, which made crimes against the deer and Deer Parks a capital offence punishable by death. Four local men were hanged at Reading in June 1723 for their part in the murder of a Windsor Forest gamekeeper's son during an attack on the gamekeeper's home.
The Royal Collection © 2010, Her Majesty Queen Elizabeth II.

HOW DO I GET THERE?

Public transport: Regular SWT trains stop at Virginia Water, Egham and Staines. Taxi service available from all stations to the Great Park and Savill Building. It is possible to walk (about 1 mile – 20 minutes) from Virginia Water Station to the Wheatsheaf Hotel and Virginia Water, and is signposted left from the Station Parade exit into Christchurch Road. The Staines to Frimley bus service no.500 stops at Staines Bus Station (Elmsleigh Centre), Egham (Arndale Way), Royal Holloway College (A30) and the Wheatsheaf Hotel on the A30.

By road: M25 Junction 13, then A30 West towards Basingstoke (3 miles), or M3 Junction 3, then A322 (Bracknell) 1 mile, then A30 East towards London (5 miles) will take you to the Wheatsheaf Hotel. The **Royal Landscape** (Wheatsheaf) **Car Park** is adjacent, and gives direct access to **Virginia Water.**

A small car park for the northeastern arm of Virginia Water, plus a road leading to the **Valley Gardens Car Park** and access to **Smith's Lawn** will be found on the left hand side of Wick Road just 400 yards from it's junction with the A30, a short distance from Royal Holloway College.

For the **Savill Garden and Obelisk Pond**, continue by car along Wick Road, around the sharp right-hand bend into Wick Lane, up to the Main Entrance 0.75 mile ahead, on the left. Pedestrians are advised not to use Wick Lane from beyond Cheeseman's Gate to Savill Garden – it is unpaved, unlit and narrow.

To get to the **Blacknest Car Park**, turn off the A30 onto the A329 towards Ascot opposite the Wentworth Club west entrance. The Car Park is one mile ahead on the right hand side.

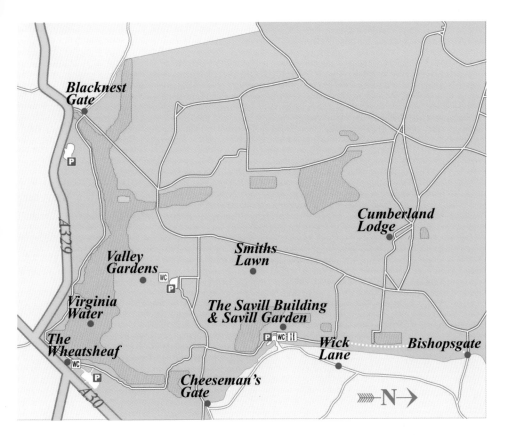

The map shows the following labels:

Blacknest Gate, P, A329, Valley Gardens, WC, P, Virginia Water, The Wheatsheaf, WC, P, A30, Cheeseman's Gate, Smiths Lawn, The Savill Building & Savill Garden, P WC, Wick Lane, Cumberland Lodge, Bishopsgate, N→

'THE ROYAL LANDSCAPE' is currently developing initial project tasks in the Southeastern corner of the Great Park, both in and around the named locations depicted in the map above.

In your walks around the Great Park you will see references to 'The Royal Landscape'. This is the name given to the project which first began in 2004 and is vigorously seeking to promote, enhance and protect the natural resources, history and facilities of this historical and beautiful place. This is an ongoing and hopefully perpetual project, which principally uses the records of the extensive works of William Augustus, Duke of Cumberland (1721-1765) as the starting point for actively managing the landscaping history of the area. Combined with reference to both previous and subsequent works, and with equally significant consideration being given to the conservation and preservation of the Natural History, flora and fauna within the Park, this has all the makings of a worthy and valuable contribution towards the effective care and management of the Great Park. This is a major step forward, and of benefit to all who visit now, and for the future.

HRH WILLIAM AUGUSTUS, 1st DUKE OF CUMBERLAND, c1758 Sir J.Reynolds
The second surviving son of George II and a respected military commander, William Augustus was his father's 'favourite', and remained so until the wave of public revulsion over the massacre after the Battle of Culloden dimmed his popularity. In 1757, his signing of the treaty of Kloster-Zeven lost him the favour of the King; William promptly resigned all his military commisions, taking refuge in his works at Windsor Great Park. Image © Devonshire Collection, Chatsworth. Reproduced by permission of Chatsworth Settlement Trustees.

The beautiful award-winning and innovative Savill Building, located in Wick Lane, is an important focal point for visitors to the Great Park. Here you will find everything you need for your visit. An information desk, restaurant, gift shop, plant shop, WC/restrooms, even an art gallery! A popular choice as the starting point for the majority of visitors, with on-site parking, and excellent access to the main points of interest in the local area – the Savill and Valley Gardens, Virginia Water, Obelisk Pond, and Smith's Lawn. Tarmac roads connect all of these areas, with gravel tracks and grass rides being the main access provision around the Gardens and Lakes themselves. A tarmac road runs around the majority of Virginia Water, with the North Bank and the Northwest Arm being the exceptions. A mobile tea and coffee shop is situated lakeside close to the Wheatsheaf Hotel, and in Summer an ice-cream vendor can also be found on the road just in from Blacknest Gate. There are public lavatories located at the Wheatsheaf Hotel, and these are accessible from the Car Park. Toilets are also located inside the Savill Building, or at the Valley Gardens Car Park (see p56).

OBELISK RIDE: the view to Cumberland Gate from Obelisk Bridge

A brief note about **Thomas Sandby** (1723-1798; left) and his brother **Paul Sandby** (1731-1809; below) who were the 'instruments' by which many of the changes to the landscape that Duke William instigated were actually recorded for us to see today. Both men were exceptional artists, with a flair for intricate detail, and this accuracy in their paintings and sketches is what allows us to look closely at many of the projects taking place at that time. Thomas, an architect as well as an artist, was employed by Duke William, and became Deputy Ranger himself under Henry Frederick, the second Duke. As such, he had influence and input into many aspects of the project.

'**Thomas Sandby**' by Sir William Beechey
© National Portrait Gallery, London

Paul, on the other hand, recorded the events and characters of the day with pencil, paint and paper – and what records they present! The attention to detail in their work is phenomenal, and particularly in Thomas' landscape views of the 1750s. Over 250 years later, we are fortunate indeed that two such talented men were at Windsor at that time. Their legacy, in the recording of the creation of the landscape as envisaged by the Duke of Cumberland (and much more besides) should be regarded as our 'window' to the Great Park of the 18th Century, and an unrivalled treasure from the past.

'**Paul Sandby**' by Francis Cotes
© Tate, London 2010

Savill Garden and Obelisk Pond

The futuristic-looking Savill Building (above) was opened in June 2006 by HRH Prince Philip, The Duke of Edinburgh, Ranger of the Great Park. The building has a story all of its own, and Royal Landscape's publication 'The Savill Building' is a must-have if you have a serious interest in modern building design and technology. Take a look at the interior roof (below) – the 'gridshell' is made with Great Park-grown larch, with an outer overlay of English oak.

The intricate construction, even to the casual observer, is quite remarkable. The inspired combination of wood, glass, light and space works very well, and when combined with the excellent facilities inside and the Savill Garden outside, makes the trip to Wick Lane really worthwhile.

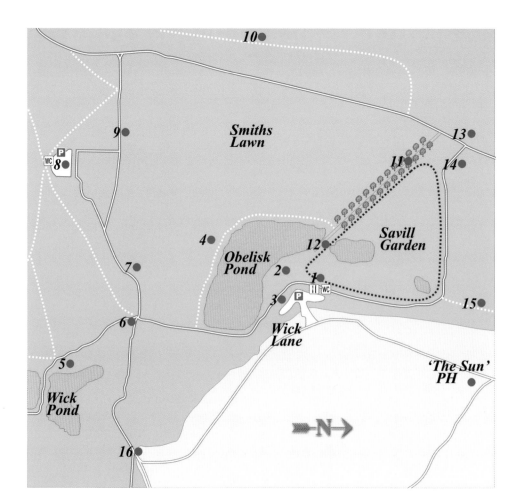

KEY:

1. The Savill Building
2. The Obelisk
3. Play Area
4. Sandpit
5. Totem Pole
6. Carter's Bar
7. Flying Barn
8. Valley Gardens Car Park

9. Guards Polo Club
10. Prince Consort's Statue
11. Obelisk Ride
12. Obelisk Bridge
13. Cumberland Gate
14. Garden House
15. Rhododendron Ride
16. Cheeseman's Gate

P Parking

● ● ● Savill Garden perimeter fence

White dotted lines indicate gravel paths or tracks

WC – Public Toilets

Arriving at the Savill Building, the first thing you notice is just how well the Building sits unobtrusively within the area around you. Going inside only heightens the experience. It's not often that a modern contemporary building makes such a positive impact on an area, but this one certainly does. You will also notice the abundance of car parking space (a separate Coach Park is sited next to the Car Park), and there are plenty of signposts, maps and information plates provided to guide you along the various routes. The Main Entrance to the Savill Building, and to Savill Garden itself, is straight ahead. Entrance to the Savill Building is free, and the Ticket Desk for the Savill Garden is inside. The pay-on-exit ticket machines for the Car Park are also located here, just outside of the Building. Facing the building, the tarmac road in front of the Main Entrance takes you left to the Obelisk Pond, Valley Gardens, the southern end of Smith's Lawn, and eventually to Virginia Water. To the right, the road leads to the northern end of Smith's Lawn, and onwards to Cumberland Lodge, Royal Lodge, the Village and the Deer Park.

The Savill Garden had been a respected local tourist attraction for a long time prior to the advent of the new Building, and the changes made in the past few years have only served to enhance the reputation. Originally the 1932 concept of (Sir) Eric Savill, a small part of this area of the Great Park was developed into what would become known as the Bog Garden. The Garden aroused considerable interest from King George V and Queen Mary, after which their Majesties visited the Garden in 1934. During the visit, Her Majesty was happy to point out to Eric Savill that 'its very nice, ..but isn't it rather small?'

This was effectively the go-ahead for Eric Savill to expand his ideas, and the Garden itself. The War years of 1939-45 halted most of the work, with only a skeleton staff of workers keeping the Garden ticking over. The end of hostilities brought men back home to the Park, and the Garden once again began to develop under the continued guidance of Eric Savill and his new Assistant, Thomas Hope Findlay, known as 'Hope' to the local Villagers.

In 1951, King George VI, a keen gardener himself, requested that henceforth the Garden should be known as the Savill Garden, and knighted Eric Savill in 1955. After Sir Eric's and Hope Findlay's retirements, the Garden continued to develop, and now encompasses an area of some 35 acres, within which you will see a truly stunning array of plants, trees and shrubs from around the world. The Garden is sub-divided into a number of 'mini-gardens', each one planned to a particular theme. As with Virginia Water, its impossible to see it all from any one point, and so your walk around the Garden will be one of continued delight as you move from area to area, with your senses greeted by new and delightful colours, scents and scenes around every corner. The Garden is more than capable of showing itself off to visitors even in the dreariest of Winter months, so don't let a grey day deter you from visiting.

MAGNOLIAS fill the Valley Gardens with heady scent in early Spring.

Rather than my attempting to advise and inform you of the many and varied horticultural delights awaiting you, I would suggest that on arrival you speak to the helpful staff at the Information Desk, who will be able to advise on the current Garden highlights. Also, take a look at the new video-screen information service just inside the Main Entrance, and finally, the Royal Landscape publishes its own Guide to Savill Garden and Valley Gardens which you can use to be your in-depth companion on your walk around what must be one of the country's finest botanical Gardens. Sir Eric and Hope would be very proud of it indeed!

THE OBELISK MONUMENT: the Monument was erected c1750 on the order of George II to commemorate his son's crushing defeat of the Scots forces at Culloden in 1746. In earlier times, the Monument would have been a very prominent landmark, although the large mature trees now surrounding it tend to block the view of the Obelisk from other areas of the Great Park.

In order to take a relatively short but pleasant stroll around the landscape adjacent to the Savill Building I would suggest the following route. Facing the Savill Building from the Car Park, take the road down to the left, and after only a short distance, the road leads out onto a grassy expanse dotted with mature trees of all shapes and sizes. Standing head and shoulders above them all is the Obelisk Monument.

Erected in about 1750 by George II, the Obelisk Monument commemorates the Duke of Cumberland's victory over the Scots in 1746 at Culloden Field, a battle which became infamous for 'Butcher' Cumberland's harsh treatment of the vanquished, inflicted by his own army. The well known garden flower the 'Sweet William' is named after the Duke, although the Scots refer to a weed, (the Common Ragwort), as 'Stinking Billy'! The engraving of the word 'Culloden' was changed by order of Queen Victoria to 'Cumberland' (apparently, Queen Victoria was not proud of her illustrious ancestor's military exploits!) Around the Monument there are a number of picnic benches, and across the road is a newly-built play area for the younger visitors – very handy for Mum and Dad when they want a break. The long grass avenue, known as Obelisk Ride, stretching downhill away from the Monument will take you to Cumberland Gate, at the northern end of Smith's Lawn.

OBELISK POND, FROM THE PONDHEAD: the Obelisk Monument can be seen in the treeline just right of centre.

From the Monument, follow the tarmac road downhill towards the Obelisk Pond. Obelisk Pond was created in 1750 as another part of the Duke of Cumberland's grand scheme. Originally, the Pond was also known as Hurst Lake, due to its proximity to Hurst Hill, on which the Obelisk Monument now stands. The pondhead, over which today's tarmac road now passes, blocked off yet another of the many streams flowing through the Great Park, thereby flooding the valley and creating the Pond. Higher up the watercourse, the original stream has been remodelled to form the two Lakes now within the Savill Garden. The outflow from Obelisk Pond flows roughly southwards, entering Wick Pond, and then flows into the Wick Branch of Virginia Water. The water in Obelisk Pond is of very good quality, and the Pond was once used as a base for a trout rearing scheme.

OBELISK BRIDGE: originally built c1750, the bridge was rebuilt by Sir Jeffry Wyattville in 1833, but retains the original stone floodgate underneath. Renovation work was undertaken on the bridge in early Autumn 2009. As you stand on the Bridge and look to the west (with the Monument behind you), you will see the view along Obelisk Ride to Cumberland Gate, pictured on p21. The later creation of Cumberland Gate at the northern end of Smith's Lawn effectively cut off the continuation of the Ride, which originally extended up to Cumberland Lodge itself.

Continue your walk across the pondhead, and then turn right onto the gravel track which follows the edge of the Pond. This will lead you to a large excavation in the ground about 200 yards ahead on your left, known as the Sandpit. An equestrian cross-country eventing course has a jump sited here, and another sited over on the far edge of the Pond near to the pondhead outflow. Carrying on around the Pond, you will reach the Obelisk Bridge (p29), located on the avenue downhill from the Monument, and from thence you can complete a full lap of the Pond by walking back uphill along Obelisk Ride to the Obelisk Monument.

Upon arrival back at the Obelisk Monument, if you wish to extend your walk a little further, rejoin the tarmac road and turn right. By walking back to the pondhead and going straight on past the gravel track, you will come to a junction in the road (Carter's Bar). From here you can go left to Cheeseman's Gate; ahead (left fork) to Wick Pond, the Totem Pole and Virginia Water, or ahead (right fork) to the Valley Gardens. A hard right turn takes you up through the birch trees and onto Smith's Lawn. The Valley Gardens and Smith's Lawn are covered on p55-66 of this Guide, and Virginia Water on p31-54. Maps of both areas are provided near the start of the relevant chapters.

SAVILL GARDEN: certain plants are sometimes overshadowed by the profusion of Summer blooms, but a clear Winter's day is a perfect time for admiring other plants, such as these colourful birch trees and shrub dogwoods.

Virginia Water

For a look around Virginia Water just by itself, I recommend that you start at the Royal Landscape (Wheatsheaf) Car Park situated next to the A30 London Road. Details of 'How to get There', parking and nearby facilities can be found on p18.

Virginia Water – a brief history:

Virginia Water was created in 1752/3 under the supervision of William Augustus, Duke of Cumberland, assisted by his architect, Henry Flitcroft. Work began with the construction of a pondhead, thus damming some of the streams that ran through the area. The original pondhead was sited adjacent to where the Ruins stand today, and extended across to Botany Bay Point, the sloping headland on the opposite shore. As part of the Duke's plans for this area of the Great Park, there were to be a number of significant features, the lake aside. These included two towers, ornate buildings, boats, plantations, bridges, waterfalls (cascades) and grottoes. Even by 18th Century standards, this was landscaping on a truly grand scale!

VIRGINIA WATER, from Shrubs Hill: Thomas Sandby c1753 (RL 14640)
The pondhead is on the right of the picture, and the Manor Lodge on the far left. Note the lack of woodland; many thousands of trees would be planted over the next few years.
The Royal Collection © 2010, Her Majesty Queen Elizabeth II.

The Duke continued with his grandiose projects right up to his early death in 1765, at the age of just 44. He was succeeded as Ranger by his brother, Henry Frederick, under whose stewardship the lake was to suffer the calamity which struck on the 1st September 1768. A great storm erupted over the area, and the deluge that followed caused the destruction of the pondhead and Cascade, and the emptying of the lake. Mrs Delany, a writer of the time, reported that the house which had stood beside the pondhead, (known as Dalton's Lodge) was carried off 'as clear as if no house had ever been built there'. Several drownings were also reported in the aftermath.

Detail from 'VIRGINIA WATER FROM SHRUBS HILL' Thomas Sandby c1753
(RL 14640 - detail) This image is an enlargement of the last small group of trees on the far right of the complete image on p31. The pondhead shown in this view was destroyed in the storm of 1st September, 1768; Dalton's Lodge is the house depicted just right of centre.
The Royal Collection © 2010, Her Majesty Queen Elizabeth II.

It wasn't until King George III took an interest in the lake in 1781 that an attempt was made to build a new pondhead to the east of the old one, but it, too, failed in 1784. By 1790, today's existing pondhead was successfully constructed, and by the resultant flooding of additional land, thus creating the Wick Branch, the lake was extended to today's dimensions.

The vast majority of visitors to Virginia Water, whether arriving by car or by public transport, will commence their walk from the Royal Landscape (Wheatsheaf) Car Park adjacent to the Wheatsheaf Hotel on the A30 London Road. For the purposes of this Guide, I shall begin my description of the lake from this point, and if you are making your way to the lake from an alternative starting point, just have a look at the map on p34, locate your position, and join the walk from there.

WHEATSHEAF HOTEL: a familiar landmark, set alongside the A30 Great West Road. This is the second version of the Inn; the first one, which once stood a short way off to the NW, was damaged by the flood of 1768. The core of this newer building dates from 1770, with later 19th Century additions.

To begin your tour, exit the Car Park towards the lake. The Wheatsheaf Hotel is to your left, and the mobile tea and coffee bar is situated here on the right. Walking down the path through the trees out onto the tarmac road gives the visitor their first clear look at Virginia Water itself. You are standing on what is actually the retaining earth bank of the lake, and what you are seeing is not the entire lake - it was purposefully designed to keep its full extent hidden from the viewer, which means, to really see it all, you've got to walk around all four and a half miles of it!

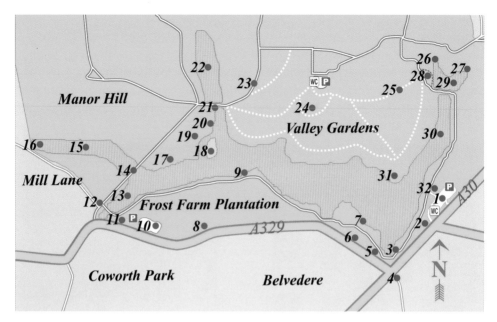

VIRGINIA WATER

KEY:

1. Royal Landscape (Wheatsheaf) Car Park
2. The Wheatsheaf Hotel
3. The Cascade
4. Wentworth Golf Club
5. Virginia Lodge
6. The Ruins
7. Landing Stage
8. World's End Gate
9. Perch Bay
10. Blacknest Car Park
11. The Belvedere PH
12. Blacknest Gate
13. Blacknest Arm
14. Five Arch Bridge
15. Northwest Arm
16. China Island
P Parking

17. Dockyard Cottages
18. Fishing Temple
19. Virginia Water Cottage
20. The Boathouse
21. Site of Hermitage
22. Johnson's Pond
23. Breakheart Hill
24. Plunket Memorial Pavilion
25. Canadian Avenue
26. Eton Bridge
27. Larch Bridge
28. Totem Pole
29. Wick Pond
30. Wick Branch
31. Botany Bay Point
32. Mobile Tea and Coffee Bar
WC – Public Toilets

NOTE – public toilets are located at the Wheatsheaf Hotel, at the end of the building nearest the Car Park. Toilets are also available at the Savill Building and the Valley Gardens Car Park (see map p24) White dotted lines indicate gravel, grass or dirt paths and tracks.

VIRGINIA WATER, LOOKING NORTHWEST: the view from the lakeside road just in from the Wheatsheaf Car Park.

Following the lakeside road to the left will take you downhill, crossing the small stone bridge over the starting point of the River Bourne, towards the lake's most famous and popular spot – the Cascade.

The waterfall, pictured on p36, was rebuilt on this spot by 1790 using the enormous heath (or sarsen) stones brought from Bagshot Heath nearby, and which once formed the original 1752 waterfall. Also included in the reconstruction was a Grotto (cave), with its entrance on the left hand side. The entrance to the Grotto is now sealed off, but still discernable as you look straight at the Cascade. A recent survey revealed the Grotto is still intact within, and complete with a second, smaller chamber and viewing 'window' situated behind the fall of water.

Water exiting from the lake is the source of the River Bourne, which flows roughly northeast towards its confluence with the River Thames, close to the town of Chertsey. To see the waterfall working at its spectacular best, a visit here on the first sunny day after a period of prolonged heavy rain would be the ideal choice.

THE CASCADE: pictured here in late Autumn, the Cascade is the most popular spot on the lake; the sealed entrance to the Grotto (once referred to as 'the Robber's Cave') is located to the top left of the waterfall.

Just beyond the Cascade, the road snakes up a short steep hill and levels out in front of Virginia (Water) Lodge, which you can now see up to your left. This Thomas Sandby-designed house dates from about 1784, and replaced the one lost to the 1768 flood, (which can just be seen to the right of the pondhead in Sandby's painting on p32) but is better sited on higher ground. The house was originally designed to be a fine Gamekeeper's lodge with kennels and in the 1830s, a pheasantry was added. After 1861 it played host to a 'grace and favour' occupant who was allowed to change the layout of the building, enabling it to be used after her death to house three separate individuals at the same time. The house reverted back to a single dwelling after 1920, and has been used as accommodation for a number of Estate workers' families since that time.

VIRGINIA (WATER) LODGE: the replacement for Dalton's Lodge, this house occupies a fabulous setting near the Cascade, and has a commanding view of the lake, looking towards the Northeast (Wick Branch) Arm.

With the Lodge behind you, you can now take in the view to the Northeastern extremity of the lake, (pictured below) where you will find the Totem Pole, the Wick Stream and Wick Pond (sometimes referred to as Little Virginia), the small lake that feeds into Virginia Water from the east.

THE NORTHEASTERN ARM, or WICK BRANCH, VIRGINIA WATER.

Continuing on past the Lodge will bring you to a pleasant open area, where you will see the 'Ruins' to your left. The stonework is what could be described as a 'folly', a popular landscaping feature of the Georgian era. This involved constructing an artificial edifice or building, but with such authenticity as to make it appear to be a genuine relic. The stones and columns used here were brought from the ancient Roman city of Leptis Magna, which once flourished on the North African coast near Tripoli. They were shipped to England in 1817, but not erected on this site until 1826, under the direction of Jeffry Wyatt (later Sir Jeffry Wyattville). There were also a number of statues located within the Ruins, but these eventually fell prey to Victorian vandalism, and were removed for safekeeping – so safe, in fact, that some of them are still lost, and have never been relocated to this day!

THE 'RUINS' AT VIRGINIA WATER: recently renovated, and the largest reconstructed antiquarian edifice of its kind in the UK, the Ruins also extend below the road bridge into the grounds of Fort Belvedere.

As part of the original Cumberland landscaping, a tower, known as the Belvedere, was built on the higher ground some distance behind where the Ruins now stand. The grounds were embellished with tree-lined vistas to the Fishing Temple and the Clockcase (a second tower, located on high ground to the east of the lake), plus an avenue of magnificent cedar trees which angled down towards the lake at this point. Until recently, a last remaining 'giant' of this avenue stood by the Ruins, and a few still survive within the grounds of the Belvedere. A colony of herons once lived in the cedars, and a few may still be seen on your walk around the lake. The introduction of commercial forestry practices within the Belvedere area, incorporating dense woodland planting, has all but eradicated the vistas, but fortunately, by means of the detailed maps and drawings which survive, there are plans to restore some of the original views currently lost to us. The Belvedere has its own place in history – it was home to King Edward VIII, who could sometimes be seen out on the lake in his speedboat in the early 1930s, and who signed the Instrument of Abdication at Fort Belvedere on the 10th of December 1936.

'THE NEW BUILDING ON SHRUBBS HILL' Canot, after Thomas Sandby c1754
(RCIN 814377) The triangular shaped Belvedere, which at this time had a clear view over the lake. Much of the adjoining area of Bagshot Heath had an unenviable reputation as the haunt of highwaymen, such as the debonnaire Claude Duval, who had a reputed hideaway in nearby Windlesham. Duval was captured, and hanged at Tyburn in 1670. The Great West Road, situated close to the tower, was frequented by many stagecoaches, bringing the chance of rich pickings for those who were prepared to risk their lives to steal and rob from the coach passengers.
The Royal Collection © 2010, Her Majesty Queen Elizabeth II.

A VIEW ACROSS TO BOTANY BAY POINT: the original 1752 pondhead (destroyed in 1768) stretched across today's lake from just left of the photo to the bank opposite. In 1866, the Rev. F.J.Rawlins wrote his Notes on Virginia Water, and noted a fish-rearing shed located on the far bank from which trout were stocked into Obelisk Pond, and salmon into the River Thames!

To the right on the lakeside are four large stone plinths, which mark the location of a now-disused landing stage. The lake once had its own flotilla of Royal pleasure boats permanently stationed here, complete with its own resident Commander, dating right back to the time of the lake's creation, and only finally ceasing in 1936, when what was left of the flotilla was officially decommissioned and the sailing vessels removed. Looking straight across the lake, you can see the sloped area known as Botany Bay Point. When the lake was first created, the original pondhead stretched across to Botany Bay Point from a spot to the left of the stone plinths. After its collapse in 1768, a new relocated pondhead was built in 1784 by Thomas Sandby, which also collapsed, earning him the nickname 'Tommy Sandbanks'. The position of the final rebuild in 1790 allowed newly purchased land to flood and create today's Wick Branch, and to submerge the original site of the 17th Century hamlet of Virginia, which gave the lake its name (off to the right of the landing stage). The remains of the 1752 pondhead were revealed once again during World War II, when the lake was drained down, in order to deter German pilots from using it as a visual reference point.

Continuing around the lake will bring you to Perch Bay. Look across the lake towards the North Shore - on the opposite bank, and to the left, a stone stepped terrace at the water's edge marks the location of what was once Manor Lodge. The site is now known as the Fishing Temple, and is one of the private areas of the Great Park to which public access is denied. Although it is unclear from this vantage point, the Fishing Temple is, in fact, on a moated island, accessed only from the far bank. There is also a grace–and–favour Victorian cottage which now stands adjacent to the site of the original 13th Century Manor Lodge. (A better view of this area can be obtained when your walk eventually brings you to the far shore). The Fishing Temple takes its name from George IV's ornate construction placed where the stone terrace is now, and from where he would regularly venture out onto the lake in one of the many sailing vessels available, so as to indulge in his passion for angling. The picture on p43 shows the second remodelled version of this building.

'VIRGINIA WATER FROM THE MANOR LODGE' Thomas Sandby c1754 (RL14646)
On the right of the painting, the 'Mandarin' afloat on the lake – the dilapidated hulk of this Chinese Junk was brought up the Thames to Old Windsor and transported overland to the lake, where it was extensively and decoratively refurbished in 1753.
The Royal Collection © 2010, Her Majesty Queen Elizabeth II.

HM KING GEORGE IV: Sir Thomas Lawrence c1822 (RCIN 405680)
The 'Fisher King', and the subject of numerous unflattering cartoons during his reign, many of which portrayed him and his female companion, Lady Conyngham, out on the Lake indulging in the King's favourite pastime of fishing.
The Royal Collection © 2010, Her Majesty Queen Elizabeth II.

George IV had a marked, singular influence on the Great Park. He led an increasingly reclusive life, and took great care to ensure that his desire for privacy was never compromised – even going to the lengths of having servants 'hidden' at various points on his routes around the Park, in order to ensure that nobody else would wander into his path either by accident or by design. George IV was frivolous with his spending, lavishing exorbitant sums of money on his projects, such as the forerunner of today's Royal Lodge and the Fishing Temple, plus the vast amount of cash that was spent on refurbishing Windsor Castle itself, and building the Brighton Pavilion! He also reclaimed the two other areas of land adjacent to the lake from which it was possible to see him, and thereby compromising his obsession with personal privacy. These now heavily-forested areas (Clockcase and Belvedere) remain in the possession of the Crown to this day, although the two tower buildings which stand there are now both privately leased. The vista from the Belvedere tower to the site of the Fishing Temple is one of the views to be restored sometime in the near future, as part of the Royal Landscape project.

'THE BOATHOUSE, FISHING TEMPLE AND TENTS' William Daniell c1829 (RCIN 500176)
The Royal Collection © 2010, Her Majesty Queen Elizabeth II.

As you continue along the tarmac road you have the extensive Frost Farm Plantation to your left. Passing opposite the Fishing Temple, over on the far bank you will see a pair of cottages. These are the Dockyard Cottages, and are the homes of current Great Park employees. As with the Fishing Temple, these homes are private, and visitors are asked to respect the occupants' privacy when passing by.

A short distance further along will place you in the perfect spot to view the Five Arch Bridge, a graceful structure dating from 1827, when it was built to replace an earlier stone bridge designed by Thomas Sandby. Prior to that, there had stood a bridge which, in its day, was a remarkable piece of civil engineering. It was known as the Great Bridge; a single arch built in 1753, and it was made entirely of wood, with brick abutments. What made it so remarkable was that it was designed to allow the replacement of any single piece of the structure without major dismantling of the rest of it. Unfortunately, for a bridge, it was exceptionally steep (to allow the Duke's boats to pass underneath) – a problem which often rendered it unsuitable and dangerous for horses and pedestrians alike.

'THE GREAT BRIDGE OVER THE VIRGINIA RIVER': P.Sandby after T.Sandby c1754 (RCIN 500179) The Royal Collection © 2010, Her Majesty Queen Elizabeth II.

The Great Bridge (pictured above in 1754) was not destined to last long. It was subject to continuous repair; its foundations succumbed to the same flood that destroyed the pondhead in September 1768, and it was derelict by 1780. Sandby's new bridge, constructed in 1789, went the way of its predecessor, and had to be replaced by the structure you now see before you. Designed and built by Jeffry Wyatt (of Windsor Castle reconstruction fame) the Five Arch Bridge has endured remarkably well, and still retains a sense of grace and elegance in its clean, uncluttered lines. Time marches on, however, and renovation work on the Bridge was undertaken in late 2009.

THE FIVE ARCH BRIDGE: dating from 1827, the Bridge is still a very impressive embellishment to the lake today. Beyond the Bridge lies the Northwest Arm, and the site of China Island.

Continuing your walk, you will now pass alongside the Blacknest Arm of the lake; a suitable joining point for visitors using the pay-and-display Blacknest Car Park on the A329. A footpath leads from a gateway in the Car Park the few hundred yards through the woodland to this point on the walk. The road takes a right turn at this point, crossing over the Blacknest Arm via a small inconspicuous stone bridge, constructed in 1788. The rather red-tinged water flowing into the lake from the small pond on the other side of the bridge is one of the main watercourses flowing into the lake, which were stopped by the pondhead, and thus creating the sheet of water which we are now walking around. The stream is coloured by the presence of Leptothrix and Gallionella bacterium which interact with naturally occurring iron oxides. This 'chalybeate' water, which can also be found in other streams nearby, was once the natural resource for a successful mid-18th Century mineral springwater business located in nearby Sunninghill Wells, some 1.5 miles further along the A329 towards Ascot.

Passing over the bridge leads you to the main thoroughfare of the Great Park, entering via Blacknest Gate to your left. Follow the road to the right, and you will see the Five Arch Bridge ahead. Caution must be taken here – the road is sometimes heavy with traffic, especially if polo is scheduled at Smith's Lawn. The gravel horseriding track also runs parallel to the road here, and so it is wise to keep eyes and ears open!

BLACKNEST GATE LODGE: the entrance here was created in 1752/3, and is the main access point for polo traffic going to and from Smith's Lawn during the Summer months.

Blacknest Gate was created along with the lake. The land by the Manor Lodge became flooded, and so it was necessary to divert the original road which had forded the stream by the Lodge and exited at what was, and still is, known as World's End Gate (on today's A329). Blacknest Gate Lodge was built in 1839, and is today very little altered from the original. Outside of the Gate, limited free roadside car parking is available in Mill Lane. Caution is also advised here – the narrow lane is a popular shortcut for local motorists, and combined with the visitors' cars, this scenario can make for a busy and congested road.

APPROACH TO FIVE ARCH BRIDGE: this road eventually leads to Smith's Lawn, Cumberland Lodge, Royal Lodge, into the Deer Park, Long Walk, the Village, finally terminating at Cranbourne Gate.

On reaching the Five Arch Bridge, you have a choice of where to go next. You can continue straight ahead, but to your left, you will see a lakeside grass ride meandering away amongst the trees. This ride will take you to the end of the Northwestern Arm of the lake, and the site of China Island, yet another creation from the time of the Duke of Cumberland. The ride is a pleasant, tranquil threequarter-mile diversion, but can sometimes be wet and muddy.

What remains of the island itself is currently overgrown with rhododendron, and not accessible. The ride crosses a feeder stream via a small bridge beyond this point, and you can then backtrack on the opposite bank, coming out on the far side of Five Arch Bridge. China Island was created in 1753 for the dual purpose of having a mooring point for some of the smaller boats in the Duke's flotilla, and also as the site for a 'teahouse' built in the Chinese style, which was in vogue at that time.

The teahouse fell into disrepair after the death of the Duke, and was subsequently restored and used as a summerhouse. It eventually saw use as a gamekeeper's home before being finally demolished in about 1870.

'THE BUILDING ON CHINA ISLAND, 1829-1836' William Delamotte (RL 17509)
The stream formerly known as the Redbrook flows into the lake at this point. Once connected to the shore via bridges, the lake is now heavily silted up at this point, and the island also appears much smaller today than in this view.
The Royal Collection © 2010, Her Majesty Queen Elizabeth II.

Passing over the Five Arch Bridge, you can now see the Dockyard Cottages to your right, just beyond which is the entrance to the out-of-bounds enclosure known as the Fishing Temple. Located within is the site of the original 13th Century Manor Lodge, (subsequently to become the site of the actual Fishing Temple) and today's Boathouse and Virginia Water Cottage. The road turns half-right at this point and passes next to Johnson's Pond, on your left. Behind the iron fence to your right, the water from Johnson's Pond flows out and over a waterfall into Virginia Water.

A small, wooden rustic hermitage, dating from 1827, was built right above the waterfall, but was demolished sometime in the 1860s.

DOCKYARD COTTAGES: these Estate workers' homes back onto what is known locally as the 'Match Stretch' of the lake, due to the York Club Angling Section once holding regular competitions over on the far side. The natural heathland in front of the cottages is one of only a few such remaining areas, the type of which once predominated in the southeast corner of the Great Park prior to the commencement of landscaping in the 18th Century.

The road climbs steeply up Breakheart Hill towards Smith's Lawn, which in Spring is a mass of beautiful bulbs, magnolias and delicate flowers. A superb display of azaleas clothe the hill on the right from early Summer onwards, with hydrangeas providing the display on the left in early Autumn. The gravel track on your right at the bottom of the hill leads you into the Valley Gardens (left fork, going uphill) or along the North Bank of the lake (right fork, close to the water's edge). Following the right-hand track takes you into a quieter area of the lake. Many visitors seem to prefer to remain on tarmac roads, especially those with small children in prams. It is easily possible to get around this part of the lake with pushchairs, but it is best to take note of the prevailing conditions before starting out – heavy rain prior to your visit can sometimes leave it rather waterlogged in places.

BREAKHEART HILL: looking up from Johnson's Pond, the hill is cloaked with a profusion of colour in Spring and Summer. The Valley Gardens spread out uphill to the right, (on what is actually High Flyer's Hill) with Smith's Lawn at the crest of the hill.

As you walk along the North Bank gravel path, to your left you can see into the wooded slopes and valleys that make up the Valley Gardens. There are a number of rides and paths that lead off into the Gardens, some of which can be soft underfoot and a little steep in places. (The Valley Gardens themselves are dealt with in more detail on p55-66). A short distance ahead on your right you can see the white-painted Boathouse, and set further back, Virginia Water Cottage, situated adjacent to the moated island.

THE BOATHOUSE: standing on the site of original boathouses dating back to the time of William Augustus, Duke of Cumberland, this ornate little Boathouse dates from c1860, and has room inside for two small boats plus accommodation on the upper floor for a Boatman.

Continuing along the gravel track, you will notice a number of individual mature beech trees bordering the lakeside. These are the last remnants of the original Cumberland plantings on this side of the lake, and make for a perfect foil to the ornamental species which adorn the slopes of the Valley Gardens off to your left. As you approach the end of the North Bank, younger beech trees increase in number to form a more substantial plantation, and close to the junction with Canadian Avenue and Wick Pond the gravel track crosses the eastern end of the line of the ancient Roman road which once led from Staines (or Pontes, as the Romans called it) westwards towards the Roman town of Silchester (Calleva Atrebatum) along a route still known today as the Devil's Highway. Looking westwards at this point, the faint outline of the Roman road embankment is, apparently, just visible here, with a short row of oaks lining its right-hand edge – you do have to look very carefully to see it, though!

VIRGINIA WATER COTTAGE: a flotilla of boats was always a significant feature of Virginia Water since its earliest days, and an official Keeper of the Boats was appointed right up until the decommissioning of the 'fleet' in 1936. There was a separate house for the Keeper, which was located over towards the Fishing Temple site. This house was demolished and a replacement (Virginia Water Cottage) built in the 1870s.

Proceeding on, the track then crosses the Northeast corner of the lake at Wick Pond, adjacent to one of the most prominent landmarks of the Great Park – the Totem Pole.

The Totem Pole was a gift from the people of Canada to HM Queen Elizabeth II. At 100 feet high, one foot for each year, it marks the centenary of British Columbia, proclaimed a Crown Colony on November 19th 1858 by Queen Victoria. Repainted in 1985, it was carved by Chief Mungo Martin of the Kwakiutl tribe. The figures on the pole, from the top down, are as follows: Man with large hat, Beaver, Old Man, Thunderbird, Sea Otter, The Raven, The Whale, Double-Headed Snake, Halibut Man and Cedar Man.

THE TOTEM POLE: a unique feature of the Valley Gardens, the sudden dramatic appearance of the Totem Pole rising majestically above Surrey's leafy and tranquil environment can often come as something of a surprise! It also enhances the Canadian 'presence' in this part of the Great Park, first established here during World War 1. Work on re-landscaping the area immediately around the Totem Pole commenced in March 2010.

The pole was carved from a 600 year old, single log of western red cedar and weighs 27,000 pounds. It was erected by the 3rd Field Squadron of the 22nd Field Engineer Regiment Royal Engineers for their Colonel in Chief, Her Majesty The Queen, in June 1958.

WICK POND: a feeder for the main lake, Wick Pond has two small bridges, known as Eton Bridge (towards the Valley Gardens) and Larch Bridge (closest towards the A30 main road).

Adjacent to the Totem Pole is Wick Pond. This particular lake receives its water from the Wick Stream, and is sometimes referred to as Little Virginia. Wick Pond has an outflow leading into Virginia Water over a small waterfall. This part of the main lake (the Wick Branch) was added during George III's final rebuilding phase of the late 1780s, and was made possible by the Crown's purchase of the required land from the Parish of Egham. The area hereabouts was known as Egham Wick, hence the name given to the pond and to the Wick Branch portion of Virginia Water. A number of smallholdings, buildings and orchards were located within this area, all demolished and submerged as a result of the creation of the Wick Branch extension to the lake.

From here, by following the tarmac road alongside the Wick Branch, it is but a half-mile walk back to your starting point at the Wheatsheaf Car Park, and maybe a stop for a welcome hot drink and a snack at the mobile tea and coffee bar.

SMITH'S LAWN and VALLEY GARDENS

HOW DO I GET THERE?

Public transport: Regular SWT trains stop at Virginia Water, Staines and Egham. Taxi service available from all stations to the Great Park, although taxi drivers are only authorised to take you as far as Savill Building, Bishopsgate, Cheeseman's Gate or Blacknest Gate, from where it is a 10-20 minute walk to either Smith's Lawn or the Valley Gardens. The Staines to Frimley no.500 bus service (see p18 for bus stop details) does not stop by the end of Wick Road on the A30. The nearest stop is Royal Holloway College, from where it is a 20 minute walk via the A30 London Road to the Car Parks in Wick Road or to Cheeseman's Gate.

By road: M25 Junction 13, then A30 West towards Basingstoke (2 miles), or M3 Junction 3, then A322 (Bracknell) 1 mile, then A30 East towards London (6 miles) will take you to the junction with Wick Road. A small car park for the northeastern arm of **Virginia Water**, plus a road leading to the **Valley Gardens Car Park** and access to **Smith's Lawn** will be found on the left hand side of Wick Road just 400 yards from it's junction with the A30, a short distance from Royal Holloway College. Please note that vehicular access to Smith's Lawn on polo days should only be via Blacknest Gate, with controlled parking available at Smith's Lawn itself. Parking in Wick Road is available, close to Cheeseman's Gate, through which pedestrian access can be gained. It is a pleasant 10 minute walk from here to the top of Smith's Lawn at Flying Barn, with the Valley Gardens over to the left, and Guards Polo Club ahead on the right. Lastly, you can park at the Savill Garden Car Park, from where it's a 10 minute walk via the Obelisk Monument and Obelisk Pond to the Valley Gardens.

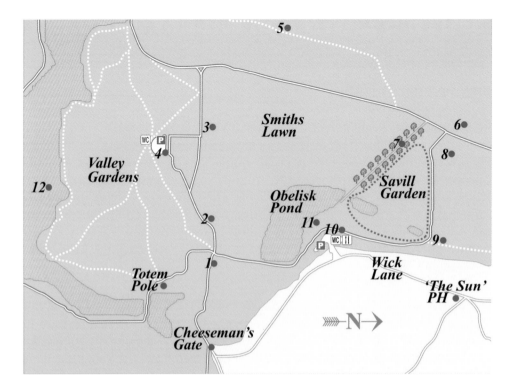

KEY:

1. Carter's Bar
2. Flying Barn
3. Guards Polo Club
4. Valley Gardens Car Park
5. Prince Consort's Statue
6. Cumberland Gate

7. Obelisk Ride
8. Garden House
9. Rhododendron Ride
10. Savill Building
11. Obelisk Monument
12. Virginia Water

P Parking

WC – Public Toilets

● ● ● Savill Garden perimeter fence
White dotted lines indicate gravel paths or tracks
(also see map p24 for additional information)

SMITH'S LAWN

FACILITIES: Smith's Lawn has no public facilities. Seasonal mobile tea and coffee shops can sometimes be found onsite at the Guards Polo Club; next to the Obelisk Monument, and inside the Valley Gardens just beyond the Public Car Park. Toilets are located in the adjacent Valley Gardens Staff Car Park, or at the Savill Building (see map above).

With a Car Park at the Valley Gardens, or the Savill Building Car Park just a short distance away, it is your choice as from where you wish to start your walk around the Valley Gardens and Smith's Lawn. From the Savill Building Car Park, just follow the tarmac road towards Obelisk Pond, walking across the pondhead and up to the junction (Carter's Bar) 200 yards ahead. Turn right here, and follow the road uphill through the silver birch trees until the ground levels out alongside a cottage and yard known collectively as Flying Barn. The Flying Barn takes its name from an 18th Century agricultural device (a barn on wheels) which was in use at nearby Norfolk Farm, one of 'Farmer' George III's projects in 1791, and not from the Lawn's connections to aircraft dispersal and aircraft repair during World War 2, both of which did take place here. Flying Barn marks the eastern extremity of the original area encompassed by Norfolk Farm, and now of Smith's Lawn, the origin of the name of which is unclear.

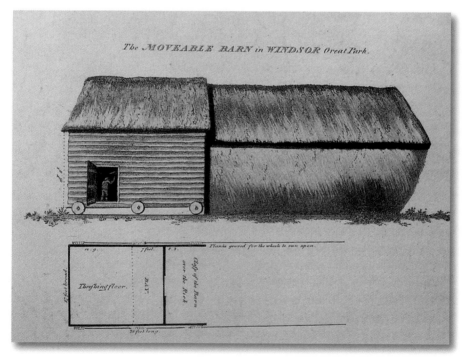

'THE MOVEABLE (or FLYING) BARN': William Pearce, 1794 (RCIN 700912)
For an idea of scale, note the figure standing in the doorway. Following the demise of George III, and the resultant loss of interest in his farming projects, the Barn fell into disuse, and c1830 was converted into a dwelling which was occupied by the Estate Fisherman.
The Royal Collection © 2010, Her Majesty Queen Elizabeth II.

Assuming you would like to look at Smith's Lawn itself, follow the road straight ahead, past the Guards Polo Club on your right, and up to the T-junction 200 yards further ahead. The Estate green waste recycling centre is located on the left, and produces tons of compost each year for use within the Gardens and the Great Park. Turning left at the junction will take you down Breakheart Hill to Johnson's Pond and Blacknest Gate.

FLYING BARN COTTAGE: on the left of picture, and built on the site of where the original Flying Barn was left to decay, this cottage dates from 1876, and faces westwards towards the Guards Polo Club, and the site of the 'long hut' accommodation, once provided for the RAF's WW2 Tiger Moth training staff.

Turning to the right, you can now see the full expanse of Smith's Lawn stretching out before you. As you walk across the Lawn, on your right you will be able to see a better view of the Guards Polo Club and the Royal Box. From March through to September, the Lawn is an area of constant activity. The preparation and maintenance of the grounds is a never-ending task. Teams of workers will be out here in all weathers ensuring that the playing surface remains at the peak of perfection. In dry periods, water is pumped from Obelisk Pond up to the Lawn, from whence it is sprayed via huge sprinkler systems over the sward. Cutting of the grass is also a constant task, with both tractor-powered gang mowers and the use of automatic mowers employed. Equestrian events predominate in this area of the Great Park, and the Guards Polo Club hosts many prestigious polo events during each playing season, with the Queen's Cup and the Cartier-sponsored International Day seeing thousands of visitors attending.

GUARDS POLO CLUB and THE ROYAL BOX

The Guards Polo Club was formed in 1955, and is the largest Polo Club in Europe, with 12 grounds. HRH Prince Philip is the Club President, and many members of the Royal Family, including HM The Queen, come to Guards to watch the polo matches. Polo is a very exciting and entertaining spectator sport, and also very competitive. It is definitely not a sport for the faint-hearted! With ponies and riders only feet away from the spectators standing behind the picket (safety boundary) fencing, you can physically feel the excitement as the mass of horses and riders, and the thunder of hooves, sweep past! If you are here on a 'Polo Day', it is customary at the end of each 'chukka' for all the spectators (on request) to go out onto the pitch and help tread in the divots thrown up by the hooves of the ponies, in readiness for the next chukka.

On the left of the road, set back against the treeline, is the Prince Consort's Statue (below). Erected in 1887, the statue was the gift of the Women of the British Empire to Queen Victoria. A gap in the treeline once 'framed' the statue against the western horizon beyond, and the approach to the statue followed an avenue of trees on the line of today's road, with a smaller crescent-shaped avenue which led up to the statue itself.

THE PRINCE CONSORT'S STATUE: standing on its pink granite plinth, the statue is set against a backdrop of two plantations known as Cork Clump and Harewarren Clump, which were first planted up in the early 18th Century.

Walking across the Lawn up to and just beyond where the road takes a slight right hand bend, brings you to the point from which the top picture on p61 was painted. In the picture you can see both Cumberland Gate Lodge and the house known as 'Roundwood' opposite.

ABOVE: 'PLANES OF THE US AIR FORCE ON SMITH'S LAWN, 1944': Charles Cundall (RCIN 409253)   The Royal Collection © 2010, Her Majesty Queen Elizabeth II.

BELOW: CUMBERLAND GATE: today's view from the same vantage point as in the painting above, with the gabled house visible in both pictures.

Smith's Lawn has a short history as an airfield, it being the place from where the Prince of Wales (later Edward VIII) learnt to fly. Smith's Lawn was used during World War 2 as a dispersal point for various smaller military aircraft, and Vickers Armstrong had two small factories close by. HRH Prince Philip also flew from here in the early 1950s. Looking back across the Lawn towards Guards Polo Club, the hill directly beyond the Clubhouse is known as 'High Flyers Hill', which itself forms part of the Valley Gardens. At Cumberland Gate, if you continue straight ahead, the road will take you past Cumberland Lodge and on towards the Deer Park. To your right at the Gate is Obelisk Ride, and set back to the left of the Ride is the house known as 'The Garden House', which was the retirement home of Sir Eric Savill, creator of the Savill Garden.

Walking along Obelisk Ride up to the Obelisk Monument will allow you to head left back to the Savill Building. Alternatively, you can head right, passing Obelisk Pond and on to Carter's Bar, turning right here to return to Flying Barn, from whence it is but a short walk to the entrance to Valley Gardens. If you wish to remain on tarmac road rather than grass, you can take the right turn into the small lane passing in front of The Garden House, which will lead you to the front of the Savill Building and Car Park, with the Obelisk Monument and Obelisk Pond both straight ahead, just beyond the Savill Building.

VALLEY GARDENS

The entrance to Valley Gardens and the Car Park is situated alongside a small group of Estate workers' cottages just across from the rough-mown grass area adjacent to the Guards Polo Club. If you have driven your car in via the Wick Road entrance, then this is where you will be directed to. The Car Park has public toilets on-site, and a mobile tea and coffee stall is sometimes parked just off from the Car Park as you walk into the Gardens themselves.

The Valley Gardens are another creation masterminded by Sir Eric Savill. Work began here after World War 2, and a key factor for Sir Eric was to make the best use of the natural topography of the landscape, and select plants that would thrive in the sandy, poor, free draining soil. There are streams flowing down towards Virginia Water, and the valleys through which they flow make for miniature landscape and planting projects in their own right. The Valley Gardens are a place where garden enthusiasts can come along and glean ideas to take home for their own projects, combined with a fabulous year-round floral display, plus a wide variety of trees, plants and shrubs. With a total of 250 acres to see, there is something here for everybody who enjoys just being out in a garden.

The walkways, paths and rides combine to form a natural maze, and at certain times of the year, when the displays reach their most colourful crescendo, the sight and smell of the Valley Gardens can literally take your breath away.

THE PUNCHBOWL: a visual delight - ablaze with colour in late Spring.

The best way to enjoy the Gardens is just to walk wherever your feet take you. Don't worry about following a map or route - it is virtually impossible to get lost inside the Gardens, but it is easily possible to spend a few hours simply savouring and enjoying the landscape and the planting. There are a number of key landmarks set within the Gardens that you will encounter on your walk. The visual highlight in early May has to be the Punchbowl, with its fabulous display of azaleas in full flower. To ensure you see it at its best, a good idea is to telephone the Visitors' Reception Desk at the Savill Building, or check the Royal Landscape website, to see how well the display is progressing. It is such a popular attraction that the Gardens Staff are nearly always able to give you an up-to-date report, or may possibly advise that you to wait a while before visiting. Wandering along the pathways and rides will eventually lead you to the Plunket Memorial Pavilion (pictured below), from where you can enjoy a splendid view down a grassy valley to Virginia Water. The Memorial was constructed in 1979, and is dedicated to the memory of Patrick Plunket, Deputy Master of the Royal Household.

THE PLUNKET MEMORIAL: a peaceful setting from which to just sit down and take a break for a few minutes, and simply savour the view down to the lakeside.

If you are seeking to view specific types of plants or trees, it may be useful to first visit the Savill Building Reception Desk, from where you can find the locations of the various 'themed' areas such as the Heather and Dwarf Conifer Garden, the Rhododendron Garden, the Hydrangea Garden or the Pinetum. The Heather Garden, located on the site of an ancient gravel works, is often overlooked by visitors whose eyes are immediately drawn to the stately trees and overwhelming array of colourful seasonal shrubs just ahead of them. However, if you take the time to wander around this miniature woodland, you will find a remarkable collection of evergreens and heathers which can brighten up even the dullest of days, particularly in late Winter.

CANADIAN AVENUE: the Avenue leads you down towards the Totem Pole and Wick Pond, and is a fabulous place to visit for an Autumn leaf display.

A walk to the northeastern corner of the Valley Gardens will take you to Canadian Avenue and the Totem Pole. A visit here in Autumn will reward you with a memorable display of tints and colours. The avenue of red oaks, possibly planted by the Canadian Forestry Batallion which was stationed at Smith's Lawn during World War 1, show themselves off in their finest array during the months of 'mists and mellow fruitfulness'. We all know that some Autumn displays are not quite as good as others, but if you are fortunate enough to visit here when the growing seasons have been kind, then in the Valley Gardens you will see an Autumn display to rival the best the UK has to offer. The Totem Pole is the furthest point away from the Valley Gardens Car Park, and from here you can retrace your steps through the Gardens, or you can follow the signposts along the tarmac road from the Totem Pole back towards the Savill Building. At Carter's Bar (see map p56), turn left and walk back up the hill to the Polo Club and the Valley Gardens Car Park, or proceed straight across towards Obelisk Pond and back to the Savill Building and Car Park.

AUTUMN COLOUR IN THE VALLEY GARDENS

THE DEER PARK and LONG WALK

HOW DO I GET THERE?

Public transport: FGW trains stop at Slough, then change trains for Windsor Central. SWT trains stop at Windsor Riverside, Datchet and Staines. Taxi service available from all stations to the Great Park. The White Bus service operates between Windsor (Guildhall), Queen Anne's Gate and the Village in the Great Park. The 71 bus service between Windsor (Guildhall) and Staines (Elmsleigh Centre) stops at Shaw Farm Gate, and it is a 200 yard walk to the Long Walk from this point. It is a 15 minute walk from Windsor Central Station to the Deer Park entrance at Double Gates, routing via High Street, Park Street, Cambridge Gate and along the Long Walk (crossing the A308).

By road: M25 Junction 13, then A308 (Slough, Windsor) then A332 (Ascot) to Picnic Area Car Park. You can also turn left off A308 (after Runnymede) onto the A328 (Englefield Green); at the top of the hill turn right, follow the signs for Cumberland Lodge, and park outside Bishopsgate, although, be warned, it can get very busy here. M4 junction 6, then A332 (Windsor), then A308 (Staines) then A332 (Ascot) to Picnic Area Car Park. You can also park at Ranger's Gate, and walk to the Deer Park via the Village. If you park in Windsor Town Centre, it is a 15 minute walk to the Double Gates on the Long Walk from here. M3 Junction 3, then A322 (Bracknell), turning right after 1.5 miles onto A332 Swinley Road, 2.5 miles to Ascot, then A332 to Windsor (at Ascot, do not follow Great Park/Smith's Lawn!), then A332 Windsor Town Centre to enter the Great Park at Forest Gate, parking at the Picnic Area Car Park 1.5 miles ahead. Alternatively, at M3 junction 2 join M25 (J12, for Heathrow) then exit M25 at junction 13 (Staines), following routes as above. Car Parking is free at the Picnic Area, Ranger's Gate and Bishopsgate.

FACILITIES: With the exception of the Car Parks, there are currently no organised facilities available. The nearest public toilets and shops are in Windsor or Englefield Green. You may prefer to start your walk from Savill Building, where all facilities are available. Facing the Savill Building, follow the tarmac road to the right. At the T-junction at Cumberland Gate, turn right towards Cow Pond, following the road straight ahead for 0.75 mile, and entering the Deer Park through the gate pictured on p78 adjacent to Bishopsgate and Royal Lodge Gates (also, see map p84).

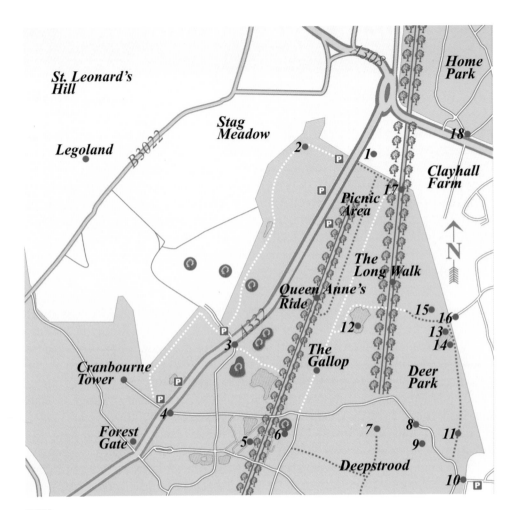

KEY:

1. Queen Anne's Gate
2. Cavalry Exercise Ground
3. Ranger's Gate
4. Cranbourne Gate
5. The Village
6. Watch Oak
7. Copper Horse
8. Stone Bridge
9. Spring Hill

10. Bishopsgate
11. Cooke's Hill
12. Prince of Wales Pond
13. Bears Rails Pond
14. Scout Camp
15. Wychemere
16. Bears Rails Gate
17. Double Gates
18. Shaw Farm Gate

P Parking

●●● Green dotted lines indicate grass paths

White dotted lines indicate gravel or dirt paths and tracks

🌳 Tree plantations (roundels and coverts)

The Gallop – rough horse riding track. See p109 for detailed map of the Village.

THE LONG WALK: viewed from just below the summit of Snow Hill and the Copper Horse, and looking towards Windsor Castle. As a 'grand entrance' to the ancient fortress over two miles distant, this must surely be one of the most magnificent and imposing approaches in all of Europe.

The subject of thousands of photos, postcards, video, television shots and individual memories, the view from the Copper Horse to a distant Windsor Castle at the far end of the Long Walk (pictured above) would probably rank as the most familiar and recognisable view of both the town of Windsor and the Great Park itself. The area of the Great Park that we are going to look at in this Section only extends down the Long Walk towards the Castle as far as the intersection with the A308 Albert Road, running between Windsor and Old Windsor. Northwards beyond this point we enter an area with restricted access, (the Home Park and Shaw Farm) excepting the Long Walk itself, which can be followed all the way up to Cambridge Gate, just short of the Castle. A left turn at the Gate will take you along Park Street and into the Town Centre, where you will be able to visit the Castle, as well as restaurants, pubs, shops, riverside walks and public gardens. Pay-and-display car parking and public toilets are also available across the Town.

As you can see from the information and directions on p67, you have a wide choice of starting points for this particular area. I would recommend that you start from the Picnic Area Car Park on the A332 (Ascot), or the small Car Park on the right immediately opposite Queen Anne's Gate itself. You can then take a shortcut through the wooden gate close to Queen Anne's Gate (photograph below) and follow the pathway across to the Double Gates and the Long Walk itself. This choice gives you free parking, and places you right in the Deer Park itself once you pass through the Double Gates towards the Copper Horse. The pathway which you will follow from the Car Park to the Double Gates is a remnant of the ancient public trackway between Clewer and Egham, and which also originally crossed the northern extent of Moat Park. Formerly a deer park in its own right, and with a large house located in the woodland to the west beyond Swan Pond, this expanse of open ground opposite the Picnic Area Car Park is known today as the Cavalry Exercise Ground.

QUEEN ANNE'S GATE: with the easy access to Double Gates and the Long Walk over to the right of the picture. Free parking and the quick access towards the heart of the Great Park make this a popular choice with visitors.

The Long Walk was the creation of Charles II, begun in 1680. Its total length is about 2.5 miles from the Castle to the Copper Horse, and it crosses the Great Park boundary at the Double Gates. Originally, the Long Walk did not terminate directly in front of the Castle as it does now, as the area between the Double Gates and the Castle was in the possession of a number of freeholders. It wasn't until the end of 1683 that the Long Walk was fully extended to its final length after the acquisition by the Crown of the private properties which stood in the way, although certain neighbouring landowners' rights of access to cross the Long Walk remained in place until the mid 1820s. The first tree planting scheme was a double row either side of the avenue, using a grand total of 1,652 English elms, the survivors of which eventually succumbed to a combination of old age and Dutch Elm Disease, and were finally felled in 1943/4. A gravel surface was added in 1710 on the order of Queen Anne, so as to allow horse-drawn carriages better access. Double Gates Lodge dates from the early 1680s, and the present Lodge on the same site dates from 1909.

DOUBLE GATES: the Long Walk is bisected between the Copper Horse and the Castle by the Double Gates and by the A308 Albert Road, which was introduced as part of the major road restructuring scheme devised in 1849 by Robert Tighe, who also co-wrote 'Annals of Windsor', a most concise and detailed history of the Town, in 1858.

The avenue was replanted with a mix of London plane and horse chestnut, and the idea was to see which species fared best, and remove the other. As it turned out, they both did well and were retained. There was a selective thinning of both species in 1979, although in recent years the chestnuts have fallen victim to a new disease known as Chestnut Leaf Miner, possibly exacerbated by the somewhat temperamental extremes of British weather. It is to be hoped that both species will prove strong enough to weather anything that Nature or Man may throw at them. The London planes, in particular, seem to thrive on neglect and poor conditions – one only has to look at the 'lungs of the Capital', the parks of Central London, with their abundance of mature giant planes, to see this for oneself.

VIEW TO THE COPPER HORSE: a herd of red deer quietly browse over the late Summer pasture of the Review Ground.

Turning right onto the Long Walk and passing through Double Gates places you in an area that was formerly part of the Lower Walk, one of the parks created to cater for the Royal passion for deerhunting. The stocks of both red and fallow deer were severely depleted during the English Civil War, with animals being culled not only by troops from both sides, but from the local populace as well. These were hard times, and anything, be it meat, fish or fowl, was 'fair game'. It was the same situation for the wooden fencing (pales) around the deer parks – the majority of it was taken away for fuel. The deer population were decimated for the duration of the Civil War, but were re-introduced fairly quickly following the Restoration of Charles II in 1660.

RED DEER: The red deer living within the deerpark enclosure are used to seeing people walking around. However, visitors should always be aware that these are wild animals, which can be unpredictable at all times, especially during the rutting season (Sept-Nov), and should be treated with great respect and caution.

RED DEER: this stag displays its autumn/winter coat, including the short neck mane, and a fine set of antlers, although not quite up to the standard which would be regarded as a 'trophy' set. The velvet coating of the antlers has been rubbed away, revealing the white bone at the tips. Stags shed their antlers each Spring, and you may possibly find one on your walk through the deer park.

The timid hinds outnumber the stags by a considerable ratio, and the more mature stags (with the largest antlers) will each have a considerable 'harem' of hinds during the mating season, known as the rut. Every Autumn, the males will lock antlers with each other in a battle for control of the females. The juvenile bucks may also attempt to challenge more senior males, but usually with little success! The roaring call of the males becomes a familiar sound across the Deer Park at this time of year.

RED DEER: two hinds keeping a wary eye on the photographer. Hinds are capable of producing young after their second Autumn. The gestation period is between 34 and 38 weeks and the hind will usually have a single calf (or fawn), although two are possible. The spotted calves will join the herd after only two weeks; are fully weaned after two months, and they will accompany their mothers for the next 10 months, until the mating season returns once again.

After the 1660s, the mixed herd of fallow and red deer remained a constant feature of the landscape. Animals were imported from afar as Scandinavia and Germany to top up the herds. There were also periods of severe local disturbances and heavy poaching activity, especially in the early 18th Century. The gamekeepers were kept constantly busy with trying to eradicate the poachers' activities across the Forest, but with limited success. However, the introduction of the 'Black Act' in 1723 certainly made an impression – it carried the death penalty for convicted poaching offenders!

In the Victorian era, under the control of Prince Albert, the Prince Consort, the red deer herd was able to multiply successfully, and create what became known as the 'Windsor Park' strain. Numbers of red deer from Windsor were sent to New Zealand and Australia in the 1860s to found a deer farming industry, which catered for deer hunting. From the first consignment of six animals, only three animals survived, yet they, and the small numbers which also followed, formed the basis of the deer hunting industry which flourished thereafter.

The fallow and red deer remained a permanent feature of the Great Park until 1941, when the fallow deer were culled, and the red deer herd was reduced by 50%. By 1950, when it was decided that the land was needed more for permanent farming than for deer pasture, the last of the herd were removed to Richmond Park and Badminton. The red deer you see today are the descendants of a small number of stags and hinds that were re-introduced from Balmoral to the Great Park in 1979, and which have successfully multiplied under the care and attention of the Estate Gamekeeping Department.

STAGS' HORNS:

A small group of stags laze away a late winter's afternoon on the grassy slopes to the south of the Prince of Wales Pond. Behind them, an ancient oak stands vigil, a monument to the passing of centuries, and also to the heritage of this place as a Royal deer park, and still the domain of England's once most prestigious and highly respected animal. The oak tree displays advanced die-back of its upper branches, and the bare, dead branches are referred to as 'staghorn' tops.

Walking up the Long Walk towards the Copper Horse, the open ground off to your right is known as the Review Ground. It was a popular spot in Victorian times for the attending of Military Reviews, sometimes involving hundreds of troops and cavalry parading, re-enacting charges etc, and was often succinctly used when entertaining diplomatic visitors as a British Empire 'show of strength'. Just beyond the Double Gates you will see a number of brick culverts marking the course of the little river known as the Battle Bourne crossing the Long Walk. Following the river off to your right, and further on via the river's left fork, and following this separate feeder stream, brings you to the Prince of Wales Pond, pictured below.

PRINCE OF WALES POND

The Battle Bourne can be traced right back through the Great Park to the woodland adjacent to Sandpit Gate. This little watercourse once linked a total of eight ponds. Two of the ponds at the top of the watercourse were breached and dried up, leaving a string of six connected ponds. The brook meanders roughly northeastwards through the Village and Deer Park before flowing into the River Thames at Old Windsor. If you choose to wander up the Long Walk, rather than across the Review Ground, about 1000 yards ahead you will reach a gravel path crossing the Long Walk. Turn right for the Prince of Wales Pond, or turn left towards a fenced wooded copse, entering the area of the ancient manor of Wychemere. Wychemere was added to the Great Park in 1359 by Edward III. It had a manor house of its own, which was subsequently used as a hunting lodge. The house had a moat around it, which still survives, hidden in a smaller (but out of bounds) wooded enclosure set back in the field to the left of the ride just beyond the first copse. Wychemere manor house was demolished in 1395.

BEARS RAILS: with the Scout Camp visible in the distance.

Bears Rails occupies an area once within the manor of Wychemere itself. It has been suggested that the name derives from a fenced enclosure designed to retain bears (there have been a number of wild animal enclosures located within the Park over the centuries), and the name was in use by 1607. Ahead on the left is a metal gateway into and out of the Deer Park, with a small group of workers' cottages and Bears Rails Gate beyond. There is no public car parking here, other than that provided for those attending organised events at the Scouts Camp which you can see off to the right, beyond Bears Rails Pond. Keep an eye out up in the trees for the flocks of beautifully coloured ring-necked parakeets. First recorded in SE London in 1969, they have bred very successfully and have now colonised the local area. Following the road around to the right towards the Scout Camp brings you to the start of a gravel track which leads off to the left. I would recommend that you carry on over to the right, avoiding the track, and walk along the edge of the Scout Camp fenceline heading away across the grass, alongside the area known as Old Windsor Wood, which was added to the Great Park in the 1730s.

There are a generous number of ancient oaks here, and the area is strangely reminiscent of how one would expect the ancient forest to have once looked. The grass track takes you uphill through open parkland and the profusion of ancient oaks until it rises quickly up to the crest of Cooke's Hill, close to Bishopsgate. At the top, the ride meets up with the tarmac road forming the route between Cranbourne Gate and Blacknest Gate. At this point, you are still within the fenced deer enclosure, about 2.5 miles away from the Car Park, and if you are feeling particularly energetic, you may choose to turn left and continue your walk out of the Deer Park via the exit at Bishopsgate and Royal Lodge Gates (pictured below) and walk onwards towards Smith's Lawn (see map p84).

EXIT FROM THE DEER PARK: with Royal Lodge Gates in the background.

Turning right and following the road for 400 yards towards the Copper Horse takes you past a short but majestic avenue of beech trees which once gave access to Royal Lodge; a colourful plantation of copper beech; down the curving Spring Hill between individual copses of oak, beech, chestnut and false acacia, offering an excellent view of the Castle over the forest canopy, crossing over the Stone Bridge (built in 1829), and finally up to the top of the Long Walk.

A VIEW TO WINDSOR FROM SPRING HILL: from this point, the copper beech plantation, with a plaque inscribed 'Queen Victoria 1866' is just behind you.

Upon reaching the Long Walk, you will see the Copper Horse at the top of Snow Hill to your left. Walk up the grass mound, turn around, and just take a moment to savour the panorama stretched out before you (if you have a pair of binoculars, be sure to take them along). Looking towards the Castle, and across the Thames Valley, the hills in the distance are the southern edges of the Chilterns. The town of Slough lies off to the left, and you will also be able to see the gothic spires and crenellations highlighting St George's Chapel within the Castle, with the Round Tower to its right. Further to the right, you can make out the spires of the churches in Old Windsor, Datchet and Wraysbury, after which is the shimmering Queen Mother Reservoir, with Langley beyond. Next, the towns of Egham and Staines, both partly obscured by the treeline, and lastly, Heathrow Airport, with its tall tower and the Terminal Five building, completes the view across the horizon. Turning your back to the Castle, you are now looking at the Copper Horse, King George IV's somewhat ironic memorial to his father, King George III.

THE COPPER HORSE: the iconic statue of Windsor Great Park. It was incorrectly rumoured that the sculptor, Westmacott, had killed himself when it was pointed out that he had omitted to affix stirrups to the statue. The 1977 Silver Jubilee celebrations were centred on this point, with the first of the chain of huge bonfires stretching across the country being built here, and lit by HM Queen Elizabeth II.

According to today's historians, theirs was not a happy father and son relationship, and especially so just before the King's 'madness' took a firm hold. Our knowledge of this is inclined to make us question why George IV ever bothered to have a statue of his father erected in the first place. The inscription adds further weight to the irony. "Georgio Tertio Patri Optimo Georgius Rex", which roughly translated reads "George the Third best of fathers King George (IV)".

The slightly inappropriately-named Copper Horse is the creation of Richard Westmacott. Work on the Horse began in London in 1824, using 25 tons of old brass cannons as the working material – and not pure copper. Due to the sheer size of the statue, it was cast in sections, prior to transportation to Windsor for reassembly. The Horse was ready to be moved by late 1828, but the base for the statue caused a separate and lengthy delay, due to a number of differing choices for the style of the base, and the material to be used. It was not until March 1830 that the Treasury eventually approved the expenditure on the final choice, and Sir Jeffry Wyattville was then appointed to oversee the construction of the pedestal, which was completed in the summer of 1831. The sections of the Copper Horse were then brought from London to Windsor, and during the move one leg section of the Horse was damaged, and needed to be re-cast.

The Copper Horse was finally erected on the new plinth in late October 1831, some 16 months after the death of George IV. The son of the "best of fathers" never actually got to see it for himself!

Take a walk around to the rear of the Copper Horse, crossing the riding track, and walk down between the two wooded areas either side of you. You are now looking downhill into an area known as Deepstrood. If you look to the left, in the near-distance you will see a group of buildings emerge from the treeline. To the right of the small church (the Royal Chapel), the white painted building that you can see is Royal Lodge, the former home of HM Queen Elizabeth, The Queen Mother. The origins of Royal Lodge stretch right back to at least 1662, although not in the guise in which you see it today. The building went through a series of changes, being known firstly as the Garden House; then the Dairy House; the Deputy Ranger's Lodge, during which time it was the home of Thomas Sandby, and finally, when the Prince Regent (later George IV) took control of it, the building was renamed Royal Lodge. As with all of George IV's projects, costs appeared to be no object, and a vast amount of money was lavished on this building between 1813 and 1830. No sooner had George IV died, than his successor, William IV, had the majority of the house pulled down and the materials recycled in other building projects within the Great Park and the Little (Home) Park.

Walking back into the Deer Park, you can now choose to complete the circuit by going back down the Long Walk to Double Gates and the Car Park, or, as a pleasant diversion (especially if it's dry underfoot) you can walk down from the Copper Horse to the road at the top of the Long Walk and turn left, exiting the Deer Park via a pedestrian access gate about 400 yards ahead. Follow the road straight ahead for another 200 yards until you reach the intersection with Queen Anne's Ride, next to the fenced copse known as Watch Oak. Turning right and walking down the Ride towards Windsor will take you directly back to the Picnic Area Car Park and Queen Anne's Gate.

DEEPSTROOD: looking North from Ox Pond: shrouded in a blanket of snow, here we can see a few of the fields which make up the area of Deepstrood, with the Copper Horse on the brow of the horizon. The area off to the right of the photograph was once the location of the 18th Century Sawyer's Yard and the Wheelwright's Workshop, (recorded by Paul Sandby) and the forerunners of today's Prince Consort's Workshops located in the Village, about 0.5 mile off to the west.

THE VILLAGE and MEZEL HILL

HOW DO I GET THERE?

Public transport: SWT train services to Windsor Riverside or Datchet, or FGW train services to Slough, changing for Windsor Central. Taxi services available to the Great Park from all stations (please note - taxis are not authorised to enter the Great Park, and will set down or pick up at main gated entrances only); the White Bus service operates to/from the Great Park, and stops at Windsor (Guildhall), Queen Anne's Gate, Rangers Gate, the Village Shop or Cranbourne Gate. For the athletic and physically fit, it is also possible to walk from Windsor to Queen Anne's Gate and thence along Queen Anne's Ride to the Village – approx 45 minutes (about 2.5 miles)

By road: M25 to Junction 13, then A308 (Windsor), then A332 to Ascot entering Great Park at Queen Anne's Gate. M3 to Junction 3 then A322 (Bracknell), turning right after 1.5 miles onto A332 Swinley Road, 2.5 miles to Ascot, then A332 to Windsor (at Ascot **do not follow** Great Park/Smith's Lawn!), then A332 Windsor Town Centre to enter the Great Park at Forest Gate. M4 to Junction 6, then A332 (Windsor), then A308 (Staines), then A332 (Ascot), entering the Great Park at Queen Anne's Gate. The most convenient car parking and pedestrian access for the Village is at Cranbourne Gate and Ranger's Gate, with small, free car parks opposite each Gate; Also, 2 small car parks close to Queen Anne's Gate Lodge, with a larger car parking area on the other side of the road (within the Picnic Area itself), all giving pedestrian access to Queen Anne's Ride, and thence a 1.5 mile walk to the Village (see map p109)

FACILITIES: With the exception of the Car Parks, there are currently no organised facilities available. The nearest public toilets are in Windsor itself, or if you are at the Cumberland Lodge end of the Park, you can walk to the Savill Building, where all public facilities are provided. There is a central Village Shop and Post Office, which you are welcome to use, subject to opening hours. As with the Picnic Area, please be advised that the local Byelaws do not permit the lighting of fires or barbecues.

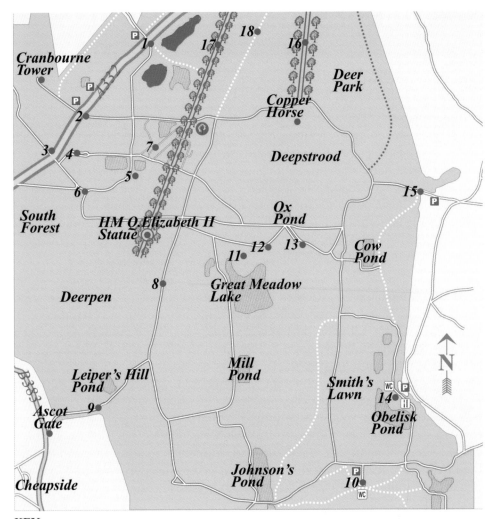

KEY:

1. Ranger's Gate
2. Cranbourne Gate
3. Forest Gate
4. Forest Lodge
5. York Club
6. Sandpit Gate
7. The Village
8. Dukes Lane
9. Prince Consort's Gate

[P] Parking
● ● ● Green dotted lines indicate grass paths
White dotted lines indicate gravel or dirt paths and tracks
See detailed map for the Village on page 109

10. Valley Gardens Car Park
11. Mezel Hill
12. Royal School
13. Cumberland Lodge
14. Savill Building and Garden
15. Bishopsgate
16. The Long Walk
17. Queen Anne's Ride
18. The Gallop

WC – Public Toilets
🔵 Watch Oak (roundel)

This is also a residential and working area, and so it is requested that visitors show respectful consideration when walking around, and to strictly observe any access restrictions or given instructions.

Although it is possible to access this location from any number of places around the perimeter of the Great Park, the easiest way to visit the Village, Mezel Hill and the other interesting outlying places within the area is to use the access points at Ranger's Gate and Cranbourne Gate on the A332 Windsor-Ascot main road. The walk around here can all be done on tarmac roads, and with only a couple of hills to contend with. There are many route variations available, and I suggest you browse this chapter and the maps on p84 and p109 before starting your walk; decide what you want to see, and the best way of getting there. A full circuit to see everything described in this section is approximately 6 miles, and dependent on your walking speed, could possibly take most of the day. Remember also that there are authorised cars and commercial vehicles using the roads, and therefore keeping a close eye on the children, and the dogs on a lead, are wise precautions.

RANGER'S GATE: with Ranger's Lodge beyond. The principal entrance to the Village.

CRANBOURNE GATE: also with pedestrian access to the Village from this point.

Starting from either Gate, enter the Park and follow the road for 400 yards to the crossroads. Coming in from Ranger's Gate, you will pass Ranger's Lodge on your right (photo p85), and entering via Cranbourne Gate you will see out to your right a large Georgian house known as Forest Lodge (photo p87). At the crossroads, you can choose to follow the route as described, or alternatively, study the maps as suggested, and make your own choice as to where you go from this point onwards.

At the crossroads, follow the sign for the York Club, which will give you a view of Forest Lodge uphill to your right, and the group of buildings and cottages comprising the Prince Consort's Workshops over to your left. Forest Lodge dates from c1772, although there had been a small cottage on the site previously. The house was designed by Thomas Sandby, and was originally known as Holly Grove. This miniature private estate, and the wedge shaped piece of land it sat on, became a problem during the 1750s for the Duke of Cumberland, as it neatly separated a direct access link between Cranbourne Lodge and Cumberland Lodge, the Duke's own two homes. The land widened out from a point at Ranger's Gate at the bottom of the hill, uphill to a line between today's Forest Gate Lodge and southeastwards to just short of Sandpit Gate. This necessitated the repositioning in 1797 of the main road between Ranger's Lodge and the

FOREST LODGE: the north face of the house, viewed from the road to Cranbourne Gate. This house also has a large walled garden, paddocks, ponds and many outbuildings. A cottage, first recorded in 1697, was built here within an encroachment (land used without consent) in Windsor Forest. The present house was built in 1772 for John Deacon, who also further enlarged the estate.

present site of Forest Gate Lodge (see map p109, and p121), thereby creating the road layout we have today. This awkward situation remained unresolved until 1829 when the Crown finally purchased the Holly Grove estate from the owners. The house has undergone a number of redevelopments, but retains the basic Sandby-designed core. Once used as the home for the Deputy Ranger of the Great Park, Forest Lodge is now a private residence. Following the road towards the York Club will take you to another crossroads, where you can turn left and walk around to the Village Shop situated just beyond the lower pond. The two ponds are the Isle of Wight Pond on your right, and the Shop Pond on your left. Both are fed by a watercourse (the Battle Bourne) dropping from the forest slopes up to the right behind Forest Lodge. These are ponds 3 and 4 in the chain of six of the existing ponds along the length of the Battle Bourne, the first two being inside the private grounds of Forest Lodge itself. Passing between the ponds brings you to the York Club on your left, and on your right, the Queen Elizabeth II Coronation Plantation of oak trees planted in 1953. The York Club (or York Hall) is the hub of the Village's social life. It has a thriving membership, with a good number of Sporting sections combined with excellent facilities, including bowls, cricket, golf and football. The Isle of Wight Pond, across the road from the York Club, is stocked with Rainbow Trout for the added enjoyment of the Fly Fishing Section membership.

THE ISLE OF WIGHT POND: the name 'Isle of Wight' first appeared on John Norden's maps drawn over 400 years ago. This is also the only pond in the Great Park to contain rainbow trout.

THE YORK CLUB: the social and sporting activity centre of Windsor Great Park.

The York Hall was built in 1945-7 by the Estate employees themselves, using the steel framework of one of the redundant Vickers-Armstrong factories which had been sited at Smith's Lawn during the War. The new building replaced an earlier wooden structure which had served as a Clubhouse, and which had stood outside Cumberland Lodge. The York Club was formally opened in July 1951 by King George VI and Queen Elizabeth, and this ceremony was also the occasion upon which the Savill Garden was formally named as such by the King. Walking past the York Club leads you to the Bowls Club on the left; continuing on up the hill with the golf course also on your left leads you to Sandpit Gate and the kennels.

Sandpit Gate is first mentioned in 1389, and has been recorded in paintings and sketches since the 1750s, including some drawings of the interior made at that time by Paul Sandby. George IV created a Royal zoo, or menagerie, situated here between 1824 and 1830, after which all the collected exotic wild birds and animals, including kangaroos, zebras, buffalo and llamas, were given to the newly-opened zoo at Regents Park by George's successor, King William IV.

SANDPIT GATE LODGE: once a busy thoroughfare on the old route through the Park between Staines, Egham and the West, the Gate is now quiet, save only for the barking of the dogs.

The house was revamped in the early 1800s to a design by James Wyatt, and the kennels were built in 1914-16 for the Royal hunting dogs. Today, the house is the residence of the Head Keeper of the Great Park. Follow the road around to the left of the house, and you can get a good view off to the right over the extensive area known as the Deerpen (not to be confused with the Deer Park)

Leaving Sandpit Gate and walking down the hill with the Deerpen to your right takes you to an intersection with Queen Anne's Ride. Looking to your left reveals the Castle, nearly 3 miles distant, and immediately to your right is the latest addition to the monuments of the Great Park, the equestrian themed statue of HM Queen Elizabeth II, beautifully sculpted by Philip Jackson in 2003.

THE HM QUEEN ELIZABETH II STATUE: shown here in late Winter sunshine, is located towards the southern extremity of Queen Anne's Ride. The lime trees set around the statue are the oldest survivors of the original planting, and are adorned with large clumps of mistletoe.

If you walk up to the monument, and look beyond, you can see that Queen Anne's Ride actually continues past this point into the Deerpen, terminating close to Prince Consort's Gate on Dukes Lane.

Queen Anne's Ride, or Queen's Walk as it was originally known, is first mentioned in 1708. Initially planted with elm and lime, it was principally designed to allow Queen Anne herself to indulge in her passion for hunting, albeit from the relative comfort of a horse-drawn carriage, or 'chaise'. Queen Anne was too large and unfit a woman to actively engage in following the Hunt from the saddle, and this was her solution to the problem. The length and direction of the Ride allowed for quick and direct access to the Forest, and to other deer hunting grounds beyond the Great Park boundary, such as Swinley Forest to the southwest. The original avenue of trees did not fare too well, and replanting was already under way in some places as early as 1813.

QUEEN ANNE'S RIDE: the view northwards from the HM Queen Elizabeth II statue. The Millstone statue, which celebrates the replanting of the Ride, can just be seen at the apex of the Ride. Windsor Castle is almost 3 miles distant from this point.

In 1993, a generous donation of 1000 oaks was received from the Association of High Sheriffs, and despite opposition from certain local quarters, the avenue was felled, and a full replanting scheme undertaken and completed. The newly planted trees have established very well, and should continue to flourish and eventually restore the Ride to its original and majestic splendour.

From the Statue, walk back out onto the road, turn right and continue until you reach the forked junction. Take the right hand fork and then turn right at the intersection 50 yards ahead onto Dukes Lane, a pleasant walk going south from this point for about one mile. About 800 yards along the Lane, just after a wooded copse, is a turning to the left leading to Manor Hill, which is out of bounds. This is the spot on Dukes Lane known appropriately as the 'Change' where the Royal Family and their guests exchange cars for horse-drawn open carriages during Ascot Week, before proceeding to the Racecourse via Ascot Gate.

THE 'CHANGE' at DUKES LANE: HM Queen Elizabeth II's open carriage, drawn by four grey horses and preceded by two outriders, leads the 2009 Ladies' Day carriage procession towards Ascot Gate and onwards to the Racecourse. (photograph © A.J.O'Connell, 2009)

Access to this point during Race Week is strictly controlled, and a limited number of tickets are available on request from the Estate Office for each Race Day. Be quick, though – they get snapped up straight away! From the Change, continue along Dukes Lane, and you will pass Leiper's Hill Pond on the right, (set inside the Deerpen perimeter fence) just before leaving the Park at Prince Consort's Gate. The road continues beyond this point down to Ascot Gate, and provides access into Cheapside village some 300 yards further along. The woodland off to the right, behind the cottages, is the southernmost tip of South Forest.

PRINCE CONSORT'S GATE: with the Deerpen off to the right, and South Forest beyond.

Retrace your walk back along Dukes Lane, with the Deerpen and its dense game coverts stretching out on the left, and also passing the fields on the right known (in sequence) as Rosy Bottom, Red Cross, Slann's Pen, and just after the wooded copse, Holly Bush. In this particular area keep your camera and binoculars handy, as there is always a good chance of seeing a wild Roe deer, or maybe a little Muntjac deer, and even a 'Mad March Hare'. It is also a great place to spot birds of prey, including Red Kites and Buzzards. Your chances of seeing these creatures are greatly increased if you are in the area either early in the day, or during the early evening.

Back at the crossroads by the cottages, turn first right, and follow this road gently downhill, passing the next right turn to Great Meadow Pond, Norfolk Farm, Mill Pond and Johnson's Pond (all out of bounds), and followed by the Works Depot just ahead on your right. The row of quaint cottages just beyond the Depot (also on your right) were built in 1936, and are nowadays mainly occupied by retired Estate workers. This area is known as Mezel Hill, and the line of ancient oaks on the roadside is the 'ghost' of the original main route through the Great Park between Egham and Sandpit Gate, first recorded in the 1650s, which was also joined at the brow of the hill that you are currently walking up to the ancient track that once led into Deepstrood, over Snow Hill, and onwards to Windsor and the Castle.

MEZEL HILL COTTAGES: with the ancient oaks lining the old main road to Sandpit Gate.

Mezel Hill is the wooded rise which you can see behind the row of cottages; it was formally planted in the late 1740s with a rectangle of trees with intersecting avenues, as part of the 'improvements' made by the Duke of Cumberland. Apparently, the massive workforce required for the task comprised mainly of an army of soldiers who had previously served under Cumberland until the end of the hostilities in Scotland. They emptied the spoil from the works associated with the construction of Great Meadow Lake onto an existing rise in the ground, thereby artificially heightening the hill. The same method of spoil disposal was utilised on the far side of the new Lake at the proposed site of the Doric temple, upon what is now known as Temple Field.

Just after the cottages, you will come to Park Farm Cottage and the Royal School. Queen Victoria and Prince Albert, the Prince Consort, founded the School in 1845 in order to provide education for the Great Park children who, according to Sir James Kay Shuttleworth, Queen Victoria's advisor on education, had been raised in a "half-wild manner"!

THE ROYAL SCHOOL: first opened in 1845, the School is highly regarded by the local and wider community. Construction of a new School Hall within the grounds of the old Vinery has recently been completed. The majority of the Great Park children have taken their first steps in Education within this building.

Queen Victoria took an active personal interest in the School right up to her death in 1901. This gave the School a private 'under Royal patronage' status, and kept it outside of the control and influence of the State Schools system until after 1901. The School, however, does retain a unique 'Crown Aided' status to the present day. As a First School, the majority of the younger children of the Estate workers attend here before moving on to other schools in the district, although places are available each year to children living outside the Great Park.

On passing the School, you will see a high red brick wall with a gated entrance on the right. This is the Vinery, part of the original Kitchen Gardens of Cumberland Lodge, and was formerly the site of a greenhouse containing an enormous Black Hamburg vine, planted in 1815. By 1846, it was capable of producing in excess of 2000 bunches of table grapes every season, and was only finally removed as part of the War Effort in 1942, when the greenhouse was subsequently used for growing tomatoes.

Part of THE KITCHEN GARDENS, viewed through the fallen wall: most of the previous incumbents of Cumberland Lodge were keen on developing and improving this garden, especially in the mid-18th Century, when many new and 'exotic' fruit trees were added. There were once 3 small ponds located off to the top right in the garden, but now infilled.

Just up from the entrance to the Vinery, part of the wall of the Kitchen Garden collapsed in 2008 and allowed a view across the Vinery's grounds to Great Meadow Pond. The area within had not been used for vegetable and fruit production for many years, and had subsequently been heavily planted with Norway spruce trees. A huge amount of brushwood was cut and bundled from the Vinery in 1977, to be used as fuel for HM The Queen's Silver Jubilee Bonfire, which was built close to the Copper Horse. With the spruce trees now conveniently removed, it is possible to see the Kitchen Gardens laid bare once again. The long building visible to the far right of the Garden is the rear facade of a range of buildings now converted into private dwellings. This is part of the the Cumberland Lodge Mews and cottages complex, which comprises of two refurbished and converted buildings on opposite sides of a cobbled courtyard.

CHAPLAIN'S LODGE: home of HM The Queen's Canon of the Royal Lodge and Chapel. The house stands on the approximate site of a 17th Century 'Banquiting House', of which no visible evidence remains. Old maps also show an icehouse sited somewhere on the north face of the hillside, towards Ox Pond, but its actual location remains undiscovered.

At the top of the hill is a junction consisting of four roads including the road you have just walked up, a driveway into Chaplain's Lodge, and a gravel trackway. As before, you have a number of choices as to where to go from here, and so I suggest you have a look at the map on p84 before proceeding. Stand on the grass island, with Chaplain's Lodge off to your left.

Turning left out onto the main road leads you back downhill via a fork in the road to either Dukes Lanes (left fork), or to the centre of the Village (right fork). The trackway straight ahead of you passes downhill alongside the fence line of Royal Lodge, with Ox Pond on the left at the bottom of the slope. This track continues on into Deepstrood, and leads up to the back of Snow Hill and the Copper Horse (see p81-82). It is also a remnant of the original route between Windsor Castle and Sandpit Gate, along part of which you have just walked up and continued along the routeway which predated the Long Walk, through what was then known as the Lower and Paddock Walks.

Turning right out onto the main road takes you towards Bishopsgate (left at T-junction 400 yards ahead).the two parallel roads behind and to your right take you into Cumberland Lodge; the left one to the Lodge itself, and the right one to the Mews Courtyard and Cottages (which is private). I suggest that you take the left of the two, and proceed along the newly planted avenue of limes, known as the Queen Mother's Avenue. Over to your right you can now get but a brief glimpse of Great Meadow Pond (due to the Pond's location in a low-lying, out of bounds area).

GREAT MEADOW POND: portrayed in the 'Watercolour of Windsor Great Park', by Thomas Sandby c1752. Ranger's (Cumberland) Lodge is on the centre horizon, with Mezel Hill to the left. Picture © Anglesey Abbey, The Fairhaven Collection, (The National Trust).

Great Meadow Pond was the first of the Duke of Cumberland's aquatic projects within the Great Park. Work began c1747 using the existing Mistle Pond as a starting point, with the construction of a pondhead on the outflow of its feeder stream. The flooding of the area above the pondhead created the new 'Great Lake', as it was first known. Designed to be a prominent focal point from Ranger's (later Cumberland) Lodge, the Lake had the usual accoutrements expected with high class landscape design at this time.

These included a stone Doric temple on the South shore, an ornate Chinese bridge, a boat house, and the obligatory sailing vessels stationed on the water. The surrounding landscape contained a number of mature trees and new plantings, but was far more 'open plan' in form than it is today, with wide grassy spaces, including a grass 'riding' upon which you could walk right around the Lake, combined with extensive views of the Lodge and the newly created panorama available from all sides.

The outflow of the Great Lake flowed southwards towards the Cawseway Ponds, and from 1795 it powered a corn mill, sited just below the Mill Pond in Norfolk Farm. The Cawseway Ponds were joined together to create a single piece of water known today as Johnson's Pond, the outflow from which flows onwards into the area which was to become Cumberland's masterpiece - Virginia Water.

GREAT MEADOW POND: with the Lodge just visible on the skyline in the centre of the photograph. This lake was the first of the great water features created in the 18th Century. This photograph was taken from the shore of the lake at the central vantage point framed between the foreground trees in Thomas Sandby's 1752 painting, shown on p98.

To return to the directions for the Queen Mother's Avenue on p98, continue walking along the Avenue towards Cumberland Lodge. Remaining outside of the Lodge Car Park, turn left onto the track that veers around the garden perimeter fence towards the tennis court, and follow the path out onto the Limetree Avenue. Looking to your right, you can now see the main entrance and front view of Cumberland Lodge.

LIMETREE AVENUE, CUMBERLAND LODGE: avenues such as this one were a fashionable addition to the landscape from the late 17th Century onwards. The Avenue is the creation of Hans Willem Bentinck, 1st Earl of Portland, the close friend and confidante of HM King William III. Bentinck was made Ranger of the Great Park in 1697, and lived at Cumberland Lodge until he fell out of favour with the King in 1702. He was very interested in gardening, and went to France (as Ambassador) in late 1697. Returning in the summer of 1698, Bentinck, influenced by both French and Dutch garden influences, had the Avenue laid out and planted. Over 300 years later it stands today (albeit with a few gaps) as a fitting memorial to him.

Cumberland Lodge has a fascinating history, and for those with a deeper interest in such things, I would recommend purchasing a copy of Helen Hudson's book about the Lodge (see Bibliography p139). The house dates from the early 1650s, just after the end of the English Civil War. Following the execution of Charles I in 1649, many Parliamentarian Army soldiers chose to accept parcels of land in lieu of owed wages, which were then bought and sold between them. One such officer, Captain John Byfield, thereby acquired 640 acres of formerly Royal Parkland upon which he built Byfield House, here on this site. John died soon after, but his widow married a lawyer, John Barry, who had children of his own, and the extended family continued to reside in the house.

All was fine until the Restoration of King Charles II in 1660, whereupon the new King wanted all his father's former lands returned. This usually included any buildings that now stood on land previously held by King Charles I. After a period of time possibly spent living in Groom's House the will of the King could no longer be ignored, and the Barrys were finally ousted by 1670. The house and land returned to Royal ownership and control, with use of the Lodge granted by Royal Warrant, initially to Sir Edward Nicholas, the Ranger originally appointed by King Charles I, but thrown out of office by the Parliamentarians.

The house has witnessed a steady stream of Crown-appointed tenants since that time. Some of them are very famous in the realms of English history; some are less well known, but had a major influence over this area in which they lived. After Sir Edward Nicholas died in 1669, and once the Great Park was wholly 'restored' to a deer park , the next tenant was Baptist May, a close friend of the King. Probably its most famous and influential incumbents have been John Churchill, the victor at the Battle of Blenheim, and his wife, Sarah (the Duke and Duchess of Marlborough) who lived here between 1702 and 1744 (the Duke dying here in 1722, and the 'redoubtable' Sarah at Marlborough House, London in 1744). They were followed shortly after by William Augustus, Duke of Cumberland, who was appointed Ranger in 1746, and lived here until his death in 1765.

After 1671, the house was referred to as either Ranger's Lodge, Windsor Lodge or the Great Lodge, only becoming known as Cumberland Lodge at the end of the residencies of the two successive Dukes of Cumberland between 1746 and 1790.

THE GREAT LODGE, EAST FRONT: Thomas Sandby, 1754. (RL 14627)
The Lodge was (and remains) the largest building within the Great Park. At the time of this drawing the Duke of Cumberland created a menagerie here, with wild exotic animals in abundance, some of which are depicted in the picture (the collection even included lions and tigers). There was, however, one particularly unfortunate incident involving the death of a local child, who died after being attacked by one of the Duke's captive tigers.
The Royal Collection © 2010, Her Majesty Queen Elizabeth II.

The first Duke of Cumberland was passionate about the racing and breeding of racehorses, and duly set up a stables and stud complex split between the Great Lodge and Cranbourne Lodge, some two miles away to the West. The Mews (the long building on the right of the Queen Mother's Avenue) was the original base of operations. The Duke began by effectively doubling in size the available stabling at the Lodge, with the enlargement of the original range of stables under the direction of Henry Flitcroft. The completed layout contained stabling for 50 horses, coach-houses, accommodation for the grooms, a slaughterhouse, brewery and liquor store. The clock tower on top of Flitcroft's' extended building (the present-day Conference and Guest area of the Mews) is original, made by J.Davis, a Windsor clockmaker, and dates from 1750.

CUMBERLAND LODGE: the main entrance is located under the elongated bay window. The building has been continually renovated and extended over the years, and now bears little resemblance to the original c1652 house. However, if you look closely at the picture above, and compare it with Sandby's painting on p102, you can see the original building is included the left-hand portion of today's Lodge, albeit with a different roofline. Counting across the windows (5 left, large bay window and entrance, 5 right) reveals the extent and 'blueprint' of the original Byfield House.

In November 1869, a serious fire destroyed the northern range of the main building, which had been added to the original house by William Augustus, Duke of Cumberland. The far right-hand block of the building (above) is the rebuilt wing. Further works have included the removal of ivy which once covered much of the building, and the repointing of all exterior brickwork across the front of the house.

The residence attached to the end of the Mews nearest to the Lodge itself is known as Groom's House (p104), and was until recently the home of the Principal of Cumberland Lodge. The Mews is now used as a conference centre, with guest lodgings above. Use of the Lodge was granted to Amy Buller and the Foundation of St Catherine's in 1947. Amy's experiences in Germany between the two world wars inspired her to write a book, 'Darkness over Germany' in 1944, and to conceive the idea of founding a place for students and professionals from around the world to meet and discuss a multitude of ethical, moral, social and spiritual subjects, but all with an additional underlying theme of the retention and involvement of basic Christian principles.

It is a subject of local lore and superstition that the Lodge, Groom's House (right) and one of the rooms in the Mews are subjected to active and continuous hauntings, and there are reports, recollections and stories reputedly made by individuals who could be considered to be very reliable and authentic witnesses indeed!

GROOM'S HOUSE: dating from c1655.

THE MEWS: built by Henry Flitcroft for the Duke of Cumberland c1747, with the original 1704 stable block created by the Duke of Marlborough incorporated within. The older portion of the building is situated to the left of the main entrance, extending across to Groom's House. Examples of original stable boys' graffiti can still be seen scored into the brickwork. In the early 1900s Dr.W.G.Grace played cricket out on the pitch which was sited on the open ground facing the building, and in the 1940s, the forerunner of the York Club stood just to the right of the Mews.

Turning away from the main entrance, and walking straight down Limetree Avenue (ignoring the left fork 75 yards ahead) leads you to an intersection with the road running between Cranbourne Gate and Blacknest Gate (see map p84).

The Avenue continues on the other side, but the lime trees have been replaced by red oaks. At the end of this Avenue is an opening allowing access to Cow Pond, an ornamental lake formally created from an existing pond in the early 1700s. Cow Pond holds an abundance of small carp, plus a few goldfish, all of which will avidly feed on any pieces of bread that manage to avoid the attentions of the resident duck population. The display of water lilies is also worth viewing, with a good number of varieties and colours on show throughout the Summer.

COW POND: an ornamental early 18th Century lake located at the end of Limetree Avenue, and, in high Summer, a pleasant spot to take a short break on your walk.

At the time of writing, work is underway to recreate a pathway which once existed right around the Pond. The Royal Landscape team will achieve this by the removal of the invasive rhododendrons, cutting back the alders, plus the bridging of a wet, boggy area at one end of the Pond. When completed, this should restore the bankside access back to how it once was. Over in the far right hand corner, the lakeside path joins up with the gravelled Rhododendron Ride, allowing for a pleasant walk to Bishopsgate (turn left) or to the Savill Building (turn right).

Returning along the Red Oak Avenue to the road, to your left you can see a group of Estate workers' cottages lining the road, and about 200 yards beyond, the entrance to Smith's Lawn at Cumberland Gate. Turning right onto the road and continuing straight ahead will lead you past the King George VI Coronation Plantation of oaks (planted in 1937) on your right, passing the left turning for the Village Shop and the Royal School, and up to a right hand bend in the road with a horse track crossing it at this point. Look back towards Cumberland Lodge; you are now standing where a majestic double-row avenue of trees once formed the approach to Cumberland Lodge, connecting it to Bishopsgate. Walking on, you arrive at a crossroads, where turning right will lead you to the Park entrance/exit at Bishopsgate. The gatehouse dates from 1902, and the Rhododendron Ride to the Savill Building begins through a small gateway just off to the side of the house. Looking to your left, you will see the double-gated entrance to Royal Lodge.

BISHOPSGATE: the exit from the Great Park to Englefield Green, Egham and Staines. An access gate onto Rhododendron Ride is located to the right of this photograph.

ROYAL LODGE GATES: with Estate workers' homes on either side within the fenced boundary. The houses in the picture are the result of an architectural restyle and rebuild dating from 1949, after one of the original houses built in late 1940 was destroyed by a direct hit from a German bomb just after completion.

Straight ahead of you is the entrance to the Deer Park, and you can now choose to continue your walk through here, passing the Long Walk and the Copper Horse on your way to the Village, or you can retrace your steps back towards Cumberland Lodge, following the sign at the next right turn for the Royal School, and back to the grass island by Chaplain's Lodge (see p97). However, in order to see as much as possible, I would recommend that you continue into the Deer Park, and follow the road for about 1 mile to the pedestrian exit adjacent to The Gallop (photo p110) at the far side. Details about what you will see en-route through the Deer Park can be found on p78-82, and also on the map on p68.

THE VILLAGE

It often comes as a great surprise to visitors to find an entire community secreted away within the boundaries of Windsor Great Park. Many local people are also completely unaware of what lies within much of the Great Park, and would find much to savour and enjoy if they would only take the time to grab a map or a guidebook and have a good walk around – after all, its right on the doorstep, and the vast majority of it is free to enter!

The Village, as an area of Great Park industry, has a history dating back to the 1830s, when the woodyard and carpenter's yard formerly sited in Deepstrood (see p82) were relocated to the site of today's Prince Consort's Workshops. The earliest houses date from 1858, and the area has since developed into a close-knit community of both specialist and multi-skilled workers and their families.

The 'communal hub' is shared equally between the Village Shop (p111-112) and the York Club (p87-88), and in an age where many facets of traditional Village life have now passed into memory, it is refreshing to know that in a few places such traditions live on. In the suburban jungle which I call 'home', I cannot name more than five families in the long road where I now live, but I guarantee that in this Village, just about everyone knows everybody else! Just walking around the Village and the Great Park renders it self-explanatory to visitors as to why so many individuals and families see no need to ever move beyond the Park boundaries. It is simply beautiful here, and compared to modern day urban and City life, it could well be classed as 'idyllic'. From my own long and personal relationship with the Great Park, I would certainly vouch for that.

If you began your visit at either Ranger's Gate, Cranbourne Gate or the Picnic Area and followed the guide as described on p83-89 you will have already touched the fringes of the Village. If you are now ready to have a closer look at the area, I would recommend that the you take a few moments to carefully peruse the map on p109 before starting your walk. Once again, please take care to remember that when walking around, this is both a residential and working area, and it is politely requested that all visitors show respectful consideration to those for whom this area is 'Home', and to strictly observe any access restrictions or given instructions.

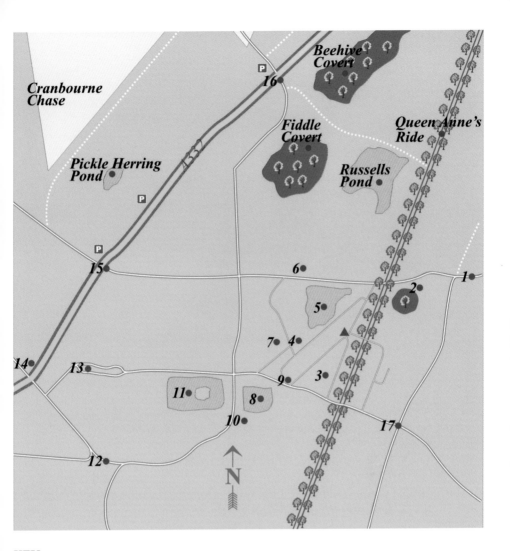

KEY:

1. Exit from Deer Park
2. Watch Oak
3. Richardson's Lawn
4. Prince Consort's Workshops
5. Prince Consort's Pond
6. Russell's Field Farm
7. Estate Office
8. Shop Pond
9. Village Shop

10. York Club
11. Isle of Wight Pond
12. Sandpit Gate
13. Forest Lodge
14. Forest Gate
15. Cranbourne Gate
16. Ranger's Gate
17. Timber Lodge

P Parking

▲ - Public Telephone

White dotted lines indicate gravel paths or tracks

WINDSOR CASTLE and the DEER PARK, from THE GALLOP: a beautiful viewpoint for the Town and Castle, seen on a hot, late Summer's day. The dense shade afforded by the ancient oaks hides groups of red deer, seeking some slight relief from the heat. The gravelled track is called 'The Gallop', and will take you back towards Double Gates and the Long Walk. You can access The Gallop at this point in the photograph at location no.1 indicated on the map on p109.

At this point, if you have followed the guide from p107 and walked through the Deer Park via the Long Walk and Copper Horse, you will now be exiting the Deer Park on the Village side. You will see a fork in the road, and the track known as The Gallop starting just inside the Deer Park to your right. Look at location No.1 on the Village map on p109 and choose where you want to go next. Turning left and going over the crossroads at Timber Lodge (400 yards ahead) takes you back to the junction for Dukes Lane, Mezel Hill and Sandpit Gate (p93). However, I would suggest that you continue straight ahead for 200 yards, passing a fenced wooded copse on your left (Watch Oak), just after which the road bisects Queen Anne's Ride. At this point, again you have a number of options. If you have suitable footwear, or if it is dry underfoot, you may wish to turn left and wander along Queen Anne's Ride, either to see the Millstone (100 yards) or the HM Queen Elizabeth II Statue (0.75 mile), or maybe turn right and enjoy an alternative green route back to Ranger's Gate via Russell's Pond (see map p109, and p114).

Rather than guide you around this part of your walk, here's a summary of the places you will see in the immediate area, all of which are identified on the Village map.

I shall start this part of the guide at the most well-known location within the Village - The Windsor Great Park Post Office and General Store (to give it its full, correct name). Affectionately known as the Village Shop, it is located adjacent to Richardson's Lawn at the heart of the Village, with the York Club located just opposite.

THE WINDSOR GREAT PARK POST OFFICE and GENERAL STORE

Although Windsor's supermarkets form the backbone of today's shopping options, "the Shop" still has an essential role to play. It offers a wide range of goods, has a daily delivery of fresh bread and rolls, and has that most valuable of commodities, a Post Office.

With only a limited public transport service available, the Village Shop can often prove to be a lifeline, especially for the older residents. Visitors to the Shop will be warmly welcomed by the Proprietors, who offer a wide choice of refreshing cold drinks, ice-cream, traditional and herbal teas, coffee or hot chocolate, as well as freshly made sandwiches, scones and cakes, all of which you can enjoy whilst sitting out in the Tea Garden if you so wish. Please don't be tempted, however, to feed the swans which regularly wander over from the Shop Pond nearby – they can inflict a nasty nip if you are not careful, especially on small hands. If you would like to feed the swans, take some bread over to the Pond and throw it onto the water.

Richardson's Lawn is the grass triangle adjacent to the Village Shop, with houses around two edges and with the oldest homes dating from 1905. Most of the homes, however, were built during 1948, and those constructed over on the far side of Queen Anne's Ride (running behind the Lawn) are referred to as being located in the 'New Village', and date from both 1954 and 1965.

RICHARDSON'S LAWN: just in case of need, the public telephone is located at the far end of the road shown on the left of this photograph.

The 'business end' of the Village is centred on the Prince Consort's Workshops complex. Following expansion of the early Woodyard in the 1850s, the area was renamed Prince Consort's Workshops after Prince Albert's death in 1861. The older buildings date from 1858-62. Wheeler's Lodge, a large detached cottage on the opposite side of the complex, was added in 1890, and became the centre of operations. A fire in 1906 destroyed some of the workshops, (and many Estate records with it) and was rebuilt with new store sheds, which are in use today.

WHEELER'S YARD: renamed Prince Consort's Workshops in 1861, this is the original layout as depicted in 1858 by Samuel Sanders Teulon. The building just above the left corner of the picture was destroyed by fire in 1906. The double gabled cottage centre left of picture is visible today at the entrance to the Workshops close to the Shop Pond.

The old 'Tyre Shed' was demolished to make way for the new Estate Office, which opened in 1975 and is located to the right of the double gabled cottage indicated in the picture above. Please be advised that the Workshops and Office complex is out of bounds to all visitors, unless you are specifically here on Estate business or in an emergency.

Nestled between the Workshops and Richardson's Lawn is the Prince Consort's Pond, sometimes referred to as the Reading Road Pond, which is pond 5 in the chain of six along the Battle Bourne. There is a large head of wildfowl resident here, along with some wild carp, all of which will eagerly come close to the bank for a free lunch - if you have something to offer them, that is!

RUSSELL'S FIELD FARM: a busy working farmyard environment, especially during Harvest, with a large number of grain and grass storage facilities located within.

Across from the Workshops is Russell's Field Farm (above), and to its left, the site of the old sawmill, which closed in 1984, with the work being transferred to a second Estate sawmill located in Swinley Forest, close to Ascot.

From the Farm it is but a short walk back to either Cranbourne Gate or Ranger's Gate. You also have the option of the grass route along Queen Anne's Ride, (see map p109) turning left past Russell's Pond (no.6 in the chain of six ponds) and walking uphill on a gravel track between Fiddle and Beehive coverts, and finally exiting alongside Ranger's Gate.

CRANBOURNE CHASE & THE PICNIC AREA

HOW DO I GET THERE?

Public transport: SWT train services to Windsor Riverside, or FGW train services to Slough, changing for Windsor Central. Taxi services available from all stations to the Great Park (please note - taxis are not authorised to enter the Great Park, and will set down or pick up at main gated entrances only); the White Bus service operates to/from the Great Park, and will stop at Windsor (Guildhall), Queen Anne's Gate, Ranger's Gate or Cranbourne Gate. For the more athletic, it is also possible to walk from Windsor Central Station to Queen Anne's Gate and the entrance to the Great Park at the Picnic Area, routing via High Street, Sheet Street and Kings Road (which becomes the A332 (Ascot) at the roundabout next to the Long Walk), and takes approximately 30 minutes (about 1.5 miles).

By road: M25 to Junction 13, then A308 (Windsor), then A332 to Ascot entering Great Park at Queen Anne's Gate. M3 to Junction 3 then A322 (Bracknell), turning right after 1.5 miles onto A332 Swinley Road, 2.5 miles to Ascot, then A332 to Windsor (at Ascot do not follow Great Park/Smith's Lawn!), then A332 Windsor Town Centre to enter the Great Park at Forest Gate. M4 to Junction 6, then A332 (Windsor), then A308 (Staines), then A332 (Ascot), entering the Great Park at Queen Anne's Gate. Car parking for Cranbourne is free, with 3 small car parks on the hill between Ranger's Gate and Cranbourne Gate; 2 small car parks adjacent to the Aeromodelling Club grass strip and Queen Anne's Gate, with a large car parking area opposite within the Picnic Area, close to the Deer Park and the Long Walk.

FACILITIES: With the exception of the Car Parks, there are currently no organised facilities available. The nearest public toilets and shops are in Windsor itself. The Picnic Area is self-catering, so remember to bring your own lunch and drinks! (Be advised that, as with the rest of the Great Park and Forests, the local Byelaws do not permit the lighting of fires or barbecues).

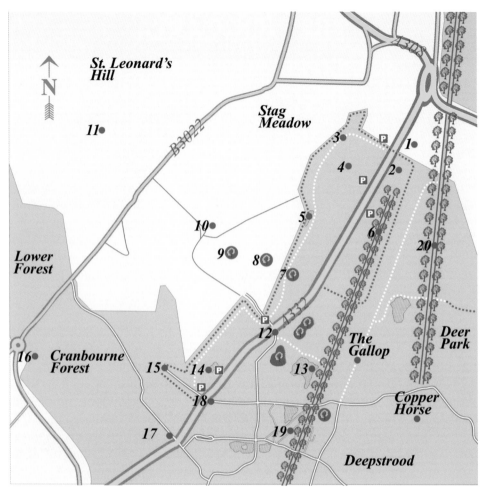

KEY:

1. Queen Anne's Gate
2. Picnic Area
3. Queen Mary's Plantation
4. Cavalry Exercise Ground
5. Swan Pond
6. Queen Anne's Ride
7. Brookers Corner
8. Star Clump
9. Bromley Hill
10. Flemish Farm
11. Legoland
12. Ranger's Gate
13. Russell's Pond
14. Pickle Herring Pond
15. Cranbourne Tower
16. Site of Bay Ponds
17. Forest Gate
18. Cranbourne Gate
19. The Village
20. The Long Walk

P Parking

● ● ● Green dotted line indicates Boundary of Picnic Area and public area of Cranbourne Chase
White dotted line indicates gravel, grass or dirt paths or tracks

● Tree plantations (roundels and coverts)
The Gallop – rough horse riding track

Assuming you are visiting for the whole day, I suggest you park your car in the signposted Picnic Area near to Queen Anne's Gate. The fencing for the Deer Park forms one edge of the Picnic Area, with the Long Walk visible further in. You also have the wide expanse of Queen Anne's Ride, laid out in 1708, on your side of the fence starting from here, heading south right into the heart of the Great Park.

QUEEN ANNE'S GATE: the A332 entrance to the Great Park nearest to Windsor.

It is almost 2 miles to the statue that you can just see on the horizon, but makes for an invigorating walk on a clear sunny day. A walk along Queen Anne's Ride will take you past Russell's Pond (1 mile on your right), through the middle of the Village (1.5 miles) passing the Millstone on the way, and the final uphill leg leads you up to the new statue of HM Queen Elizabeth II.

FOREST GATE: the A332 entrance to the Great Park nearest to Ascot.

Queen Anne's Ride itself continues on beyond the statue into an area known as the Deerpen (not to be confused with the Deer Park), but this area is restricted, and off limits to the public. Queen Anne's Ride is covered in more detail on p90-92.

From the Picnic Area, and looking across the (sometimes very busy) A332 main road, you will see the large open expanse of ground known in olden times as Moat Park; today, it is known locally as the Cavalry Exercise Ground. This area of the Great Park is more suited to those who wish to partake in dog walking and biking activities, as there is not much in the way of 'items of interest' to view, (as you would find at Virginia Water, for instance) with the exception of Cranbourne Tower and the ancient oaks. Over here you will find the local

Aeromodelling Club's grass strip, which is normally in use by Club members on most fair weather days. The kite flyers also frequent this area, and if you are into aircraft spotting, the final approach paths into Heathrow Airport are directly overhead at this point when the wind is from the east; the aircraft are only 1500 feet high as they fly over. Moat Park is predominately rough pasture, and there are a number of well-worn grass pathways criss-crossing the area. Beginning from the car park on the opposite side of the road to Queen Anne's Gate Lodge, the path tracks northwest next to a line of private residences towards a belt of woodland known as Queen Mary's Plantation.

The River Bourne (also known as the Maple Bourne) flows behind the trees, and the scant remains of the old moat and island, upon which the Duke of Cumberland built his Moat Island Cottage (pictured below), are located here next to a dog-leg in the river's course. The Cottage was rebuilt as two dwellings in 1793, and eventually demolished in 1896. There is a purpose-built track across the open ground from the front of Queen Mary's Plantation that will take you all the way to the Car Park opposite Ranger's Gate further along the A332.

MOAT ISLAND COTTAGE: F.Vivares after T.Sandby c1754. (RCIN 500180)
Another of Duke William Augustus' creations; sometimes used by the Duke as a tea room, but in a different style to the one located on China Island at Virginia Water. The course of the Maple Bourne was altered to form the moated island upon which the cottage stands, and the outfall and bridge can be seen in the right hand corner of the picture.
The Royal Collection © 2010, Her Majesty Queen Elizabeth II.

On the way across, you will pass Swan Pond (below), and as the ground rises uphill, you will enter a grove of oaks on a point known as Brookers Corner. The two large clumps of trees standing in the field to your right are Bromley Hill and Star Clump (the nearer one). The stream at the bottom of the valley here marks the extent of the public access – the fields and Clumps are off limits.

SWAN POND: a small and silty pond which receives its water from the Maple Bourne, before outflowing towards the site of Moat Island Cottage, and onwards to the River Thames.

The track exits the trees and proceeds downhill towards Ranger's Gate. At this point you can either backtrack across the open ground direct to Queen Anne's Gate (running parallel to the road), or you can continue your walk into Cranbourne Chase from Ranger's Gate Car Park, another 400 yards ahead. From this Car Park, looking across to the opposite side of the A332, you will see Ranger's Gate (see p85). Ranger's Lodge, set well back on the right and inside from the Gates themselves, dates from 1795 although it is now much altered from the original.

Ranger's Lodge is currently the official residence of the Deputy Ranger of the Great Park. This is also regarded as the 'Main Gate' into the Village and the Estate Office and Workshops complex. Access through the double gates on foot or bike is allowed, but not by vehicle, except for residents and official visitors.

RANGER'S LODGE: H.B.Ziegler's drawing of the Lodge as it looked in 1839, when he drew all of the Lodges in the Great Park for HM Queen Victoria.

RANGER'S LODGE: the same house today, but much altered. The tower would have stood on the corner where the sunny wall meets the shaded wall in this photograph.

THE LINE OF THE OLD ROAD: with the A332 to the left, the two lines of ancient oaks clearly reveal the former route of Sheet Street, until its rerouting to the left of the photograph in 1797.

The road by the Ranger's Gate Car Park leads up to Flemish Farm, which is itself off limits to visitors after passing the gravel track into Cranbourne and reaching the white gate. The main road (the A332) used to follow a slightly different track at this point to what it does today. It formerly passed in front of the far side of Ranger's Lodge, until the road was moved to its present position. The double line of ancient oaks from Queen Anne's Gate to this point actually mark the route of the original Sheet Street road, which is best seen (and clearly visible) from inside Ranger's Gate, looking over the field boundary uphill to the right of the small gatehouse. The road was rerouted in 1797 after the expansion of Forest Lodge, further up the hill (see p86-87).

Walking onwards through Ranger's Gate and following the road past Ranger's Lodge will bring you to the crossroads with the road from Cranbourne Gate (see p86). From this point it is your choice as to where you wish to go next, and it is possible to return to the Picnic Area from within the Village. Have a look at the map on p109 and locate your position at the crossroads. To get back to the Picnic Area, walk past Russell's Field Farm and, (as you are approaching from the opposite direction), turn left (not right!) onto Queen Anne's Ride at Watch Oak, as described on p82.

CRANBOURNE

Standing on the Car Park road (with your back to Ranger's Gate) and looking towards Flemish Farm, to your left is the start of the secluded and ancient forest area known as Cranbourne Chase. The woodland in front of you is the site of a 13 acre plantation created in 1580 by Lord Burleigh, in response to the country's need for ships' timber. This is probably the earliest recorded 'deliberately created' plantation in England, and a few of the original oak trees still survive within the remotest areas of the Chase. There is a left turn onto a gravel path about 200 yards away from the Car Park on the road towards Flemish Farm which will take you on a meandering course along the edge of the ancient woodland, bringing you out close to another prominent landmark, Cranbourne Tower. You can also walk through the wood, entering via a gate in the field behind the Car Park, and you may well encounter a herd of gentle English Longhorn cattle which reside there.

LONGHORN CATTLE: a mild mannered, ancient breed which was common in England until the 1700's. New breeds displaced the Longhorns as 'favourites', as Longhorns were unable to compete in terms of milk yield, although they remained excellent animals for meat production.

In the Late Middle Ages, this area was known as Cranbourne Rails. There has been a building recorded here since 1486, when Gilbert Mawdesley was appointed Keeper of Cranbourne Walk, (a 'Walk' being essentially an enclosed deer park) including a building referred to as 'the toure (sic-tower) on the hethe'.

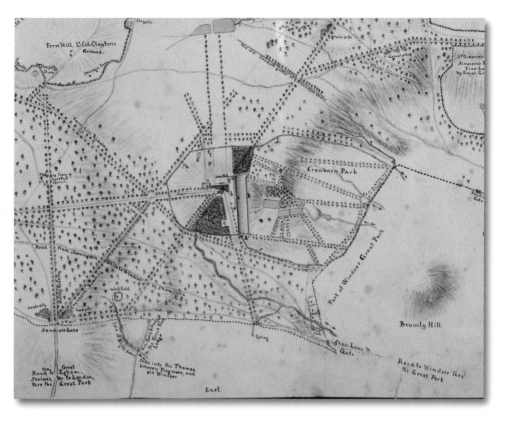

PLAN OF CRANBOURNE CHASE c.1752: (RCIN 711332 – detail)
North is to the right. The main entrance is at top, between the Bay Ponds (see map p116), the outlines of which today lie hidden in the woodland just off the Squirrel Roundabout on the B3022 Windsor to Ascot Road.
The Royal Collection © 2010, Her Majesty Queen Elizabeth II.

Henry VIII and his daughter, Queen Elizabeth I, both hunted here during their respective reigns. John Norden's 'Survey' of 1607 shows 'Cranbourne New Lodge' on this site, but without a tower. The house and its grounds were remodelled on a number of occasions, especially from 1665 onwards, and played host to some famous and notable people, including Anne Hyde (the mother of Queen Anne), and John Evelyn (the horticulturalist and diarist) throughout its comparatively short history. Samuel Pepys, the renowned 17th Century diarist, visited here on a number of occasions, describing it as 'a very noble seat in a noble forest...otherwise a melancholy place, and little variety save only trees'.

CRANBOURNE LODGE c1765: Thomas Sandby. (RL 14635)
This is the view from the East of the house, with the main entrance and the avenue leading to the
Bay Ponds located on the opposite side.
The Royal Collection © 2010, Her Majesty Queen Elizabeth II.

Cranbourne Lodge underwent further changes in 1700 with the arrival of Richard
Jones, 3rd Viscount and 1st Earl of Ranelagh, who was also Paymaster General
of the Army. He spent large amounts of money on the property, most of which
went on landscaping rather than building work. His exuberant spending became
the cause of Parliamentary concern in 1703, mainly due to his involvement in
the small matter of £72,000 of public funds not ending up where they should
have! Principal access to Ranelagh's house was gained from the West, entering
past the Bay Ponds, and along an impressive avenue of trees which led up to the
house, at a distance of almost one mile. There were a number of extensive
avenues laid out as part of the landscaping scheme, and remnants of them can
still be traced in the modern day landscape. Ranelagh's death in 1712 saw most
of his estates sold off, but in 1731 the Crown took Cranbourne back into its
possession. The house was successively granted to a number of people thereafter,

but remained separated from the Great Park by the wedge-shaped piece of land between Ranger's Gate and a small house which once stood on the site of today's Forest Lodge, the large house located to the southeast of Cranbourne Tower.

NEW RISE: the view to the North from a point just behind Cranbourne Tower.

In its heyday, the grounds of Cranbourne were beautifully landscaped, with ornamental lakes, bowling greens, long avenues of trees and extensive views of the surrounding countryside. Thomas Sandby, artist, architect, and a future Deputy Ranger, recorded these 'Views' in six watercolours painted in 1754. Thomas lived in Cranbourne Lodge in the late 1750s, and his first child, Elizabeth, was born here in 1758. One man, in particular, who lived here for a number of years was William Augustus, Duke of Cumberland, who was to play such a significant role in the shaping of all that we see today in Windsor Great Park. Cranbourne was his temporary residence from 1751, whilst building work was carried out at the Great (Cumberland) Lodge. The Duke's equestrian interests led to the creation of stables at Cranbourne, and as a result of his endeavours in the field of horse breeding, the famous racehorse, Eclipse, was foaled in the paddock just to the southwest of the house on the 1st of April, 1764. What followed was what can only be described as the start of a racing legend!

"ECLIPSE FIRST – THE REST, NOWHERE!!"

Eclipse was the product of the pairing of the sire, Marske, with the dam, Spiletta, neither of which were regarded as special horses in themselves. Marske won three races in total, and Spiletta ran in only one race, which she lost. By 1763, both horses were owned by the Duke, and stabled at Cranbourne. Following Eclipse's arrival in 1764, all three horses were sold off at the dispersal sale following the Duke's death in 1765, with Eclipse going for 75 guineas to William Wildman, a meat salesman who kept racehorses as his hobby. Why Eclipse should turn out to be so successful is one of those strange quirks of fate or evolution, but successful he was. He was certainly different from other horses; he was temperamental; tall at 15.3 hands high, and was described as 'the largest boned bloodhorse ever bred'. Today, he is a direct male-line ancestor for some 95% of the world's Thoroughbreds. Eclipse's racing career began on the 3rd of May, 1769, and after winning the first race, the second race of the day was the occasion for Captain Dennis O'Kelly's famous challenge (quote, top of p126) to the betting masses gathered at Epsom Downs.

'ECLIPSE' 1770: by George Stubbs (1724 - 1806) © private collection/The Bridgeman Art Library

The horse was trialled before the day's racing, with O'Kelly watching, and he already knew that the horse was something special. So confident was O'Kelly, he bet that not only would Eclipse win the race, but also that the other four horses would all be 'nowhere' - at least 240 yards behind (by a 'distance', in betting parlance) when Eclipse passed the post – and that's exactly what happened! Eclipse sailed over the line with the others 'nowhere' near him. O'Kelly purchased a half share in Eclipse from Wildman for 650 guineas in about June 1769, and bought the other half share in May 1770 for a second payment of 1100 guineas. Eclipse ran in a total of 18 races, the last on the 4th of October 1770 at Newmarket. He retired unbeaten, and was then placed in O'Kelly's stud farm near Epsom. From this point, Eclipse sired 344 winning horses, amassing a total of 862 race wins between them. He also made Dennis O'Kelly a rich man! Eclipse died of colic on the 27th of February 1789, at O'Kelly's Cannons estate in Edgware, London. The body of Eclipse was the subject of an in-depth post mortem to try and discover more about the workings of this exceptional animal. His well-preserved skeleton changed hands on a number of occasions, finally to end up in 2003 at the Royal Veterinary College in Hatfield, Herts, where it can be seen today.

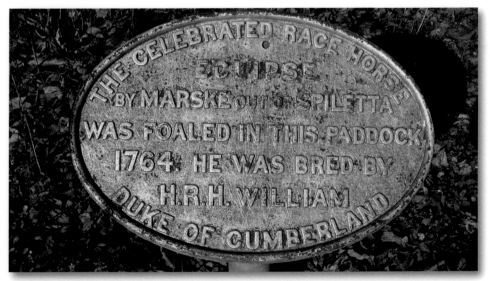

ECLIPSE'S CELEBRATORY PLATE: the plate is situated to the southwest of the Tower, adjacent to the edge of the site of the original paddocks.

Cranbourne became a focus of national interest for the last time in 1814-16 when, in a dispute over potential suitors, HRH Princess Charlotte, the only child of her father, the Prince Regent (later George IV) was ordered to remain at Cranbourne. With a similarity to the acidic relationship between George III and George IV, Princess Charlotte also endured a difficult relationship with her father.

Charlotte was a very popular national figure, and following her repatriation into Court life, and her subsequent marriage to Prince Leopold of Saxe-Coburg Saalfeld, her personal life appeared to have been happily changed for the better. Tragedy was to quickly occur, however, when in November 1817 after a difficult childbirth at her marital home at Claremont, Princess Charlotte died along with her stillborn son. She was mourned by the nation on a grand scale, and a beautiful memorial to her was erected within the nave of St George's Chapel at Windsor Castle. The Royal Obstetrician was blamed (somewhat unfairly) for the calamity, and he committed suicide 18 months later.

One of the last recorded views of Cranbourne was drawn by S. Hollyer, published in 1820 (pictured below). It shows the current octagonal tower, which was built in 1808. Upon the succession of William IV, it was decided that Cranbourne was too badly dilapidated to warrant the extensive and expensive repairs it needed, and in 1830, the decision was taken to demolish the building with the exception of the tower itself. A single storey dwelling was added to the Tower, and has been used as private accommodation for various Park employees ever since.

CRANBOURNE LODGE c1820: S.Hollyer after H. Perry. (RCIN 700925)
The view towards the main entrance located on the west front. The curved driveway has long since disappeared from the current landscape.
The Royal Collection © 2010, Her Majesty Queen Elizabeth II.

Should you just wish to view Cranbourne Tower itself, and do not wish to walk through the woodland, drive along the A332 past Ranger's Gate towards Ascot, passing a small Car Park which offers access to see the curiously named and tiny Pickle Herring Pond, up to the final Car Park at the top of the hill opposite Cranbourne Gate. This will allow you to walk directly up to Cranbourne Tower via an adjacent tarmac road.

CRANBOURNE TOWER: once a prominent visible landmark, the Tower is now difficult to see from anywhere other than the southeastern side towards Cranbourne Gate.

Following the demolition of the main building in 1830, the Tower (above) is now all that remains of this once-grand house. From its rooftop, the view should be even better than that afforded at the Copper Horse, but many of the adjacent trees are now reaching such lofty heights as to become an intrusion on the surrounding panorama. A large underground reservoir is situated adjacent to the Tower. Built around 1850, it features a large and ornate pump house sitting above ground. The reservoir was one of the supplies for Windsor Castle, receiving water all the way from the Pumping House on the River Thames close to Romney Island in Windsor. It replaced a water system that had first originated in the 16th Century, with water being transferred to Windsor from Blackmoor Wood, near Ascot, through a series of lead and wooden pipes and conduits.

CRANBOURNE TOWER: the west front.

The photograph above is of the West front of the Tower, with the single storey accommodation set in front. The original house would have stood immediately in front of the Tower when viewed from this point, extending off to the right, and almost as far out as the foreground shadows. This would also have been the principal approach to the house from the main entrance at the Bay Ponds. Cranbourne Chase is now gently reverting 'back to Nature', although ghosts of the original landscape features, such as the ponds, sections of the tree avenues, outbuilding foundations and a single wall, still exist, hidden amongst the dense, ever-encroaching forest that surrounds the Tower.

In conclusion...

I trust that your visit to the Great Park has been an enjoyable experience, and it would give me great pleasure if you were to choose to visit again. More importantly, I am certain that it would also please each and every member of the Windsor Great Park team who are actively involved in the day-to-day upkeep of this fabulous and quite remarkable environment. With the advent of the Royal Landscape project, I see a far more certain future ahead for this special place, and I am positive that both present and future custodians of the Great Park will do their very best to maintain, protect and enhance what has taken the best part of eight hundred years to create. In this age of rapid change in which we find ourselves, it is comforting to know that there still exists a few small pockets of our 'green and pleasant Land' that can offer a sense of escape from the hustle and bustle of modern life, and Windsor Great Park most definitely fits into this category.

Windsor Great Park has held an unrivalled fascination for me since my childhood. To be allowed to spend my younger days playing, growing up, and living in such surroundings has been one of the greatest 'gifts' I have ever received, and for that alone, my dear parents both deserve and have my utmost gratitude.

In closing, I hope that you have found this little Guide both useful and informative, and if it has made your visit to Windsor Great Park just a touch more enjoyable, then I will have happily achieved my goal.

Andrew Fielder

Index

Albert, HRH Prince, the Prince Consort 74.94.112
Anne, HM Queen 71.91
Ascot Gate 92
Bagshot 15
Bagshot Heath 35.39
Battle Bourne, River 76.87.113
Bay Ponds, the (site of) 124.130
Bears Rails **77**
Bears Rails Gate 77
Bears Rails Pond 77
Beehive Covert 114
Belvedere, Fort **39**.43
Bibliography 139
Birds of prey 93
Bishopsgate 55.67.78.98.**106**
Blacknest Gate 18.21.**46**.55.58.78.105
Boathouse, the 48.50.**51**
Botany Bay Point 31.**40**
Bourne, River (Cranbourne) 118
Bourne, River (Virginia Water) 35
Breakheart Hill 49.**50**.58
Bromley Hill 119
Brookers (Brookes) Corner 119
Burghley, Lord 122
Byelaws 10.83.115
Byfield House 15.101.103
Byfield, John 15.101
Cambridge Gate 67.69
Canadian Avenue 51.**65**
Canadian Forestry Batallion 65
Carter's Bar 30.57.66
Cascade, the 32.35.**36**
Cavalry Exercise Ground 70.117
Change, the **92**
Chaplain's Lodge **97**.107
Charles I, HM King 15.101
Charles II, HM King 15.71.72.101

Charlotte, HRH Princess 127.128
Cheapside 93
Cheeseman's Gate 18.30.55
China Island 45.47.**48**
Churchill, John, Duke of Marlborough 101
Churchill, Sarah, Duchess of Marlborough 101
Civil War 15.17.72.101
Clewer 13.70
Clockcase, the 39.43
Commonwealth Plantation 106
Cooke's Hill 78
Copper Horse, the 9.69.70.71.**72**.76.78.79.**80**.81.82.96.97.107.110.129
Cork Clump 60
Coronation Plantation 87
Cow Pond **105**
Cranbourne Chase 10.15.115.119.121.122.**123**.124.125.126.130
Cranbourne Forest 10
Cranbourne Gate 47.78.83.85.**86**.87.105.108.114.115.121.129
Cranbourne Lodge 86.102.123.**124**.125.127.**128**
Cranbourne Rails 15.**16**.122
Cranbourne Tower 117.122.125.128.**129**.130
Cumberland, Henry Frederick, 2nd Duke of 22.32.101
Cumberland, William Augustus, Duke of 17.19.**20**.22.28.31.32.39.47.48.51.86
94.98.99.101.102.103.118.125
Cumberland Gate 21.28.29.60.61.62.106
Cumberland Lodge 15.25.29.47.62.67.83.86.89.95.96.98.99.100.101.102.103
106.107.125
Cumberland Lodge Mews 96.98.102.103.**104**
Dalton's Lodge 32.37
Deepstrood 81.**82**.94.97.108
Deer, fallow 72.75
Deer, muntjac 93
Deer, roe 93
Deer Park, the 25.47.62.67.70.73.77.78.82.90.107.**110**.115.117
Deerpen, the 90.92.93.117
Deer, red **72.73.74.75**
Dockyard Cottages 43.48.**49**
Double Gates 10.67.70.71.72.76.82

Duke's Lane   11.90.92.93.97.110
Eclipse, celebratory plate   127
Eclipse, the racehorse   125.126.127
Edinburgh, HRH The Prince Philip, Duke of   23.59.62
Edward III, HM King   76
Edward VIII, HM King   39.62
Elizabeth I, HM Queen   14.123
Elizabeth II, HM The Queen   52.54.59.80.87.90.92.96
Elizabeth, HM Queen, The Queen Mother 81.89
Estate Office   10.92.113.119
Eton Bridge   54
Fiddle Covert   114
Findlay, Thomas Hope   25.26
Fishing Temple   39.41.43.44.48.52
Five Arch Bridge   44.45.46.47.48
Flemish Farm   121.122
Flitcroft, Henry   31.102
Flying Barn   55.57.58.62
Forest Gate   67.83.86.87.115.117
Forest Law   14.15
Forest Lodge   86.87.121.125
Frostfarm Plantation   43
Gallop, the   107.110
Garden House, the 62
George II, HM King   20.27.28
George III, HM King   17.32.54.57.79.81.127
George IV, HM King   17.41.42.43.79.81.89.127
George V, HM King   25
George VI, HM King   25.89.106
Great (High) Bridge   44
Great Meadow Pond   93.94.96.98.99
Groom's House   101.103.104
Grotto, the   35
Guards Polo Club   55.56.58.59.62.66
Hares   93
Harewarren Clump   60
Henry VIII, HM King   123
High Flyers Hill   50.62
HM Queen Elizabeth II Statue   90.91.92.110.117

Holly Bush 11.93
Holly Grove (see Forest Lodge)
Hurst Hill 29
Hurst Lake 29
Isle of Wight Pond 87.88
Johnson's Pond 48.50.58.93.99
Kennels 89
Kitchen Gardens, Cumberland Lodge 95.96
Larch Bridge 54
Leiper's Hill Pond 92
Leptis Magna 38
Limetree Avenue 100.105
Little Virginia Lake 54
Longhorn cattle 122
Long Walk, the 9.10.47.67.69.70.71.72.76.79.82.97.107.110.115.117
Long Walk, shortcut to the 70
Lower Forest 10
Manor Hill 92
Manor Lodge 31.41.46.48
Maple Bourne, River 118
Martin, Chief Mungo 52
Mary, HM Queen 25
Menagerie, site of 89.102
Mezel Hill 83.85.93.110
Mezel Hill Cottages 94
Mill Pond 93.99
Millstone, the 91.110.117
Mistle Pond 98
Moat Island Cottage 118
Moat Park 70.117.118
New Lodge 15
New Rise 125
Norden, John, Survey of Windsor 1607 16. map on rear inner cover
Norfolk Farm 93.99
Obelisk Bridge 21.29.30
Obelisk Monument, the 27.28.29.30.55.56.62
Obelisk Pond 18.21.23.25.28.29.30.40.57.58.62.66
Obelisk Ride 21.28.29.30.62
Old Windsor Wood 13.77

Ox Pond 82.97
Pales (see Rails) 15
Parakeets, ring-necked 77
Park Farm Cottage 94
Perch Bay 41
Picnic Area 10.67.70.82.83.108.115.117.121
Pepys, Samuel 123
Pickle Herring Pond 129
Plunket Memorial Pavilion 64
Prince Consort's Gate 90.92.93
Prince Consort's Pond 113
Prince Consort's Statue 60
Prince Consort's Workshops 82.86.108.112.113.119
Prince of Wales' Pond 75.76
Prince Regent (see George IV)
Public telephone 109.112
Punchbowl, the 63
Queen Anne's Gate 67.70.82.83.115.117.118.119.121
Queen Anne's Ride 82.83.90.91.110.112.114.117.121
Queen Mary's Plantation 118
Queen Mother's Avenue 98.100.102
Rails 15
Ranelagh, Richard Jones, 1st Earl of 124
Ranger's Gate 67.83.85.86.108.110.114.115.118.119.121.122.125.129
Ranger's Lodge 85.86.87.119.120.121
Red Cross 93
Reservoir 130
Review Ground, the 72.76
Rhododendron Ride 106
Richardson's Lawn 111.112.113
Rosy Bottom 93
Roundwood 60
Royal Box, the 58.59
Royal Chapel, the 81.82
Royal Landscape, the 18.19.23.26.43.63
Royal Lodge 25.43.47.67.78.81.82.97.106.107
Royal School 94.95.106.107
Ruins, the 38
Russell's Field Farm 114.121

Russell's Pond 110.114.117
Sandby, Paul 22.89
Sandby, Thomas 22.36.40.44.81.86.87.125
Sandpit, the 30
Sandpit Gate 76.89.90.93.94.97.110
Sarsen stones 35
Savill Building, the 21.23.25.26.28.55.56.57.62.63.64.66.67.83.106
Savill Garden, the 7.18.21.23.25.26.29.30.62.89.140
Savill, Sir Eric 25.26.62
Sawmill, site of 114
Scout Camp 77
Shaw Farm Gate 69
Sheet Street Road, original route 86.121
Shop Pond 87.112
Shrubs Hill 31.32.39
Slann's Pen 93
Smith's Lawn 18.21.25.28.29.30.46.47.49.55.56.57.58.61.62.65.78.89.106
Snow Hill 69.79.94.97
South Forest 10.93
Spring Hill 78.79
Star Clump 119
Stone Bridge, the (adj.Long Walk) 78
Swan Pond 70.119
Swinley Forest 10.15.91.114
Tighe, Robert 71
Timber Lodge 110
Totem Pole 30.37.52.53.54.65.66
Upper Pond 7
US Air Force 61
Valley Gardens 18.21.25.26.30.50.51.53.55.56.57.62.63.65.66
Vickers-Armstrong 62.89
Victoria, HM Queen 28.60.79.94.95
Village, the 25.47.67.82.83.85.86.97.108.110.111.117.119.121
Village Shop 83.87.106.108.111.112
Vinery, the 95.96
Virginia 40
Virginia Water Cottage 48.50.52
Virginia Water 18.21.25.29.30.31.32.33.35.37.41.48.52.54.55.62.64.99.117
Virginia (Water) Lodge 36.37.38

Walks (see Rails) 15.122
Watch Oak 82.110.121
Wheatsheaf Hotel, the 21.31.33.54
Wheelers Yard 112.113
Wick Branch 29.32.37.40.54
Wick Pond 29.30.37.51.52.54.65
Wick Stream 37
William I, HM King 13.14
William IV, HM King 17.81.89.128
Windsor Castle 9.13.43.69.79.90.91.94.97.110.128.130
Windsor Forest 13.17.87
Windsor Great Park, byelaws 10.83.115
Windsor Great Park, early history 12.13.14.15.16.17
Windsor Great Park, location 9.10
Windsor Great Park, overview 9.10.11
World's End Gate 46
Wyatt, James 90
Wyatt(ville), Sir Jeffry 29.38.44.81
Wychemere 76.77
York Club, the 86.87.88.89.108.111

Selected Bibliography

'Les Delices de Windsore' J.Pote 1755

'The History of Windsor and its Neighbourhood' J.Hakewill 1813

'The Royal Lodges in Windsor Great Park' H.B.Ziegler 1839

'Annals of Windsor' (2 vols) R.R.Tighe & J.E.Davis 1858

'The History of Windsor Great Park and Windsor Forest' William Menzies 1864

'Notes on Virginia Water' Rev F.J.Rawlins 1866

'A History of Windsor Forest, Sunninghill and the Great Park' G.M.Hughes 1890

'Thomas and Paul Sandby' William Sandby 1892

'Windsor Park and Forest' William Menzies jnr 1904

'Windsor, Old and New' T.E.Harwood 1929

'The 'Ruins' at Virginia Water' G.E.Chambers 1956

'The Gardens in the Royal Park at Windsor' Lanning Roper 1959

'The Story of Windsor Great Park' R.J.Elliott 1974

'Whigs and Hunters – The Origin of the Black Act' E.P.Thompson 1975

'Royal Lake' Raymond South 1983

'Cumberland Lodge' Helen Hudson 1989

'The Savill Garden, Windsor Great Park' John Bond 1991

'The Royal Stags of Windsor' D.Bruce Banwell 1994

'Views of Windsor' Jane Roberts 1995

'Royal Landscape; The Gardens and Parks of Windsor'. Jane Roberts 1997

'The Royal Gardens in Windsor Great Park' Charles Lyte 1998

'The Great Park and Windsor Forest' Clifford Smith 2004

'The Walker's Guide -Windsor Great Park' David McDowall 2007

'Gardens in a Landscape' Crown Estates Commissioners 2007

'The Savill Building' Crown Estates Commissioners 2007

'Eclipse' Nicholas Clee 2009

'Virginia Water, Neighbour to Windsor Great Park' D.Davis 2009

SAVILL GARDEN – A WINTER SUNSET: snow is an infrequent visitor to this part of the country, but when it does make an appearance, late afternoon in the Great Park is transformed into a magical world of soft light, whispering winds, clean crisp air and muted sound, broken only by the crunching footfall of the visitor, and the wild calls of the birds flying home to roost in nearby deep and dark pine woodland.

Author's Note

Whilst every effort has been taken to ensure that the information contained within this Guide is as accurate and up-to-date as possible, changes do occur from time to time.

With the essential day-to-day upkeep and maintenance required on such a large expanse of land, visitors may sometimes find certain areas or places slightly altered from the descriptive text and illustrations, or possibly off limits.

The latest online information on Windsor Great Park can be found at

www.theroyallandscape.co.uk

If you require more detailed information about the places and the history of Windsor Great Park; or if you would like to comment about this Guide, or anything else I may be able to help you with, then please feel free to email me at

info@copperhorsepublishing.co.uk

Photographic Acknowledgements

With the exception of the images listed on pages 142-144, each and every image contained within this book is hereby reproduced by the kind permission of the Crown Estate Commissioners.

The following list of illustrations are reproduced from The Royal Collection with the gracious permission of Her Majesty Queen Elizabeth II.

Page 16   'Cranbourne Rails' John Norden, Survey of the Honor of Windsor, 1607
The Royal Collection © 2010, Her Majesty Queen Elizabeth II
RCIN 1142252 Table X

Page 31   'Virginia Water from Shrubs Hill' Thomas Sandby c1753
The Royal Collection © 2010, Her Majesty Queen Elizabeth II
RL 14640

Page 32   Detail from 'Virginia Water from Shrubs Hill' Thomas Sandby c1753
The Royal Collection © 2010, Her Majesty Queen Elizabeth II
RL 14640 - detail

Page 39   'The New Building on Shrubs Hill' Canot, after Thomas Sandby c1754
The Royal Collection © 2010, Her Majesty Queen Elizabeth II
RCIN 814377

Page 41   'Virginia Water from the Manor Lodge' Thomas Sandby c1754
The Royal Collection © 2010, Her Majesty Queen Elizabeth II
RL14646

Page 42   'HM King George IV' Sir Thomas Lawrence c1822
The Royal Collection © 2010, Her Majesty Queen Elizabeth II
RCIN 405680

Page 43   'The Boathouse, Fishing Temple and Tents' William Daniell c1829
The Royal Collection © 2010, Her Majesty Queen Elizabeth II
RCIN 500176

Page 44   'The Great Bridge over the Virginia River' Thomas Sandby c1754
The Royal Collection © 2010, Her Majesty Queen Elizabeth II
RCIN 500179

Page 48   'The Building on China Island, 1829-1836' William Delamotte
The Royal Collection © 2010, Her Majesty Queen Elizabeth II
RL 17509

Grateful acknowledgement is hereby given to the following persons and Institutions for their kind permission in allowing me to use the following examples of their work, or examples from a Collection, as illustrations within this book. (Image identification references are included where known.)

Page 12 'Stag Hunting' The Book of Hours, Use of Worms (Hours of the Death) with elements of a Breviary;
© The British Library Board. Egerton 1146

Page 14 'Elizabeth I at a stag hunt' The Booke of Hunting, Turberville 1576.
© The British Library Board. C.31.g.1.(2),liii r

Page 20 'HRH William Augustus, Duke of Cumberland' by Sir Joshua Reynolds
© Devonshire Collection, Chatsworth. Reproduced by permission of Chatsworth Settlement Trustees.

- -

The right of Andrew Fielder to be identified as the author of this work has been asserted by him in accordance with the Copyright, Design and Patents Act 1988.

British Library Cataloguing in Publication Data.
A catalogue record for this book is available from the British Library.

ISBN 978-0-9564703-0-0

Designed by Andrew Fielder.

Printed & Typeset in Officina Serif and RotisSerif by Claire McGuinness, Windsor Digital Print. Email: claire@windsordigitalprint.co.uk

Published by Copperhorse Publishing, 24, St Paul's Road, Staines, Middlesex, TW18 3HH, England.

© Andrew Fielder 2010

EMERGENCY CARE of MINOR TRAUMA in CHILDREN

EMERGENCY CARE of MINOR TRAUMA in CHILDREN

A PRACTICAL HANDBOOK

Ffion CW Davies
Consultant in Emergency Medicine
Leicester Royal Infirmary
Leicester, UK

Colin E Bruce
Consultant Orthopaedic & Trauma Surgeon
Alder Hey Children's Hospital
Liverpool, UK

Kate Taylor-Robinson
Consultant Paediatric Radiologist
Alder Hey Children's Hospital
Liverpool, UK

**HODDER
ARNOLD**
AN HACHETTE UK COMPANY

First published in Great Britain in 2011 by
Hodder Arnold, an imprint of Hodder Education, a division of Hachette UK
338 Euston Road, London NW1 3BH

http://www.hodderarnold.com

British Library Cataloguing in Publication Data
A catalogue record for this book is available from the British Library

Library of Congress Cataloging-in-Publication Data
A catalog record for this book is available from the Library of Congress

ISBN-13   978 1 444 12014 1
1 2 3 4 5 6 7 8 9 10

Commissioning Editor:	Caroline Makepeace
Project Editor:	Sarah Penny
Production Controller:	Kate Harris
Cover Design:	Helen Townson

Cover image © Claire Deprez/Reporters/Science Photo Library

Typeset in Minion Pro 9.5pt by MPS Limited, a Macmillan Company
Printed and bound in India by Replika Press Pvt Ltd

What do you think about this book? Or any other Hodder Arnold title?
Please visit our website: www.hodderarnold.com

CONTENTS

Preface   vi

Acknowledgements   vii

How to use this book and website   viii

CHAPTER 1   **Introduction**   1

CHAPTER 2   **Prevention of injury**   3

CHAPTER 3   **Pain management**   6

CHAPTER 4   **Wounds and soft tissue injuries**   16

CHAPTER 5   **Head and facial injuries**   30

CHAPTER 6   **Neck and back injuries**   46

CHAPTER 7   **Fractures and dislocations – general approach**   58

CHAPTER 8   **Injuries of the shoulder to wrist**   69

CHAPTER 9   **The hand**   95

CHAPTER 10   **The lower limb**   119

CHAPTER 11   **Burns, scalds, chemical and electrical injuries**   146

CHAPTER 12   **Bites, stings and allergic reactions**   156

CHAPTER 13   **Foreign bodies**   163

CHAPTER 14   **Injuries of the external genitalia and anus**   178

CHAPTER 15   **Non-accidental injury**   183

CHAPTER 16   **Practical procedures**   188

CHAPTER 17   **Medico-legal issues**   211

Index   217

This book is written for frontline healthcare professionals who deal with children with everyday injuries. It is an easy reference guide to the first few hours of care, to help doctors and nurses in emergency departments and walk-in centres, as well as general practitioners and ambulance staff.

Despite the frequency with which children injure themselves, surprisingly little is written about minor injuries, and notably, the 'little things in life' are rarely covered in conventional textbooks. This handbook covers everything from beads up noses to a fractured femur!

In addition to the main text there is advice about child protection issues, pain management and a brief overview of the particular legal issues relating to caring for children. Each chapter is concise, illustrated heavily and the use of 'warning signs', 'stop signs' and 'top tips' help the reader spot when a 'minor' injury is potentially not so minor. The text also links to free downloadable videos and other online resources at www.hodderplus.com/emergencycare.

If you find this book useful, you may also find www.spottingthesickchild. com helpful – this online learning resource covers the 6 most common acute medical illnesses with which children present, as well as minor head injury.

Ffion Davies, Colin Bruce, and Kate Taylor-Robinson

ACKNOWLEDGEMENTS

The authors would like to thank the following people for making this book possible:

To our families, for forgiving us those laptop days.

To the children and their families, and the staff in the Emergency Department of Leicester Royal Infirmary, who allowed themselves to be filmed and photographed, in order to help us demonstrate the very practical nature of this book.

Also thanks to OCB Media Ltd, Leicester, for help with editing video clips and to Damian Roland and Melissa Cannon for help with the filming and voiceovers.

Icons throughout this book indicate where there is additional material on the accompanying website, available for free at www.hodderplus.com/ emergencycare.

 Video content

 Web links

 Case studies which relate to the text

To access this content, which includes the Case Vignettes for Chapter 15, plus an image library, video content, glossary and web links, please register on the website using the following access details:

Serial number: 6sq47u7qhz6o

Once you have registered, you will not need the serial number but can log in using the username and password you will create during registration.

CHAPTER 1

INTRODUCTION

Minor trauma is a normal part of childhood. In fact children comprise between 20 per cent and 30 per cent of all patients attending a general Emergency Department (ED). In the UK it is also estimated that in any one year around 2.5 million children visit the ED as a result of injury: this translates to around a fifth of all children *each year*. Children are therefore high users of Emergency Services, and Emergency Services spend quite a bit of their time seeing children! Children are likely to have further attendances, and the care that they receive influences their behaviour and fears at those times.

The purpose of this handbook is to enable doctors, nurses and emergency nurse practitioners to manage common minor injuries, to know when to ask for help, and to spot when the 'minor injury' has more significance and is not actually minor.

It is relevant for practitioners based in hospitals, minor injury units/ urgent care centres and primary care centres. Similarly, although aimed at a UK audience, most of it will be relevant to other developed countries. It is not an exhaustive text, and in this evidence-based world in which we now live, much is written on the basis of experience. Minor trauma is one of the poorest-researched areas of medicine and the quality of the scientific literature is generally poor.

A child's minor injury should not be seen in isolation. As healthcare professionals we need to consider our approach to the child, treating them with respect and compassion, being aware that this may be their first experience of hospital, and making sure that the take-home advice we give is sensible and practical to the whole family. The effect of something as simple as being in a plaster cast and missing school to attend follow-up appointments is seen as far from 'minor' by the family, so the term 'minor injury' is a bit of a misnomer.

It is also our responsibility to pick up safeguarding issues when a child has an injury, in other words suboptimal care or supervision, or the more subtle indicator of a lack of compassion, such as delay in seeking medical help in a child who is obviously in pain. These are welfare issues, but sadly we also see child protection issues, where injuries may have been deliberately inflicted. You can be forgiven for thinking that paediatric-trained colleagues are a bit obsessed by this, but it is vital that we detect these safeguarding issues, which are unfortunately common.

Children should be seen in a child-friendly environment, ideally audio-visually separated from adults. This area should be specifically designed for their needs with child-sized equipment, suitable play areas, and examination and treatment rooms that are bright and welcoming. It is quite easy to transform an area with brightly coloured paint and posters, and funding is often readily available from local charities. Toys can be used as distraction therapy during painful procedures and as entertainment during observation or waiting times.

Attention to these aspects really helps with the assessment and treatment of children. Most of your medical examination can be conducted through play, rather than a formal examination on a couch. Larger EDs may employ a Play Specialist. This person can prepare children for procedures, provide distraction during the procedure, and make the whole treatment quicker and less stressful for staff and patients alike!

More detailed standards for the care of children in emergency settings are available in the UK from the Royal College of Paediatrics and Child Health (a document called 'Standards for the care of children in emergency care settings', 2011).

CHAPTER 2

PREVENTION OF INJURY

| Introduction | 3 | Engineering | 4 |
| Education | 3 | Enforcement (legislation) | 4 |

INTRODUCTION

'Accidents' are a leading cause of both death and permanent disability in children and young adults in the UK. Many injuries in children could have been avoided by adequate supervision and common-sense measures, so in a sense are not truly 'accidents'. At the same time, children will always be exposed to some risk, as they must be allowed to explore their environment and have fun, experience and contextualize risk, and be physically active.

Most injuries to children under 3 years of age occur in the home or garden. At this age, children develop rapidly, and so carers often underestimate their capabilities. Although it is impossible to have 'eyes in the back of the head' when looking after small children, it is important that true neglect is not missed (see Chapter 15). Older children attend nurseries or schools, and move further from home for play and other activities. Many incidents leading to injury then occur in schools, sports facilities, out on the street or high-risk places (railway lines, derelict buildings) where bored teenagers seek adventure. There is a strong association between injury rates and social deprivation.

We can tackle accident prevention in three ways: education, engineering and enforcement (legislation)

EDUCATION

The role of teachers

Injury awareness and first aid skills can be incorporated into most parts of the school curriculum without requiring special dedicated time, if aspects of injury prevention are built into the standard curriculum. A successful example of this approach in the UK is the Injury Minimisation Project for Schools (IMPS), which is aimed at year 6 children.

Parents, carers and children themselves

Most research on injury prevention shows that it is difficult to bring about changes in behaviour. Healthcare professionals should take advantage of the motivation following acute injury to give information and advice. Parents are more receptive to advice about cycle helmets when their child has just fallen off a bike, or to the suggestion that drugs should be locked away in a drug cupboard after an accidental overdose. Many organizations (such as the Royal Society for Prevention of Accidents and the Child Accident Prevention Trust) have leaflets and websites with information. Key subjects are:

- safety equipment, e.g. stair gates, fireguards
- child-resistant containers for medicines
- safe storage of household cleaners and garden products
- safe positioning of hot objects, e.g. cups of tea, kettles, pans, irons
- safe use of equipment, e.g. not putting baby bouncers on work surfaces; always supervising the use of babywalkers
- safety on roads and railways.

The role of health visitors

Health Visitors have a key role in injury prevention. At routine assessments and in clinic visits they can give out information leaflets and discuss the development of the child in relation to injury prevention. On home visits they can give constructive advice on hazards in the home. UK guidance recommends that the Health Visitor should receive notification of all Emergency Department (ED) attendances in children.

ENGINEERING

Knowledge of child development and the potential for injury by designers, architects and engineers can help prevent accidents and death in children. If a doctor or nurse becomes aware of a hazard that has led to the injury of a child, this should be discussed with a senior doctor. With parental permission this can then be reported to the appropriate agency, e.g. Local Authority, Trading Standards Office, Health and Safety Executive, Members of Parliament, for action.

ENFORCEMENT (LEGISLATION)

The most effective ways to reduce death and disability have occurred when legislation has been introduced. Worldwide the most effective interventions have been compulsory wearing of seat-belts in cars, fencing around open water, wearing of crash helmets when on bicycle/motorbike/horse and severe speed restrictions (e.g. 20 mph) in residential areas.

Audit and research in EDs can help provide information for legislative change, local safety hot-spots, and local motivation for change – such as safety locks on the windows of all local housing authority buildings over one storey high.

CHAPTER 3

PAIN MANAGEMENT

Introduction	6	How to treat pain	9
What are we treating?	6	Procedural sedation	14
Assessment of pain	7		

INTRODUCTION

The vast majority of minor injuries cause some degree of pain. Recognition and alleviation of pain should be a priority when treating injuries. This process should ideally start on arrival to your facility, and finish with ensuring that adequate analgesia is provided at discharge.

On the whole, pain is commonly under-recognized and undertreated in children. There are several reasons for this; in particular, assessing pain in children can be difficult. For example, children in pain may be quiet and withdrawn, rather than crying. Communication may be difficult with an upset child, and it may be difficult to distinguish pain from other causes of distress (fear, stranger anxiety, etc.). Some words are better understood than others, depending on what words the family use, e.g. hurt, sore, poorly. In some cases, children may deny pain for fear of the ensuing treatment (particularly needles).

On a practical note, there is often insecurity about dosage of medication in children, which has to be worked out in mg/kg. Some medications are not licensed for use in children, although are commonly used. Lastly, severe pain in adults is treated with intravenous opiate and although this should also be true for children the psychological hurdle of cannula insertion can lead to reluctance from staff to use this route.

WHAT ARE WE TREATING?

- *Pain* This requires analgesia (see below).
- *Fear of the situation* All efforts should be made to provide a calm, friendly environment. You should explain what you are doing, preparing the child for any procedures, and let the parents stay with the child unless they prefer not to, or are particularly distressed.

- *Loss of control* Children like to be involved in decisions and feel that they are being listened to.
- *Fear of the injury* Distraction and other cognitive techniques are extremely useful (see below). A little explanation and reassurance, and allowing the child to look at the injury, go a long way to allay anxiety.
- *Fear of the treatment* Unfortunately, some treatments hurt and are frightening in themselves (e.g. stitches). There are lots of things you can do to make procedures less stressful all round; this is covered below.

ASSESSMENT OF PAIN

Pain assessment and treatment now forms an integral part of quality standards for EDs in the UK and features in most triage guidelines.

 Stop: If there is severe pain, is there a major injury or ischaemia?

Your prior experience of injuries can help in estimating the amount of pain the child is likely to be in. For example, a fractured shaft of femur or a burn are more painful than a bump on the head. After that, you will rely on what the child says and how the child behaves.

Clearly the younger the child, the less they are able to describe how they are feeling, and separating out the distress caused by pain versus distress caused by other factors is tricky. Some children with mild pain can be very upset because of the stress of the whole situation, the circumstances of the accident, their prior experience of healthcare or because their parents are upset. Having a reassuring environment and staff trained to be comfortable in dealing with distressed children makes a big difference.

Asking a child to rate their pain is difficult; they have little life experience to draw upon and may not clearly remember previous painful episodes, yet we are asking them to make a comparison of mild pain to worst pain ever! Linear analogue scales of 0–10 or comparisons with stairs or a ladder are often too abstract for a child.

Faces scores showing emotions such as those in Table 3.1 are frequently used for self-reporting of pain in children. They have value but cannot be used in isolation, as they can also be flawed. Children may misunderstand the question and point to the happy face because that is how they want to feel, or choose the saddest face for the same reasons as above – it reflects how they feel and relativity is too difficult a concept.

Table 3.1 Pain assessment tool suitable for children

	No pain	Mild pain	Moderate pain	Severe pain	
Faces scale score					
Ladder score	0	1–3	4–6	7–10	
Behaviour	Normal activity No ↓ movement Happy	Rubbing affected area Decreased movement Neutral expression Able to play/talk normally	Protective of affected area ↓ movement/quiet Complaining of pain Consolable crying Grimaces when affected part moved/touched	No movement or defensive of affected part Looking frightened Very quiet Restless, unsettled Complaining of lots of pain Inconsolable crying	
Injury example	Bump on head	Abrasion Small laceration Sprain ankle/knee # fingers/clavicle Sore throat	Small burn/scald Finger tip injury # forearm/elbow/ankle Appendicitis	Large burn # long bone/dislocation Appendicitis Sickle crisis	
Category chosen (tick)					

Taking all of these issues into account, it is clearly better to use a composite score rather than relying on one system. Table 3.1 shows a suggested pain assessment tool that is recommended by the UK College of Emergency Medicine; the assessor uses the available information to decide what category the pain is. It uses objective and subjective information, and staff experience, to give an overall score of no, mild, moderate or severe pain.

HOW TO TREAT PAIN

Having assessed the degree of pain, there is a range of ways to treat pain. This includes psychological strategies, medication via various routes and non-medication treatments. A working knowledge of all the options is useful, so that your treatment is appropriate for the child's age and preference, type of injury and degree of pain. A suggested strategy for common conditions is given in Table 3.2.

Table 3.2 Examples of strategies for managing pain in common injuries (see also Chapter 16)

Injury	Psychological strategies	Non-pharmacological adjuncts	Pharmacological strategies
Facial wound	✓	Consider procedural sedation	Oral paracetamol Local anaesthesia
Fractured femur	✓	Sling, splint, or plaster backslab	Entonox as interim measure Intranasal diamorphine or intravenous morphine Femoral or '3 in 1' nerve block
Burn	✓	Initial cooling, then cover with dressing or cling wrap	Minor – oral paracetamol and/or ibuprofen Major – intranasal diamorphine or intravenous morphine
Minor head injury	✓	Cold compress	Oral paracetamol and/or ibuprofen

Psychological strategies

Psychological strategies should be relevant to the age of child, but are useful in all situations.

Many children object to practical procedures, even if not painful. This therefore generates a lot of anxiety in parents and staff alike. Good communication, at a level appropriate to the child, and good listening skills make a big difference. Look confident at all times, since apprehension appears to be contagious!

In some clinical areas Play Specialists are available to calm children waiting to be seen, prepare them for what will happen during the consultation, provide distraction during procedures and rewards afterwards. There is no hard evidence but in clinical areas where Play Specialists are employed, staff feel that children are treated with less stress, much quicker and with less recourse to sedation or hospital admission for general anaesthesia. Without Play Specialists, it is still quite possible to provide the right environment and some basic psychological techniques to achieve the same outcome.

Preparation is useful; for example, an explanation with carefully chosen words, focusing on the endpoint, demonstrating on a doll using the same equipment, and bargaining around getting home as soon as possible or receiving rewards.

Next you need to provide distraction during the procedure. This applies from infants to teenagers and your unit should have a selection of age-appropriate toys, bubbles to blow, murals on walls, books, videos, etc. Hypnosis is successful but is a skill that has to be learned. Music is both soothing and distracting. Videos are useful, although turning one off before it has finished can be tricky! It is usually relatively easy to obtain toys, etc., from charitable funds, through local fundraising; just be aware that all purchases should be easy to keep clean with your organization's antimicrobial cleaning fluids.

It is important to perform procedures swiftly; do not explain the procedure to the child then leave them worrying about it while you go and do something else.

Experienced staff are invaluable when handling distressed children. It is important to be reassuring but sympathetic. Cuddling, stroking and talking to children helps to reassure them. Keep the momentum moving forwards and do not allow excessive procrastination or bargaining if the child is trying to avoid the procedure.

Non-medication treatments

Splintage of injured limbs, and elevation of the lower leg above hip level, or elevation of the hand in a high arm sling reduce swelling and therefore pain. When treating burns, reducing air currents with cling film or dressings is sometimes all that is needed. Regular application of ice packs (e.g. frozen peas) to soft tissue injuries reduces inflammation (avoiding direct contact of ice with skin). Small children dislike ice packs but a bowl of cool water can be tried.

Medication options

There are numerous options for analgesia, with differences between different organizations and different countries. The options here are just suggestions.

 Stop: For major injuries, seek senior advice and obtain intravenous (IV) access!

Oral medication

- *Mild pain* may be treated with paracetamol (acetaminophen) or non-steroidal anti-inflammatory drugs such as ibuprofen. A combination of both works well.
- *Moderate pain* may be treated with codeine-containing preparations in addition to paracetamol and an anti-inflammatory drug; diclofenac is a stronger anti-inflammatory than ibuprofen.
- *More severe pain* may be treated with oral morphine solution (Oramorph) but this takes around 20 minutes to start working. Intranasal opiates work quicker (see below). Intravenous opiates should not be avoided, but in many situations the intranasal opiate will give you 30–60 minutes of good analgesia and anxiolysis, during which time you can obtain venous access with less stress.

Intranasal analgesia

A useful alternative with a quicker onset of action is intranasal diamorphine (see below) or intranasal fentanyl. Intranasal diamorphine has a rapid onset of action (2–5 minutes), and is highly effective. It is now in widespread use in UK EDs and is popular for the following reasons: it acts much quicker than oral opiates, is well tolerated, avoids a needle and has marked anxiolytic effects. Its offset is 30–60 minutes, by which time

Table 3.3 Dosage of intranasal diamorphine for acute pain

Child's weight (kg)	Volume of water
10	1.9
15	1.3
20	1.0
25	0.8
30	0.7
35	0.6
40	0.5
50	0.4
60	0.3

Dilute 10 mg of diamorphine powder with specific volume of water. Instil 0.2 mL of the solution into one nostril, using a 1-mL syringe (gives 0.1 mg/kg in 0.2 mL).

dressings or splints will have been applied and the child's trust gained, so that if ongoing analgesia is needed, insertion of an IV line is much easier and less traumatic.

0.1 mg/kg is made up to 0.2 mL with saline, and dropped in to the nostril via a 1-mL syringe with the head tilted back slightly. See the chart in Table 3.3 for full dosage and administration, which ensures an end volume of 0.2 mL whatever the child's weight.

These are the commonest choices for analgesia in the UK. Figure 3.1 shows a suggested algorithm for analgesia for mild, moderate and severe pain, as recommended by the UK College of Emergency Medicine.

Inhalational analgesia
30% nitrous oxide and oxygen (Entonox) can be provided in cylinders with a facemask or intra-oral delivery system. It depends on the child's cooperation and coordination, and understanding that it is self-activated. For continuous administration of nitrous oxide see 'Procedural sedation' (below).

Topical anaesthesia
Lidocaine gel is useful for dirty abrasions that need to be cleaned. Local anaesthetic creams such as Ametop or EMLA are not licensed for use on open wounds, and have an onset of 20–60 minutes so are of limited use for urgent situations. However, if time allows, it is useful to use these before

Algorithm for treatment of acute pain in children in A&E

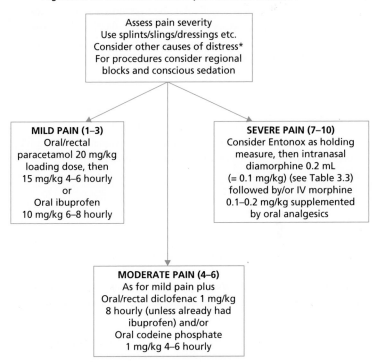

Assess pain severity
Use splints/slings/dressings etc.
Consider other causes of distress*
For procedures consider regional
blocks and conscious sedation

MILD PAIN (1–3)
Oral/rectal
paracetamol 20 mg/kg
loading dose, then
15 mg/kg 4–6 hourly
or
Oral ibuprofen
10 mg/kg 6–8 hourly

SEVERE PAIN (7–10)
Consider Entonox as holding
measure, then intranasal
diamorphine 0.2 mL
(= 0.1 mg/kg) (see Table 3.3)
followed by/or IV morphine
0.1–0.2 mg/kg supplemented
by oral analgesics

MODERATE PAIN (4–6)
As for mild pain plus
Oral/rectal diclofenac 1 mg/kg
8 hourly (unless already had
ibuprofen) and/or
Oral codeine phosphate
1 mg/kg 4–6 hourly

*Other causes of distress include: fear of the unfamiliar environment, parental distress, fear of strangers, needle phobia, fear of injury severity etc.

CONTRAINDICATIONS:
Ibuprofen/diclofenac: avoid if previous reactions to NSAIDs or in moderate or severe asthmatics
Intravenous morphine: use with caution if risk of depression of airway, breathing or circulation.

Figure 3.1 Example of a pain treatment strategy.

local infiltration of anaesthesia. Preparations safe for use on open wounds are very useful (e.g. LET cream) but are not commercially available in the UK; however, they can be made up by your local pharmacy.

Local infiltration of anaesthesia
Infiltration of local anaesthetic is painful and may not be justified if only one or two sutures are required. The pain of injection can be reduced by using a narrow bore needle (e.g. dental needle), by slow injection (see Chapter 16) and probably by buffering and warming the solution.

Regional anaesthesia

Nerve blocks are easy to learn, well tolerated by children and avoid the risks of sedation and respiratory depression. Particularly useful nerve blocks are the femoral or 'three in one' nerve blocks for a fractured femur, the infra-auricular block for removing earrings, and digital or metacarpal nerve blocks for fingers (see Chapter 16).

Intravenous analgesia

IV opiates such as morphine are used when immediate analgesia is required. There should be no hesitation in administering these drugs to children provided care is taken and resuscitation facilities are available. IV fentanyl or propofol should only be used for procedural sedation (see below).

Warning: Respiratory depression and drowsiness may occur!

Respiratory depression may be avoided by titrating from half the recommended dose to the normal recommended dose, up to as much as the child needs for an adequate dose over a few minutes, within the maximum allowed. Naloxone should be available in your department if you are using IV opiates, for reversal, if necessary. Anti-emetics are not usually required in children.

Intramuscular route

This route is best avoided as it subjects the child to a needle and holds no advantage over the IV route. Absorption is unpredictable and often slow, making repeated doses (and therefore needles) necessary, and the repeat dosage difficult to calculate.

PROCEDURAL SEDATION

A wider discussion of the various techniques for procedural sedation is beyond this handbook. Procedural sedation is practised in many UK EDs, but is not suitable for other urgent care settings. It holds benefits for the child (amnesia and avoidance of generating fear for subsequent hospital treatment), the child's parents, other parents and children who might otherwise hear screams, the staff and, most importantly, a more thorough and better technical result for the procedure itself without recourse to general anaesthesia.

Warning: Adequate monitoring, trained staff and resuscitation facilities are essential. Do not attempt procedural sedation unless your unit fulfils the basic requirements!

In the UK there are guidelines about safe sedation practice, available from the National Institute for Health and Clinical Excellence (NICE).

Link: http://guidance.nice.org.uk/CG/Wave18/52

Midazolam is a benzodiazepine that may be given orally, intranasally, rectally or intravenously. Oral midazolam at a dose of 0.5 mg/kg provides mild anxiolysis within 10–15 minutes, but has wide individual variation in effect and can cause hyperactivity. It is most useful in facilitating distraction such as when removing a foreign body. The oral route is less likely to cause a rapid peak in drug levels than the rectal route, and is better tolerated than the intranasal route, which may cause local irritation. *Note it is not an analgesic.* IV midazolam is often combined with an IV opiate for procedures such as fracture or dislocation reduction. The adverse effects of both drugs combined are higher than with a single agent and only experienced doctors should be using this combination.

Nitrous oxide 50%, with 50% oxygen administered continuously provides analgesia, anxiolysis and amnesia. Monitoring and resuscitation facilities are needed.

Ketamine is a more effective and safe alternative that provides 'dissociative anaesthesia' and has become the preferred option for procedural sedation in the UK. The UK College of Emergency Medicine has a useful guideline on its use in EDs. The USA, Canada, South Africa and Australia also have guidelines for this setting. Upper respiratory tract symptoms or abnormal airway anatomy (e.g. history of prolonged ventilation) are the main contraindications to the use of ketamine. It may be given IV (ideally) or IM (intramuscular). The IV route allows you to titrate the dose, and wears off quicker. A dose of 2.5 mg/kg IM, or 1–2 mg/kg IV, works within 3 minutes and allows you to perform procedures lasting up to 30 minutes with the child remaining undistressed.

Ketamine may cause hypersalivation, which, rarely, may cause laryngospasm. Also, children are at risk of agitation and hallucinations in the 'emergence' phase as the drug wears off, so should therefore be allowed to recover in a quiet room, although still under close nursing observation.

The UK College of Emergency Medicine guidelines also provide useful templates for monitoring, discharge criteria and parental advice after discharge.

Link: http://www.collemergencymed.ac.uk/CEC/cec_ketamine.pdf

IV propofol is also gaining in popularity but its use is not yet mainstream in the UK.

CHAPTER 4

WOUNDS AND SOFT TISSUE INJURIES

Introduction	16	Common complications	25
Basic history	16	Specific wounds and areas	26
Basic examination	18	Hair tourniquet syndrome	26
Factors involved in healing	19	Haematomas and contusions	27
General principles of wound management	21	Sprains	27
		Compartment syndrome	28
General principles of wound repair	22	Degloving injuries	29
Aftercare	24	Skin abscesses	29

For specific areas, refer to the following chapters: face, Chapter 5; hand, Chapter 9; genitalia, Chapter 14.

INTRODUCTION

Wounds and superficial injuries form a large part of paediatric trauma. Wounds, in particular, are a source of anxiety for children, parents and Emergency Department (ED) staff. Often the child is distressed by the accident itself, the parents are concerned about scarring, and both parents and staff may be reticent about the procedure of wound repair itself. The use of psychological techniques, an experienced nurse and adequate analgesia will make the procedure more endurable for all (see Chapter 3).

You can avoid most pitfalls related to wound management by stopping to ask yourself: How exactly did this happen? Are there likely to be associated injuries? What is underneath this part of the body? Is this a simple wound that is suitable for simple repair?

BASIC HISTORY

Important questions

Mechanism of injury
A precise history is needed to alert you to potential problems.

 Warning: By asking What? How? Where? you will spot important pitfalls!

For example:

- underlying injury to tendons/nerves (e.g. wound from something sharp)
- hidden foreign body (FB) (e.g. wound from broken glass)
- significant head injury (e.g. fall from higher than child's head height)
- significant blood loss (e.g. wound over blood vessel such as femoral canal)
- non-accidental injury (e.g. injury in non-mobile child).

Time of injury
Wounds over 12 hours old may be better left to heal by secondary intention. If the wound is clean, it may be repaired up to 24 hours, particularly if it is on the face or scalp. You should consider prescribing an antibiotic such as flucloxacillin if suturing an injury after 12 hours.

Tetanus immunization status
Most children in the UK will be fully vaccinated. Routine immunizations are given at 2, 3 and 4 months old, then again pre-school, and aged 14–15. This confers life-long immunity. If an immunization has been missed, the opportunity should be taken to provide it (if there are departmental arrangements to ensure communication with primary care/community colleagues to avoid duplication). In a non-immunized child this will not provide cover in time for the existing wound, so if the wound is dirty antitetanus immunoglobulin should also be given.

Concurrent illness
This is rarely an issue in children and does not affect wound repair. If the child is immunosuppressed or on long-term steroid treatment, follow-up to check wound healing at 5–7 days is advisable. Remember that children with chronic illness may be more needle-phobic.

Consideration of non-accidental injury and accident prevention
The circumstances of the accident need to be given adequate attention (see Chapter 15). However, wounds usually raise concerns more about supervision of the child than actual deliberate injury. The Health Visitor should be notified for all injuries to pre-school children. They will identify issues around accident prevention, and may subsequently visit the family at home.

BASIC EXAMINATION

Wound description

Site

When writing your notes always draw diagrams, which are clearer than a written description.

Think through the anatomical structures underlying the wound. Is there potential damage to tendons, nerves, blood vessels, the joint capsule? Bleeding can be significant from scalp wounds or concealed vessel injury, such as the groin. The skin surrounding and distal to the wound should be normal colour, have normal sensation, and distal pulses and capillary refill should be tested and documented.

Test for tendons and nerves where you can. Full strength against resistance should be tested for muscle groups and tendons. Assessment is harder in pre-verbal children. Where you cannot test, or there is the possibility of deep, serious injury, the wound may need exploration by a surgical colleague.

 Warning: If in doubt, always seek expert advice!

Site also affects wound healing (see below), so bear that in mind when deciding whether follow-up is needed.

Size

Large wounds may need suturing under general anaesthesia. Calculate the maximum safe dose of local anaesthetic for the child's weight. If this is likely to be exceeded, a general anaesthetic may be needed if there is not a suitable alternative regional block (see Chapter 16). Other than anaesthetic issues, size in itself does not affect the choice of options for closure, as discussed below.

Depth

Depth affects the likelihood of damage to underlying structures, and your options for closure (see below). The most innocent-looking wound on the surface can conceal serious complications, especially if it is a stab wound or a puncture wound. Deep wounds may need two layers of suture – an inner, absorbable layer as well as the skin sutures.

 Stop: Seek senior advice immediately for stab wounds! Treat A, B, C, D, before focusing on the wound

FACTORS INVOLVED IN HEALING

Wounds generally heal better in children than adults. Wound healing is very individual, and in growing children the appearance of the scar can change for up to 2 years. Therefore, avoid being either very positive or very negative when asked about future appearance.

Children with pigmented skins may have hypopigmentation of the affected area, either for a year or so, or long term. Those of Afro-Caribbean origin may develop keloid scars. Sun sensitivity may be a problem for 6–12 months in any race, so recommend protective creams. Many wounds itch when healing, and simple moisturisers (particularly those used for treating eczema) are useful.

Site of injury

Healing is quickest in wounds on the face, mouth and scalp, because of the richness of the blood supply, and takes longest in the lower body.

The tension across a wound is important, and is a major factor in your choice of closure techniques (see below). Delayed healing and/or scarring are most likely when wounds are under tension. It is worth considering splintage to help healing in mobile areas, for example knuckle, knee or heel wounds.

There are lines of natural tension in the body. These are called Langer's lines (Figures 4.1 and 4.2). If a wound is aligned with these lines, healing occurs quicker and is less likely to produce a scar than wounds that cross the lines.

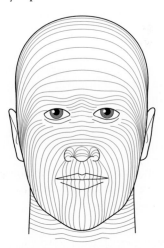

Figure 4.1 Langer's lines of the face.

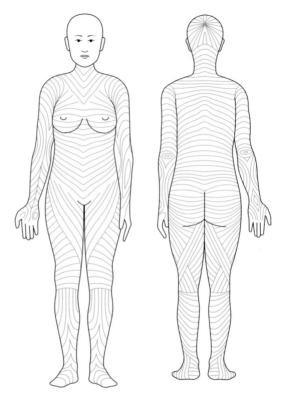

Figure 4.2 Langer's lines of the body.

Infection risk

Infection is more likely in dirty areas of the body, e.g. sole of the foot, and, obviously, more likely in dirty wounds. Organic material is far more likely to cause infection than inorganic material. Substances such as soil carry a high bacterial load. Also, bacteria multiply in a logarithmic fashion so the longer a wound remains dirty, the higher the risk. Infection risk is lower in areas with a good blood supply. The more distal the wound (from the head), the greater the likelihood of infection.

The more open a wound, the easier it is for infection to drain. This means that puncture wounds are at high risk of infection, despite looking benign (see 'Specific wounds and areas', below).

 Warning: Puncture wounds are at high risk of infection!

Lastly, wound infection may be a sign of a FB. See below for a discussion of this.

Wound edges

Wounds which heal best and scar least have healthy, straight edges. Crush injuries are more likely to produce swelling and ragged edges that are difficult to oppose, causing delayed healing and scarring. They may also damage the skin, causing haematoma formation and jeopardizing viability. Shaved edges (sometimes with skin loss) are likely to heal with a visible scar.

If wound edges look severely damaged, it is often worth waiting a few days to judge viability in children, rather than immediately debriding the edges; children can recover well. If you are unsure, ask a more experienced doctor.

GENERAL PRINCIPLES OF WOUND MANAGEMENT

Abrasions

Abrasions may be of variable depth, and can be described and treated in a similar way to burns. At initial presentation, every attempt must be made to get the wound as clean as possible using local anaesthesia if needed.

In children, abrasions may be contaminated with road tar, which has the potential to cause 'tattooing'. If the wound is inadequately cleaned, dirt particles become ingrained and cause permanent disfigurement. Forceps, surgical brushes or needles may be used. If the surface area to be cleaned is so large that the dose of local anaesthetic may be exceeded, general anaesthesia may be necessary.

If a little dirt remains, this may work its way out over the next few days and dressings and creams such as those used to deslough chronic ulcers may be helpful. Follow-up is necessary.

 Warning: Do not leave the wound dirty for more than 2 or 3 days. If difficulties persist, refer to surgeon!

Cleaning and irrigation of wounds

All wounds should be considered dirty to an extent, but those contaminated with organic material are particularly at risk of infection. Good wound toilet, with adequate dilution of the bacterial load with copious water, is far more important than relying on prophylactic antibiotics. See Chapter 16 for how to irrigate a wound. There is little evidence for antiseptic solutions being any better than water at preventing infections, and they sting more.

Exploration of wounds

Exploration of a wound should be considered when a FB, or damage to underlying structures, is suspected. However, it often requires several injections to create an anaesthetic field, and some children may not understand or tolerate this, or prolonged periods of wound exploration. Consider this before you start. Also consider how much local anaesthetic you are likely to need. If this exceeds the safe total dose for the child's weight, the child will need a regional or general anaesthetic. If you think you will need more experienced help, it is better to get this at the outset than have a child waiting halfway through a procedure, getting anxious.

Lastly, never extend a wound without seeking advice first.

Foreign bodies

See also Chapter 13. Foreign bodies such as grit and oil may cause tattooing if left (see 'Abrasions', above). If there is a FB below the wound and this is not suspected or detected, the wound is likely to become infected, or heal slowly or break down again.

Warning: Always consider the potential presence of a FB in any infected wound!

Warning: Always request a soft tissue X-ray if an injury has been caused by glass!

Top-tip: Most types of glass are radio-opaque (see Chapter 13, Figure 13.1). Fragments are notoriously difficult to spot with the naked eye, and may lie deep. If glass has been removed from a wound, a follow-up X-ray must be performed to check it is all gone. Other types of FB are not radio-opaque including plant material such as wood. However, these can often be clearly demonstrated by ultrasound.

GENERAL PRINCIPLES OF WOUND REPAIR

See Chapter 16 for application of adhesive strips and glue; anaesthesia: local infiltration and regional blocks; insertion of sutures.

Primary repair or not?

Wounds over 12 hours old (24 hours for facial or scalp wounds), those which are contaminated, contused, devitalized or bites are more likely to become infected. In these cases you will often be best advised to leave the wound unclosed, with a dressing over the top. It will heal by 'secondary intention'. This means healing by granulation from the bottom up and eventual re-epithelialization over the top. In such wounds, sutures act as an additional FB and increase the risk of infection; opposition of the wound edges (either by sutures or adhesive strips) makes the underlying wound anaerobic and more prone to infection. The outcome can be a lot more protracted, with worse scarring, than if the wound had been left open. To speed this process up, splintage may be needed (e.g. of a knee).

Wounds with skin loss should also usually be allowed to heal by secondary intention, rather than creating tension by trying to achieve primary closure. Wounds with skin loss of less than a squared centimetre tend to do well, and even larger areas will often heal in children, without recourse to skin grafting.

In certain circumstances delayed primary closure after 4–5 days is appropriate. This means not attempting any closure until that time, to minimize the risk of infection. If you are thinking of leaving a wound to heal by secondary intention, seek advice about the option of delayed closure.

 Warning: If in doubt, always seek expert advice!

Choice of technique for wound closure

Although interrupted sutures are what we often do, and are often perceived as the gold standard in wound repair, in fact the cosmetic result is as good with adhesive strips or glue, provided there is no tension on the wound. Factors such as Langer's lines (see 'Factors involved in healing', above) are more important than depth. Do not let yourself avoid sutures if they are indicated though, simply because of the practical difficulties of suturing children. A good cosmetic result is paramount.

Tissue glue has an excellent cosmetic result. It needs to be applied properly (see Chapter 16) and can sting while it is applied. It rubs off and dissolves away after about 2 weeks. Adhesive strips are often known by parents as 'butterfly stitches' and are easy to apply. They are easy to remove after a few days, especially if wetted. Glue tolerates a few splashes or a quick dunk in water better than adhesive strips. Staples are sometimes used, but patients and parents find them off-putting, and removal can be tricky. In mobile areas of the body or in fidgety children, glue with overlaid adhesive strips can be a useful technique.

AFTERCARE

Dressings and bandages

There is a lot of debate but not much scientific evidence for 'the right dressing'. There is often less focus on how to do 'the right bandage' but, in practical terms, for children this is crucial. Many bandages do not last much longer than the child leaving your treatment area, and the dressing will fall off too. For tips on longevity see Chapter 16.

The purpose of a dressing is to prevent additional contamination of the wound and to provide a barrier to air currents and friction against clothing, etc. Wounds that are oozing (blood or serous fluid) must be dressed with a non-stick dressing, so that changing the dressing in the next day or two does not hurt or disturb the wound too much. Paraffin-impregnated gauze is a suitable dressing.

After the first 24–72 hours, silicon-based dressings are particularly useful, but other non-stick dressings can be used. It is best to leave the wound undisturbed for a few days, unless it is at high risk of infection. Unfortunately, despite the tricks of the trade, children often pull dressings off, or get them wet or dirty, necessitating more frequent dressing changes.

A more detailed discussion of wound dressing is too large a topic to be covered in this book, and there is a great deal of variation, depending on local circumstances.

Prophylactic antibiotics

Good wound cleaning (see above) is more important than antibiotic treatment. Antibiotics are only necessary if there is a high risk of infection. This means wounds contaminated with organic material, or bites. An anti-staphylococcal and anti-streptococcal agent such as flucloxacillin is appropriate. Cover for Gram-negative organisms is only needed for certain animal bites (see Chapter 12), oral or perineal wounds, or those sustained in muddy areas or water.

Tetanus

See 'Basic history' (above).

Immobilization

If a wound is over a mobile area such as a joint, wound healing is often speeded up considerably, and scarring reduced, if the part is immobilized with a splint or small plaster of Paris for a week or two. In this short period of time, stiffness is not really an issue with children compared with adults.

Suture removal

If sutures are left in too long there is an increased risk of infection, and of suture marks being visible on the skin permanently. Children heal much quicker than adults, so sutures can usually be removed on day 4 on the face, and day 5 on other areas, unless under tension. The wound can always be supported by adhesive strips for a few days after sutures are removed.

COMMON COMPLICATIONS

Infection

Infection is more likely in wounds that are dirty or contain a FB, those with contused or crushed skin, puncture wounds, or those with a delay in treatment or cleaning. If a wound becomes infected, consider the presence of a FB.

It may sometimes be difficult to tell if a wound is infected, but signs include slow healing, ongoing oozing, surrounding erythema, smell and pain. Spreading cellulitis, lymphangitis or systemic upset are indications for intravenous antibiotics.

Wound swabs do not yield useful microbiological results for 2–3 days so the decision to treat is usually clinical. Treat with an antibiotic such as flucloxacillin, immobilize the wound or discourage use of the limb, elevate it if possible and remove sutures if present.

 Warning: Infected wounds should be reviewed after 2–3 days!

Dehiscence

If dehiscence occurs, seek surgical advice. Dehiscence almost always means that there is wound infection (unless there has been clear disturbance of the wound).

SPECIFIC WOUNDS AND AREAS

Puncture wounds

Innocent-looking puncture wounds are a minefield to the unwary. First they may be much deeper than initially suspected, and a thorough clinical examination of underlying structures should be undertaken (see beginning of chapter).

Second, bacteria are injected deep into tissues. The smaller the wound, the more likely it is to become infected because the overlying skin edges are opposed. Consider antibiotic prophylaxis, unless you can get the nozzle of a syringe into the puncture wound for gentle irrigation (see Chapter 16).

Needlestick injuries

Hospitals often have a needlestick policy. Children may sustain such injuries when they find discarded needles in areas frequented by drug misusers. If you have no local policy, advise parents that the risk of blood-borne infection is low, but is higher for hepatitis B than HIV. Also, post-exposure prophylaxis for potential hepatitis B infection carries minimal side-effects, unlike HIV. Seek specialist advice.

Plantar wounds of the foot

These wounds are notorious for their propensity to develop infection, particularly *Pseudomonas aeruginosa,* often after a delay of several days to a few weeks. Patients should be advised to return if pain increases, and appropriate specialist advice sought if this occurs. An antibiotic such as ciprofloxacin is often prescribed prophylactically. Find out if you have a local policy.

HAIR TOURNIQUET SYNDROME

Assessment

This odd condition occurs when one or more hairs become wrapped around the base of a digit, and gradually constrict, causing ischaemia. It usually occurs in babies, and affects fingers and toes, but may affect other areas such as the penis. It is most common in toddlers and babies. There is no history of a hair becoming entangled – you will only make the diagnosis by being aware of this condition or by very close examination. The digit may be bluish or white. A magnifying glass may be needed to see the hair(s).

Management

The hair must be released as soon as possible. Cut or unwind the hair using forceps; a stitch cutter may be able to get under the hair; fine ear, nose and throat (ENT) instruments may also help to lift it up; a commercial depilatory cream may work. Be very careful that you do not only remove part of the hair or just one of several hairs. Keep the child under observation for an hour. If you are unsure that you have successfully released the hair, call for a more experienced person. The child may end up needing general anaesthesia, a hand surgeon and an operating microscope. A deep incision may have to be made.

Warning: Be sure the digit looks healthy and reperfused before discharging the child!

HAEMATOMAS AND CONTUSIONS

A haematoma is a large bruise with a large collection of blood. A contusion just means bruising. Bruising is common in children, and normally affects the lower limbs. Bruising is less common on the trunk or face or behind the ears. If you see bruising in these areas, or see many bruises, ask how they happened.

Warning: Always assess whether bruising is compatible with the history given, and refer for a second opinion if unsure. See Chapter 15.

If there are multiple bruises, consider checking the platelet count and a clotting screen. The age of a bruise is more difficult to determine than is commonly thought, so you should never comment on the age of a bruise.

Following blunt injury, a significant amount of bleeding may go on underneath the skin surface and may not be apparent for some days. It will usually come out distal to the actual site of injury because of gravity. Fortunately, children are less prone to stiffness of the affected muscles than adults, because they heal quicker and are more determined to mobilize early.

Simple initial management of contused areas involves elevation of the affected part if possible and the application of icepacks (avoiding direct contact of the ice on the skin) at regular intervals for the first few hours, if the child will accept this. Early mobilization will help the blood dissolve. Although this is rarely a problem in small children, teenagers may need some encouragement!

SPRAINS

A sprain is a soft tissue injury such as tearing of a ligament. Children have stretchy tissues so are less prone to sprains than adults, and generally recover much quicker. This means you should be careful in diagnosing a simple sprain in toddlers and young children, since an underlying fracture is more likely.

The management of a sprain is similar to a contusion (see above). Early mobilization should be encouraged. Most EDs have advice sheets for common sprains such as the ankle, shoulder, or knee.

The mnemonic 'RICE' is often used: rest, ice, compression and elevation. However, most children are reluctant to rest or elevate their limb for very long, and there is little evidence that more than 24 hours of rest is beneficial. Also, children often find using crutches difficult. Icepacks can be applied a few times in the first 12 hours. Direct contact of ice with skin should be avoided, and packets of frozen vegetables wrapped in a tea towel are a practical choice for most households! A compression bandage may help reduce swelling but does not provide support or improve healing.

Refer to the following chapters for specific sprains: neck, Chapter 6; knee and ankle, Chapter 10.

COMPARTMENT SYNDROME

In certain areas of the body, particularly the forearm and lower leg, the muscles are grouped together in compartments, separated by fascia. Following injury, swelling occurs, and can be accommodated up to a point. Thereafter, the pressure inside the compartment rises, the blood supply via the arterioles becomes jeopardized, and the muscles become ischaemic. A vicious cycle develops, which can result in necrosis, rhabdomyolysis, contractures and even loss of limb. This is much less common in children than adults, and is usually associated with limb fractures in teenagers.

Pulses often remain present until late on in the process. Early symptoms are pain and paraesthesia. Passive stretching of the muscles is extremely painful and the limb may appear swollen. If in doubt, the pressure inside the compartment can be measured using a needle and transducer (pressures above 30 mmHg are worrying). Opening up the whole compartment with a fasciotomy may be needed.

Stop: An urgent surgical opinion is necessary for suspected compartment syndrome!

DEGLOVING INJURIES

Degloving injuries occur when the skin and its blood supply are avulsed. This occurs with a blunt, shearing, mechanism of injury and may not be obvious in the early stages, particularly if no laceration of the skin has occurred.

 Warning: It may be very difficult to spot a degloving injury, so always think about the mechanism of the injury!

Areas prone to this kind of injury are the scalp, lower leg and foot. A typical mechanism of injury would be a car wheel running over the leg. On examination, the skin is often contused and may be mobile. Swelling and/or an underlying fracture need not necessarily be present.

Initial management consists of elevation of the limb or compression for a scalp laceration. A plastic surgeon must be involved, often jointly with an orthopaedic surgeon, since microsurgery, external fixation of fractures, fasciotomy or skin grafting may be necessary.

SKIN ABSCESSES

An abscess is a contained infection that may be caused by a breach of the skin, an infected hair follicle or often for no obvious reason. They are relatively uncommon in children, and the presence of a FB should be considered. A common abscess in children is a paronychia (see Chapter 9).

Once pus has collected, it cannot be treated successfully with antibiotics, but requires incision and drainage. The abscess may be quite deep seated and require general anaesthesia to achieve enough analgesia to allow full evacuation of its contents. Axillary, perianal and facial abscesses should be referred to a surgeon.

For straightforward abscesses, incision and drainage can be performed in the ED. This is best achieved with infiltration of local anaesthesia, and a large incision made to allow the pus out and to continue to drain. A non-adhesive dressing should be applied and the patient reviewed by their general practitioner.

Head injury: introduction	30	Injuries of the ear	39
Assessment of head injuries	31	Nasal injuries	40
Management of head injuries	33	Oral injuries	41
Scalp lacerations	36	Dental injuries	42
Facial lacerations	36	Chin lacerations	43
Eye injuries	37	Facial fractures	43

HEAD INJURY: INTRODUCTION

Around half a million children per year present to the Emergency Department (ED) with head injury. Less than 1 per cent of these children will have a positive computed tomography (CT) scan. Only around 6 per cent will receive a head scan in an average UK ED. So you can see that the vast majority of children are rapidly discharged home after a brief, clinical examination. The challenge is to spot the child who may have an intracranial bleed, and require neurosurgery or admission for observation. The way to do this is to recognize the importance of the mechanism of injury, take into account the difficulty of clinical evaluation in babies and small toddlers, and recognize the importance of confusion or agitation.

 Stop: Serious head injury is one of the commonest causes of death in children.

Most seriously injured children are apparent from the mechanism of injury, and their symptoms and signs (see below). Sadly, a small group of infants die each year from non-accidental head injury.

For the purposes of this book, a minor head injury is defined as one where the Glasgow Coma Score (GCS) is *normal,* i.e. the child is alert and orientated.

ASSESSMENT OF HEAD INJURIES

Mechanism of injury

In any age group, injury severity correlates with the distance fallen. Any child falling from higher than their head height must be regarded as high risk. Infants and toddlers often fall head first because the head is large compared with the rest of the body.

Non-mobile infants may fall from a height such as parents' arms, a bed, or a baby chair put on a work surface. Skull fractures are relatively common in these cases, whereas injuries in toddlers tend to be caused by tripping over and are generally benign.

In any non-mobile infant, listen hard to the history. If the baby is said to have rolled off a surface check that the baby is developmentally capable of doing this by playing with them.

 Warning: Always consider non-accidental injury in non-mobile infants! (see Chapter 15)

A depressed skull fracture will tend to be caused by something with a small surface area striking the head, such as a golf club or corner of a table or step.

Beware in older children as the true story may be concealed (for example a teenager who does not want to confess what he/she was up to). This can occasionally catch us out.

Symptoms

When you take the history you must ask directly about the following symptoms: loss of consciousness (beware different phrases for this such as 'knocked out' or appearances such as 'floppy', 'not there', etc.), memory of events during and pre- and post injury, headache, confusion at any time, agitation or drowsiness, a seizure post injury, and vomiting.

 Link: Vomiting once or twice is fairly common, as is the child wanting to sleep for a short period. Vomiting or drowsiness beyond this point means the child needs a head CT scan. In the UK there are national guidelines for this. www.nice.org.uk/CG56

Headache is a relatively uncommon complaint in a child, so have a low threshold for CT. Any of the other symptoms listed require a head CT.

A minor head injury in some toddlers can trigger a 'breath-holding attack', which must be distinguished from loss of consciousness as a result of brain injury. The diagnosis is based on a careful history of a brief interval of consciousness and fright before apnoea, and sometimes unconsciousness. The child recovers back to normal within a minute or so. There may have been previous similar episodes such as after immunizations. Though frightening, it is an entirely benign phenomenon.

Examination

In any head-injured child, before you start assessment consider if the cervical spine needs to be protected (see Chapter 6).

 Warning: Consider an associated cervical spine injury!

Next, you need to learn how to assess a GCS (Table 5.1). This can be a bit tricky in a small child, so use the adult score but apply some common sense. If it is impossible to be accurate, describe the child's behaviour. For example, do they interact with the people and environment around them? Are they settled or agitated or drowsy? Assessing the GCS takes practice: keep a copy with you (or look at the ambulance sheet, chart on a wall or observations chart) and keep practising!

Table 5.1 Glasgow coma scale

Glasgow coma scale		Score
Eyes open	Spontaneously	4
	To speech	3
	To pain	2
	None	1
Best verbal response	Orientated	5
	Conversation disorganized	4
	Inappropriate words	3
	Incomprehensible sound	2
	None	1
Best motor response	Obeys commands, normal spontaneous	6
	Localizes to painful stimulus	5
	Flexes to pain	4
	Abnormal flexor posturing	3
	Abnormal extensor posturing	2
	None	1

Warning: If the GCS is less than 15 for more than 10 minutes after the injury, it is not a minor head injury!

After assessing the GCS you need to examine the pupils and the scalp. In a fully conscious child, if you see asymmetry of the pupils it is highly unlikely to be due to the head injury (asymmetry implies rapid deterioration due to raised intracranial pressure, which is a late sign and follows confusion).

Scalp signs may include lacerations or haematomas. Small, firm haematomas are generally benign, even if quite prominent. Larger, 'boggy' haematomas are highly indicative of underlying fracture, particularly in the under-ones.

In an infant, if there is visible bruising on the face or scalp (as opposed to the usual 'bump') non-accidental injury must be considered.

Conventionally we are taught to examine for Battle's sign (bruising behind the ears) and 'panda eyes' (bruising around the eyes) as signs of a base of skull fracture. In reality, base of skull fractures are rare in children, and these signs take a few hours to develop. Equally, fundoscopy is largely pointless. By the time the fundi show signs of papilloedema, the child will not have a normal GCS or be behaving normally.

MANAGEMENT OF HEAD INJURIES

Local policies will, for the large part, determine your management. By the time children have arrived in the ED, been observed in the play area while waiting to be seen, then undergone a simple clinical assessment, the vast majority can be sent home with advice.

The role of X-rays and CT

The correlation between skull fracture (Figure 5.1) and intracranial bleeding is less clear than in adults, and particularly so in the shaken baby syndrome (see Chapter 15), so there is an argument that skull X-rays (SXR) are largely redundant if there is access to a CT scanner and there is cause for concern.

A SXR remains useful for several reasons however. It can provide extra information without resorting to CT, which carries a high radiation dose and may require sedation. The most likely example is the child with a boggy haematoma who appears perfectly well. SXR is a useful screening tool for depressed fracture, if suspected by the mechanism of injury. If you think a SXR may help, discuss the situation with your radiologist. Different hospitals have different policies.

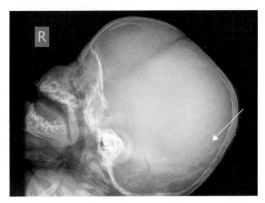

Figure 5.1 A linear parietal skull fracture.

Fractures can be difficult to identify on X-rays. Features which make a lucent line more likely to be a fracture than a suture line or vascular marking are: sharply demarcated with uniform width throughout its length – doesn't taper or fork; does not fit with expected anatomy of suture lines; crosses a suture line; straight line; matches site of injury; does not correlate with similar line on opposite side of skull.

Link: The indications for a head CT scan are described well in the UK NICE guidelines at www.nice.org.uk/CG056/. These include the mechanism of injury (see above), the symptoms we described above, and on examination a boggy haematoma or a GCS below 15. http://www.nice.org.uk/CG56

With modern scanners the child only needs to stay still for 20 seconds or so. With a parent present, a little cajoling, sandwiching the head in soft foam or the child in a vacuum mattress the scan is often possible. Occasionally general anaesthesia will be needed in order to get an adequate image.

Warning: Consult an anaesthetist or senior ED doctor for advice if the child may require sedation for a CT scan!

If the CT scan is positive for acute injury, in most centres the case would be automatically discussed with a neurosurgeon. On the whole, intracranial haematomas are much less common in children than adults.

If a subdural haemorrhage (Figure 5.2) is seen in a younger child or infant, always consider non-accidental injury as a possible cause.

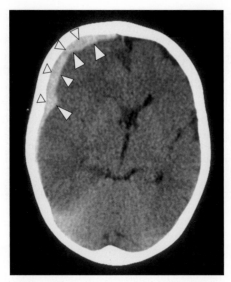

Figure 5.2 Acute subdural haemorrhage due to non-accidental injury.

Top-tip: Note the crescent shaped fresh white haemorrhage on the right causing compression of the lateral ventricle and midline shift. Intracranial haematomas gradually become isodense to brain tissue over two weeks and eventually become the same density as cerebrospinal fluid.

Discharge instructions

Children must be watched by a competent adult for the next few hours, and brought back to the ED if they become drowsy, vomit more than once or if the carer is worried (saying this means if the child is 'not himself' is better than any head injury advice leaflet). For infants, criteria for returning should be kept broad, and include poor feeding, drowsiness or persistent crying.

Parents of older children and teenagers should be advised that headache is a common symptom post head injury, and may continue for a week or two. They should only be concerned if it is severe, unresponsive to analgesia, or associated with drowsiness, change in behaviour, vomiting or confusion. Other symptoms such as dizziness, poor concentration and memory, blurred vision and tiredness are also very common and can be explained to parents as 'concussion'.

Link: Other resources: information and videos for treating children with head injuries can be found at http://www.spottingthesickchild.com.

SCALP LACERATIONS

The scalp has an excellent blood supply so small wounds can bleed a lot, causing alarm to witnesses. Most wounds will have stopped bleeding within 10 minutes, but, if not, after insertion of some sutures through all the layers, the wound will tamponade itself. Less commonly in children, bleeding may be brisk and uncontrolled by pressure bandaging. In this situation, lidocaine with adrenaline may be useful to reduce bleeding and help you see what you are doing.

For wound closure options and techniques, see Chapters 4 and 16.

 Stop: Read the following sections in conjunction with Chapter 4, Wounds and soft tissue injuries, and Chapter 16, Practical procedures.

FACIAL LACERATIONS

Facial lacerations may bleed profusely. This rich blood supply means that wounds generally heal quickly, and infection is unusual, even in bites. However, facial scars are noticed easily.

 Warning: If you lack confidence in ensuring a cosmetic repair for difficult areas, seek help!

Senior ED staff, orofaciomaxillary (OFM) and plastic surgeons are always happy to be referred difficult facial wounds in children.

Suturing of the face is traumatic for most children, and it may be necessary to use procedural sedation (see Chapter 3) or to refer for repair under general anaesthesia.

Forehead wounds may bruise in the coming days, and track down around the eyes. It is worth warning parents about this innocent complication.

Eyelid wounds

 Warning: Any wound involving the eyelid should be referred to an ophthalmologist!

Eyebrow wounds

Wounds involving the eyebrow require perfect anatomical repair with sutures to avoid a 'step' in the line of the eyebrow, which has significant cosmetic consequences. Refer to a specialist if you are not confident. Even with accurate initial repair, a step can develop later as the child grows, so parents should be warned about this.

EYE INJURIES

You should be familiar with the use of a slit lamp, and be able to test visual acuity. A modified Snellen's chart, using pictures, is available for younger children.

 Warning: Visual acuity must always be documented for eye injuries!

Topical anaesthetic drops, e.g. benoxinate, proxymetacaine, are often necessary to facilitate thorough examination, and are effective almost instantly. Duration of action is usually 20–60 minutes. Photophobia is commonly present, and a feeling of direct pressure can be comforting, so an eye patch may be offered to older children. Patients often request anaesthetic drops to take home because of the instant relief of symptoms, but this is not advisable because of the risk of secondary injury.

Many painful eyes cause blepharospasm and spasm of the ciliary apparatus. Administration of mydriatic drops to dilate the pupil, e.g. cyclopentolate, can relieve this but are best avoided in young children since they may cause systemic anticholinergic effects.

For any breach of the corneal surface, topical antibiotics, e.g. chloramphenicol, should be prescribed for prevention of secondary infection until the patient is asymptomatic. Ointment can be administered twice daily, whereas drops require application every 3 hours. So although ointment blurs vision, if is often easier to administer in children.

Corneal abrasions

Corneal abrasions are caused by the eye being scratched, e.g. by a zip or twig. Babies can sustain corneal abrasions accidentally from their mothers. It is therefore valuable to look for an abrasion if presented with a persistently crying baby. Diagnosis may prevent a series of other investigations!

Corneal abrasions tend to be very painful, or may present with a foreign body (FB) sensation. Photophobia, watering and injection of the conjunctiva are usually present.

Abrasions are easier to see with fluorescein (orange) staining under a blue light. It is not necessary for a child to cooperate with slit lamp examination: shining the blue or green light of an ophthalmoscope from a distance is less threatening.

Cover the eye with a patch and prescribe an antibiotic ointment to prevent secondary infection. Abrasions smaller than the size of the pupil, and not crossing the pupil, do not require follow-up.

Corneal foreign bodies

A small FB may enter the eye while working with tools, or simply when carried by the wind. FB detection often requires a slit lamp for magnification. Anaesthetic drops may be needed. If it is not visible on direct view, use a cotton wool bud, with the patient looking downwards, to evert the upper eyelid in case the FB is trapped underneath. At this point, if there is still none visible, an abrasion is the most likely finding (see above) or often an allergic reaction to a FB that has now been washed out in the tears (particularly if the FB was organic).

To remove a FB see Chapter 16. After removal, apply a patch and prescribe antibiotic ointment (see above) and arrange follow-up.

 See Video 19. Foreign body removal in an eye

Hyphaema

A hyphaema occurs when the eye is struck and bleeding occurs into the anterior chamber. There is photophobia and a fluid level may be visible in front of the iris, but it may require a slit lamp for detection. Hospital admission may be required. Refer to an ophthalmologist immediately.

Penetrating injuries of the globe

If a sharp object has injured the eye and you examine it using fluorescein (see 'Abrasions', above) you must be confident that penetration of the globe has not occurred if you are discharging the child. If there is an obvious tear in the cornea or vitreous extrusion, or signs such as an abnormal pupil shape or reaction or decreased acuity, refer immediately to an ophthalmologist because there is a high risk of loss of sight.

 Warning: All penetrating injuries must be referred to an ophthalmologist immediately!

Chemical injuries

Children commonly get liquids in their eyes, e.g. household cleaning fluids. Alkaline injuries are more serious than acid splashes, so use litmus paper to see what injury you have. If the liquid causing the injury has been brought in you can test it directly with litmus, rather than the eye. Alkalis permeate between cell membranes, causing deep-seated damage. Deceptively, they may be less painful than acids initially. When acid hits the eye, injuries are usually superficial because acids cause coagulation of the surface tissues, thus forming a protective barrier to further damage.

 Warning: Alkaline injuries are much more serious than acid injuries!

Alkalis are found in household cleaning products, and may be highly concentrated in substances such as oven cleaner or dishwasher tablets.

If the fluid is acidic, then irrigation using 500 mL of saline solution, via an intravenous giving set, should suffice. Anaesthetic drops may be needed before you start. No follow-up is necessary unless the child remains symptomatic. If the fluid is alkaline, irrigate immediately and for much longer with larger volumes. If symptoms return over the next hour, seek advice from an ophthalmologist as the child may need hospital admission for constant irrigation.

 Warning: Litmus paper is not useful for monitoring response to irrigation! Rely on symptoms.

INJURIES OF THE EAR

The pinna

Wounds through to the cartilage should be referred to facial or ear, nose and throat (ENT) surgeons. A blow to the pinna may cause a haematoma. If this becomes tense, necrosis of the inner cartilage may occur, causing lifelong deformity ('cauliflower ears'). If tense, consult an ENT surgeon for drainage; if not, apply a pressure bandage using a gauze pack and a 'turban' bandage, and arrange review the following day.

The tympanic membrane

This may perforate following a blow to the side of the head, but more typically following FB insertion, particularly cotton wool buds (see Chapter 13). Examination may be difficult because of pain. Spontaneous healing usually occurs, but the child should avoid swimming and be examined by their general practitioner after 3–4 weeks to ensure healing has occurred.

NASAL INJURIES

Nasal fractures

A direct blow to the nose may result in fracture. This is unlikely in children under 7 years because the nasal bone is not calcified. Many parents bring babies and toddlers who have fallen forwards and have a bleeding nose; in these cases you can be very reassuring.

Record displacement of the nose, and always document presence or absence of a septal haematoma, which looks like a dark, bulging mass.

Warning: Always examine specifically for a septal haematoma!

A similar process as happens in the pinna can occur, resulting in a 'saddle nose' deformity. If present, refer to ENT immediately for drainage. Even if you think there may be a fracture, it is not necessary to X-ray for nasal fractures as the management is symptomatic and/or cosmetic.

Advise the patient that the swelling will increase over the next few days and they may develop 'black eyes'. The only treatment is to apply icepacks in the first 24 hours. Find out your local arrangements for follow-up in an outpatient ENT clinic in 5–10 days' time. The purpose of follow-up is for consideration of manipulation of the fracture if there is deformity or nasal obstruction. This is impossible to assess in the first few days, hence the delay.

Epistaxis

As described above, nosebleeds may happen with trauma, and are mainly harmless. Spontaneous epistaxis is also common in childhood, usually caused by nose-picking. This causes staphylococcal infection in the anterior nose and scabs. When picked they bleed. If simple pressure does not work (after 30 minutes), then cautery may occasionally be necessary. On discharge it is worth a course of topical antibiotics to get rid of the underlying infection. Recurrent, spontaneous nosebleeds, or protracted bleeding, should prompt you to think of coagulation disorders or a low platelet count. You should take the relevant blood tests.

ORAL INJURIES

Injuries of the mouth area are common. Fortunately, they heal well, but there are a few pitfalls.

Lacerations crossing the vermillion border of the lip

Wounds crossing the vermillion border of the lip require perfect anatomical repair with sutures, to avoid a 'step' in the line of lip border, which has greater cosmetic consequences for this complication than for most scars. Despite accurate initial repair, a step may develop later as the child grows. Parents should be warned about this.

 Warning: Wounds crossing the vermillion border require expert repair!

'Through and through' lacerations of the lip

This means that the wound extends from the inside of the mouth to the skin outside, and is usually caused by the teeth. Careful repair with sutures is necessary to avoid cosmetic deformity, accumulation of food in the tract, or formation of a sinus. A layered repair may be necessary: do not attempt this yourself if you are unsure you have the necessary skills.

Torn frenulum

The frenulum attaches the upper lip to the gum, between the two first incisors. It contains a small artery, which bleeds profusely initially, then usually goes into spasm and stops, particularly if cold compresses and pressure are applied. Suturing is rarely necessary. It is caused by a direct blow to the upper lip. This is commonly due to a toddler falling face first onto a table, or a swing swinging backwards into a child, etc. The history should never be vague – you should be able to account for the injury with confidence.

 Warning: Check the history!

Wounds of the buccal cavity

Most wounds heal quickly by themselves. Sutures are only necessary if they are gaping or a piece of tissue will interfere with chewing. Use absorbable materials if sutures are necessary. For this, procedural sedation or general anaesthesia is often needed. Ice lollipops can help with pain. Advise soft diet, avoiding foods such as potato crisps, for a few days. Broad spectrum antibiotics, e.g. co-amoxyclavulinic acid, are frequently prescribed. Warn the parents that the wound will look yellow in the next couple of days.

Lacerations of the tongue

The same principles apply as for wounds of the buccal cavity (see above).

Penetrating intra-oral injuries

This type of injury commonly occurs if a child trips while holding something in their mouth. It is important to recognize if the object may have penetrated through the palate (usually soft palate). A small wound may hide a significant injury, which may result in a retropharyngeal abscess and mediastinitis. If in doubt, request a lateral soft tissue X-ray of the neck and refer to ENT.

 Stop: Failure to recognize perforation of the palate may result in severe illness and even death.

DENTAL INJURIES

The most important consideration in dental injuries is whether the tooth is a deciduous or permanent tooth. In general, injuries to deciduous teeth can be reviewed by a dentist the following day.

Avulsion of a tooth

When a permanent tooth is avulsed, the root starts to die within half an hour, so that reimplantation rapidly becomes unsuccessful, or if the tooth reattaches it may become discoloured. A simple first-aid measure is to keep the tooth in the mouth (saliva is protective) or in a cup of milk pending reimplantation.

As soon as possible, the tooth should be reimplanted into the socket and held in position by the child (by occluding the mouth or with a finger) or by an adult, until the on-call OFM doctor can come and fix it in position.

 Stop: Avulsion of a permanent tooth is an emergency which needs immediate action.

Wobbly or chipped teeth

Most of these injuries can be seen by the patient's own dentist the next working day. Where there is either suspicion of alveolar fracture, or significant difficulty with occlusion, discuss with the OFM service.

CHIN LACERATIONS

Wounds under the chin occur frequently when children fall forwards or come off a bicycle. They can nearly always be repaired with adhesive strips, even if they are gaping. Assess for mandibular fracture (below).

FACIAL FRACTURES

'Blow-out' fracture of the inferior orbital margin

This injury occurs when an object, e.g. small ball, hits the eye rather than the zygoma. It is uncommon in children. The contents of the orbit are pushed down through the orbital floor, since this is the weakest point. There may be an associated hyphaema (see above).

The inferior rectus muscle becomes trapped, causing diplopia on upward gaze. The classical appearance on X-ray is a ball of proptosed tissue, described as a 'tear-drop', visible in the maxillary antrum.

All 'blow-out' (Figure 5.3) fractures must be referred to an ophthalmologist immediately. It is crucial that the child does not blow their nose: this can severely worsen the entrapment of soft tissues.

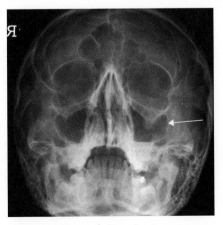

Figure 5.3 The tear-drop sign in a 'blow-out' fracture of the left orbit.

Fractures of the zygomatic complex

Fractures of the zygoma (Figure 5.4) are unusual in children, and usually associated with quite severe injury or a punch. The hallmark signs of zygomatic fracture are unilateral epistaxis, swelling and bruising of the area, subconjunctival haemorrhage (the posterior border of which cannot be seen) and reduced sensation in the distribution of the infraorbital nerve (around the cheek, nose, gum and lip on the affected side). In this age group, it is best to ask advice, the same day, from the OFM service.

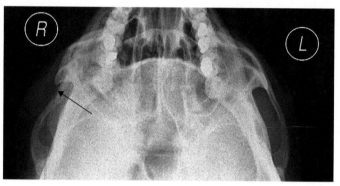

Figure 5.4 Fractured right zygoma.

Fractures of the mandible

History

Fractures of the mandible (Figure 5.5) are uncommon in children, and occur most often with a fall onto the point of the chin. They may be caused by a punch in adolescents. Remember that the mandible is a ring-type structure, so it may fracture in two places, even with one point of impact, e.g. fracture of the body with associated fracture of the condylar neck.

Examination

The hallmarks of mandibular fracture are pain, swelling, malocclusion, poor opening (except crack fractures of the condylar neck) and bruising (particularly around the gum or sublingually). There may be anaesthesia in the distribution of a mental nerve.

Management

Refer all fractures to the OFM service.

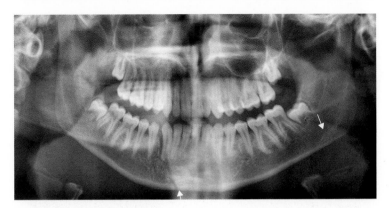

Figure 5.5 Fractured mandible.

 Top-tip: The view in Figure 5.5 is an ortopantogram (OPG), which is a panoramic view of the mandible, shot with moving imaging apparatus. OPGs can be hard to interpret. Try to trace any lucent line beyond the edge of the bone to see if it relates to an overlying structure. Figure 5.5 shows bilateral mandibular fractures involving the roots of the right canine and the left wisdom tooth.

CHAPTER 6

NECK AND BACK INJURIES

Introduction	46	Imaging	54
What is spinal immobilization?	47	Sprains of the neck and back	56
Should I immobilize the child?	51	Fractures and dislocations	
Clinically clearing the neck	52	of the spine	56
Log-roll examination of the			
thoracic and lumbar spine	53		

INTRODUCTION

Spinal injuries are rare in children, and usually associated with injury mechanisms such as pedestrians hit by a car or trampolining accidents. Although serious injury is rare, minor injury to the neck and back is common, and it is important to feel secure in assessing severity.

Stop: Is this major trauma? Stop and think. Does this need an ABC approach? See advanced trauma or paediatric life support guidelines.

Children may sustain fractures and/or dislocations of the spine, which may or may not be stable or associated with cord injury. A history of transient neurological symptoms such as numbness or tingling (seconds or minutes) is not uncommon, and usually indicates minor cord contusion.

In the cervical spine, it is not uncommon for children to sustain cord injury without fracture as a result of ligamentous injury. In fact, immediately following impact the ligaments can return to their normal position, making diagnosis very difficult. Plain films may appear normal, and the injury is only visible on computed tomography (CT) and magnetic resonance imaging (MRI). If cord injury is present, this may be called 'SCIWORA': spinal cord injury without radiographic abnormality.

Thoracic and lumbar fractures are also rare in childhood. Typical mechanisms would include falling from a height, or a vehicle crash without an appropriate seat belt.

WHAT IS SPINAL IMMOBILIZATION?

Cervical spinal immobilization in practice requires three types of movement restriction:

(1) a hard collar, which restricts flexion, extension and some lateral movement – it should be sized according to the manufacturer's guidelines;

(2) specially designed head blocks/sandbags/bags of intravenous (IV) fluids, either side of the neck, to prevent lateral movements;

(3) tape or straps across the forehead and chin (Figure 6.1).

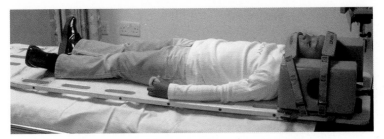

Figure 6.1 Cervical spine immobilized with collar, blocks and straps. The long spinal board should be removed on arrival at your facility.

OR

An alternative to the 'collar, blocks and tape' is another person holding the head in line with the body, in the neutral position, either from below or above (Figures 6.2 and 6.3).

OR

A vacuum mattress (Figure 6.4), often with padding around the head and neck, is a device in which the child lies in a neutral position, and which 'shrinks to fit' as the air is sucked out. This is actually the most anatomically correct way of immobilization but many organizations do not have one, and they are not very radiolucent.

Thoracic and lumbar spinal immobilization is done with the child lying either on a long, spinal board during transport, or on a firm, flat surface such as a hospital trolley after arrival.

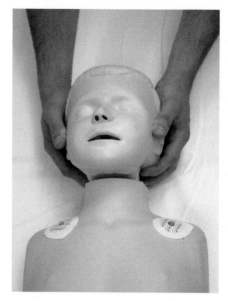

Figure 6.2 Manual in-line immobilization of cervical spine from above.

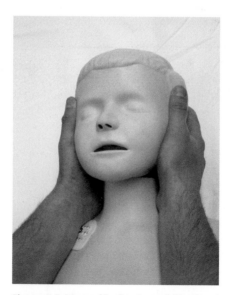

Figure 6.3 Manual in-line immobilization of cervical spine from below.

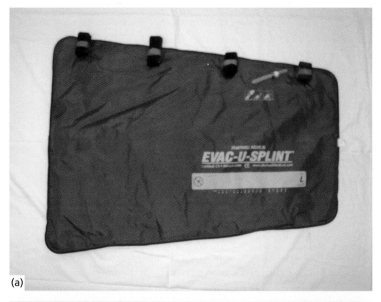

Figure 6.4 Vacuum mattress, (a) before application and
(b) after application.

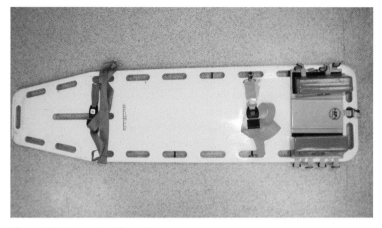

Figure 6.5 Long spinal board.

The child may arrive from the pre-hospital phase on a spinal board (Figure 6.5). This is an extrication device that is used in the pre-hospital phase. The child should be log-rolled off this hard board soon after arrival, and allowed to lie on a firm surface such as a trolley.

 See Video 1. Log roll off spinal board

Alternative devices include a 'scoop' bivalve stretcher (Figure 6.6); this undoes at the top and the bottom and pulls out from the child's sides, thus

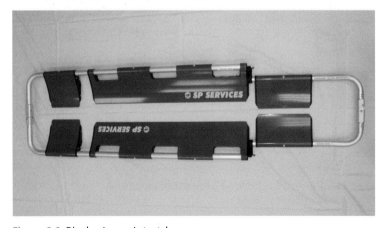

Figure 6.6 Bivalve 'scoop' stretcher.

avoiding the need for log-rolling. Also the vacuum mattress, which we mentioned above, immobilizes the whole spine.

Common sense needs to be applied. Immobilization is disorientating, uncomfortable and upsets children, making the rest of the examination difficult. If the child is very agitated and spinal precautions are necessary, immobilization may be harmful, as the body is pivoting on the neck. Either use manual immobilization (e.g. parent) or allow the child to move, ideally retaining the hard collar for some protection.

In a child with an injury that has just happened and who did not arrive by ambulance, consider the mechanism of injury. The following types of situations require initial spinal immobilization until you are in a position to 'clinically clear' the spine:

- fall from higher than child's head height
- hit by vehicle
- high-speed collision (e.g. sledge into tree)
- unwitnessed drowning
- car occupant in serious road traffic accident.

Children brought by ambulance will frequently have been immobilized already. This need not be continued if you can 'clinically clear' the neck (see below).

In many cases the child has had an injury and is complaining of neck pain but the event was a few hours or days ago and they have been mobile. In these circumstances it is not necessary to immobilize the neck. Even if there is an injury, it is likely to be stable; however, you may need imaging. Injuries can be present, but be stable; immobilization is for safety in unstable fractures or dislocations.

A stable injury, which is not uncommon in children with a mechanism of injury such as a 'clash of heads' in football, is a unifacet dislocation of one of the vertebrae. This presents with torticollis. If you see a child holding their head in a particular position, or to one side (torticollis), they may have a significant injury. Do not make them lie down in a neutral position as this may do further harm.

CLINICALLY CLEARING THE NECK

Children hate lying flat on their back, immobilized. Within 15 minutes of arrival, a clinician competent in clinically clearing the spine should assess the child to see if they can be allowed to mobilize; if it is not safe to do so they should be sent immediately for imaging.

The rules for being safe to clinically clear the neck in children aged 10 and over are covered well in the UK NICE guidelines on head and cervical spine injury.

 Link: http://www.nice.org.uk/CG56

Essentially you need to be sure that all of the following are true:

- the child is fully conscious, orientated and able to communicate with you (drugs and/or alcohol are a contraindication to clinical clearance)
- the mechanism of injury is not high risk (such as those listed above)
- there is no neurological deficit detectable in the arms or legs
- there is no distracting painful injury elsewhere
- there is no torticollis or abnormal posture of head.
- if all the above are negative, that when asked, the child is able to rotate their head at least 45 degrees to the left and the right.

 Warning: If any of the above are positive, send the child for X-rays immediately!

See 'Imaging', below, for what to do next. Once you have the images back, if they are normal films and the child has no neurological signs and is alert and orientated, the child can be freed up.

Similarly, if all the checks above are negative, at this point you are safe to remove the collar.

If your patient is reluctant to move, do not force them. Try reassurance and analgesia and reassess in half an hour. At this point, if movement is still very limited, further imaging is needed. Get senior help and reimmobilize the child.

Below the age of 10 years the same principles of assessment apply, but a degree of caution is warranted.

In those under 4 years, assessment will probably need to involve observation of how much they want to move the neck themselves, and whether they are using their arms and legs properly. In a child of this age with a minor or moderate mechanism of injury and who is alert, cervical spine injury is very rare.

The only exception to this is in non-accidental injury. However, these children will tend to be children under 2 years, and they will usually have other injuries, such as bruising, fractures or a head injury.

If you have now cleared the cervical spine, do not forget – you need to check the rest of the spine out!

LOG-ROLL EXAMINATION OF THE THORACIC AND LUMBAR SPINE

If you suspect back injury, the principles of management are the same as for the cervical spine. Consider the mechanism of injury, whether the child is alert and orientated, and check for any sensory or motor deficit in the arms and legs.

To examine the back itself you will need to perform a controlled 'log-roll' (Figures 6.7 and 6.8) ensuring the spine remains aligned (see below). Before attempting this, reassure the child that they do not need to 'help' or move, and that they will not fall off the side since there are people holding them.

Roll the child only as far as is necessary to inspect the back and palpate the whole spine for midline tenderness.

Clinical examination is quite poor at detecting thoracic and lumbar fractures. If the mechanism of injury suggests that a fracture may be possible and the child can point to a specific area of their spine, do not rely on tenderness to palpation, but consider imaging.

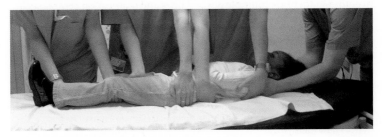

Figure 6.7 **Hand positions for a log-roll.**

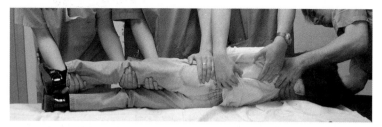

Figure 6.8 A log-roll.

See Video 2. Log roll to examine back

IMAGING

The standard X-ray views you need to request are an anteroposterior, a lateral and (if over 9 years) an odontoid peg X-ray of the cervical spine.

Interpretation of children's spine X-rays can be difficult even for the experienced.

Alignment is key. The lines you should follow are demonstrated in Figure 6.9.

Indirect evidence of injury may be seen in cervical X-rays by assessing soft tissue swelling. This is shown in Figure 6.10. The presence or absence of soft tissue swelling is also an indicator of a fracture. Any deviation from this requires radiological or senior support, before you allow the patient to move around.

Figure 6.10 shows an example of a normal variant. In younger children there is frequently pseudo-subluxation of C2 on C3, or C3 on C4.

In addition, there are multiple physeal lines and ossification centres such as the ring apophyses visible in puberty at the corners of vertebral bodies, which may be mistaken for tear-drop fractures.

If you detect a fracture look for another as it is possible to find multiple levels involved in spinal injuries.

Warning: If in doubt, continue immobilization until senior help is available!

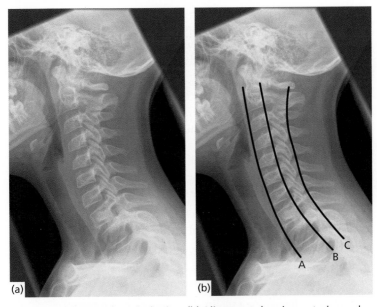

Figure 6.9 (a) Normal cervical spine. (b) Alignment showing anterior and posterior vertical lines (A,B) and the spinolaminar line (C).

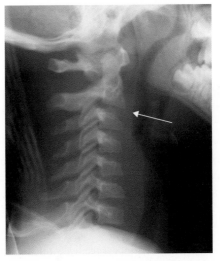

Figure 6.10 Pseudo-subluxation of C2 on C3.

CT scanning with 3D reconstruction is swift with modern scanners and is particularly useful for those ligamentous injuries that are more common in children. However, the radiation dose to the thyroid is significant, and senior radiological colleagues should guide you in your decisions.

SPRAINS OF THE NECK AND BACK

Children are generally active, so injury to the neck or back is not uncommon. Fractures are very unusual, unless the mechanism of injury is high risk (see above), but sprains are also unusual because children are supple. Children can develop torticollis after 'sleeping funny'. This can take a few days to settle so often causes concern, or in fact the child is brought to medical attention because of fears of meningitis.

Treatment for soft tissue injuries involves simple painkillers, icepacks (such as a packet of frozen vegetables) in the first day or so and exercises to avoid stiffness.

Children make a rapid recovery after a soft tissue injury so in your discharge advice make sure the parents know to return if pain lasts more than 5 days.

Be cautious in diagnosing a sprain of the thoracic or lumbar area, especially if it has gone on for longer than this time. Back pain in children under 10 years is very unusual and should be investigated promptly. Adolescents can experience occasional backache symptoms similar to those experienced by adults, but persistent symptoms in any young person should be referred for further evaluation.

In the same way as limps or bone pains are often attributed to trauma, when the cause is malignancy, for example, the same can happen in back pain. Back pain can also be caused by discitis (a staphylococcal infection in younger children), tuberculosis and repeated injury related to high-level participation in certain sports.

FRACTURES AND DISLOCATIONS OF THE SPINE

These are uncommon and largely beyond the remit of this book. Unifacet dislocation of a cervical vertebra is described above. Dislocation of the ligaments can occur in the cervical spine, and usually involves the upper three vertebrae in young children, and C7–T1 junction in older children.

Imaging

The prevertebral soft tissue can appear relatively thick in small children. Crying, neck flexion and intubation can cause apparent soft tissue widening unrelated to spinal injury. Apparent swelling can be seen in any

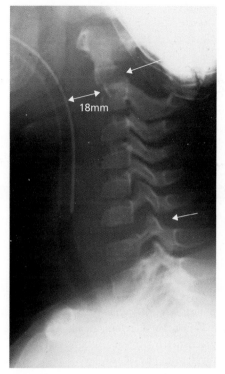

Figure 6.11 Cervical spine soft tissue swelling with fracture-dislocations at C1–2 and C5–6.

intubated child but in this case it is severe and related to obvious underlying fractures of C2 and C6 (Figure 6.11).

Top-tip: There is a useful aide memoire, the '2 at 6 and 6 at 2' rule: 2 cm of soft tissue shadow anterior to C6 and 6 mm of shadow in front of C2.

Cevical spine dislocations are possible without any bony injury, yet can be severe enough to cause spinal cord compression. This phenomenon is known as spinal cord injury without radiographic (this means plain films) abnormality (SCIWORA).

Another injury pattern is anterior wedging of the vertebrae from forced flexion mechanisms of injury.

CHAPTER 7

FRACTURES AND DISLOCATIONS – GENERAL APPROACH

Introduction	58	General principles of management	67
General principles of assessment	63		
X-rays	65	Plaster casts	68

INTRODUCTION

Before the age of 16, around 50 per cent of boys and 25 per cent of girls will sustain a fracture. Dislocations, however, are very uncommon in pre-pubertal children, apart from those with a collagen disorder such as Ehlers–Danlos syndrome.

The bones of children (Figure 7.1) differ from adults in three respects:

- A child's bone is less brittle than that of an adult due to a higher collagen to bone ratio; therefore, incomplete fractures may occur (torus or greenstick fractures).
- The growth plate (or physis) may bear the brunt of the injury (Salter–Harris classification).
- The periosteum in young children is very strong, and protects the bone from fracture, or can limit displacement if it does fracture (e.g. a 'toddler's' fracture of the tibia).

Torus fractures

A torus, or 'buckle', fracture (Figure 7.2) describes an injury where the cortex buckles with no apparent break. In practice it is best to show the image to the parents and explain that, although a fracture means a broken bone, this is not a proper break.

Top-tip: The X-ray appearances can be subtle – look for convexity of the cortex rather than concavity and be sure you look carefully at both views (see Figure 7.2).

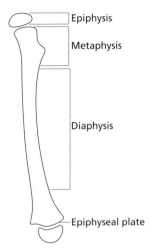

Figure 7.1 Anatomy of a child's bone.

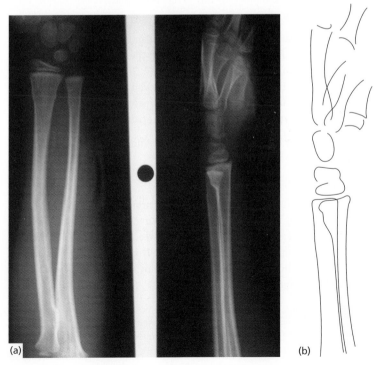

Figure 7.2 A torus fracture.

Greenstick fractures

In a greenstick fracture one cortical surface breaks, and the opposite surface merely buckles (Figure 7.3). The periosteum over the buckled side often remains intact.

Growth plate injuries

A child's bone must also have the ability to grow and achieves this by the presence of cartilaginous growth plates at the ends of long bones. The growth plate or physis (sometimes referred to as the epiphyseal plate) is a relatively weak part of the bone and is vulnerable to various patterns of fracture. These injuries were originally classified by Salter–Harris into five types (Figure 7.4).

Top-tip: With a clever choice of words, the Salter–Harris classification can be easily remembered, to mimic the name 'Salter'.

Figure 7.4 demonstrates an easy way to memorize the five types. Type II is the most common injury.

It is important that these injuries are identified and treated appropriately. This is especially true when the fracture breaks the continuity of the growth plate and the articular surface (types III and IV). Treatment of types III and IV fractures requires restoration of the perfect continuity of the growth plate and the articular surface (usually by internal fixation) to minimize the potential for later growth disturbance and traumatic arthritis.

The type V injury is very difficult to diagnose initially, and may present as abnormal growth many months later.

Metaphyseal corner fractures

These fractures are almost pathognomonic of non-accidental injury (see Chapter 15). They may be very subtle when acute, but the injury becomes more obvious as callus forms and a periosteal reaction occurs along the length of the metaphyseal cortex (Figure 7.5). This is seen when there is a delay in presentation, or a skeletal survey is done to pick up injuries that have not been brought to medical attention.

Top-tip: A 'bucket handle' fracture represents an avulsion of a ring or crescent of the metaphysis. A 'corner fracture' usually represents a bucket handle fracture seen 'end on'.

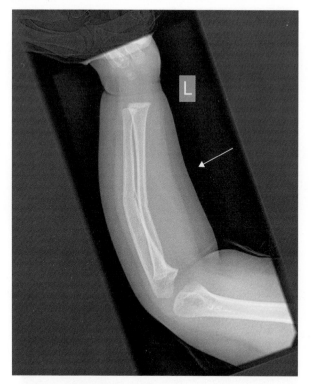

Figure 7.3 Mid-shaft greenstick fractures of the radius and ulna.

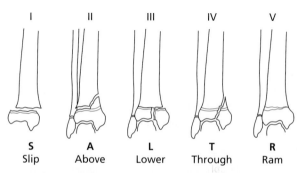

Figure 7.4 The Salter–Harris classification of physeal injuries with aide-memoire.

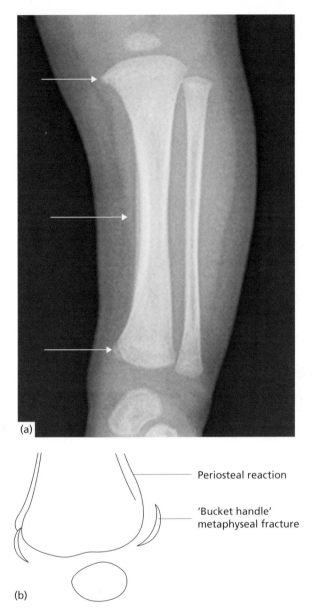

(a)

(b)

Periosteal reaction

'Bucket handle' metaphyseal fracture

Figure 7.5 Metaphyseal corner fracture characteristic of non-accidental injury. Top arrow: healing corner fracture; middle arrow: periosteal reaction; bottom arrow: acute corner fracture.

Stop: If you see a metaphyseal corner fracture, call for senior help and refer to your local child protection policy!

GENERAL PRINCIPLES OF ASSESSMENT

History

The child's age will give a clue to the injury. For example, a fractured scaphoid bone is unusual below the age of 9 years; acromio-clavicular or shoulder dislocations are rare before adolescence; a toddler's fracture occurs in toddlers!

When you take the history, the exact mechanism of injury is important for several reasons. First, it will tell you the likelihood of a fracture and therefore help you to decide whether or not you need to ask for an X-ray. For example, falling over onto an outstretched hand is more likely to break a bone than banging against something. A direct blow can sometimes cause a fracture and/or dislocation at that site, but quite severe force would be involved. More often fractures occur as a result of indirect forces. For example, a fall on an outstretched hand may lead to a fractured distal radius, a supracondylar fracture of the elbow or a fractured clavicle.

 Warning: If significant forces are involved, e.g. child hit by car, be on your guard for significant injury!

Second, it will tell you whether a specific diagnosis is likely, if you know which injury patterns are associated with the various fractures. For example, a femur will only fracture with quite severe force or an awkward twist; a clavicle will break easily; a toddler's fracture is caused by a twisting mechanism.

Lastly, if the story does not match up with your findings on examination or on the X-ray, then you must consider non-accidental injury.

 Warning: Is the history for this injury clear and does it match your findings? If not, consider non-accidental injury

Examination

When examining for evidence of a fracture or dislocation, you should look, then feel, then very gently try to move the affected area, unless it is very painful.

Look for:

- deformity (bending, rotation)
- swelling (comparing with the opposite side helps)
- bruising
- any wounds
- abnormal posture or alignment.

Children can be quite deceptively calm or indeed active, despite significant injuries. Therefore, limping, non-usage of a limb or abnormal posture should all be taken seriously.

Feel for:

- tenderness – it is important to try to localize this to the point of maximal tenderness
- deformity (comparing with the opposite side helps)
- distal pulse/capillary refill/sensation.

The more localized the tenderness, the more likely there is a fracture present. If the child is unable to localize the pain, try asking them to press around the area themselves and tell you where it hurts the most. If they are not very specific, you can then try gently pressing yourself, and offer options 'this bit or this bit?' or 'number one, number two or number three' as you try different areas. For pre-verbal children it may be difficult, but by being gentle and systematic, and sometimes repeating pressing and moving the limb while the child is distracted, you can usually localize the injury.

Move:

Give the child an opportunity to use the limb, e.g. introduce them to some toys or just ask to copy you, and watch how the limb is held or used. Think through your joint movements so you test them all; for example, elbows can supinate and pronate, as well as flex and extend. Attempt movements of the relevant joints if pain allows. Do not cause unnecessary pain, but at the same time you must persist to an extent. Try getting the child to show you rather than you moving the limb, and tell them that if they can just demonstrate a movement once, that's enough for you to know they can do it – for example, full elbow or knee extension.

Ensure you isolate the joint movement which you are trying to test, to limit pain and to limit compensation from another joint; for example, support the wrist if you move the elbow, and vice versa.

Top-tip: By being patient, trying to localize tenderness, repeating movements and using distraction, you can avoid over-ordering of X-rays or missing injuries.

X-RAYS

When to X-ray

If in doubt, have a low threshold for requesting X-rays. Young children, in particular, can have quite subtle signs for fractures such as greenstick fractures. Most parents will be expecting you to X-ray their child, but you have to use your experience, and explain the potential future risks of irradiation if you consider the X-ray to be unnecessary. Use the information such as mechanism of injury and likelihood of a positive X-ray to help you.

Top-tip: It is better to get senior advice if you can, rather than over-request X-rays.

Which X-rays to request

It is crucial to order the right X-ray view if you are not to miss fractures. If in doubt, ask a radiographer for their advice, explaining the context.

To ensure adequate X-rays are taken, always give as much information as possible on the request card. The area you specify on your request should be as focused as possible (use Table 7.1 to guide you). To diagnose and fully assess the injury, two films should be taken at right angles to each other: these are usually anteroposterior and lateral views, but usually the radiographer will decide this for you. For midshaft, longbone fractures the joint above and the joint below should be seen.

Interpretation of paediatric X-rays

Interpreting paediatric X-rays comes with practice. Fractures may be very subtle and the presence of various ossification centres around joints can add to the confusion. If in doubt about an X-ray, always seek a second opinion. It is important to note any significant angulation (greater than 20°) or displacement (greater than 50 per cent) of the distal fragment of a fracture when reviewing the X-ray.

In practice, most services should have a safety net system whereby a radiologist will report the film in the next couple of days and the patient can be contacted if something has been missed. If you explain this to the parents at the time, they will tend to leave your consultation more reassured, and if they are called back they will appreciate the call and understand the context.

Table 7.1 Requests for radiographic studies

Body area	Appropriate request	Injury or fracture (#) suspected
Upper limb	Shoulder	Ruptured acromio-clavicular joint or dislocation head of humerus
	Clavicle	# clavicle
	Humerus	# shaft humerus
	Elbow	# supracondylar, # of either epicondyle, # radial head or neck, # olecranon
	Forearm	# shaft radius/ulna
	Wrist	# distal radius/ulna
	Scaphoid views	# or dislocation of any carpal bones
	Hand	# metacarpals
	Finger	Finger down to and including MCPJ
Lower limb	Pelvis	Any hip pathology. If you are looking for SUFE add "frog leg lateral" to your request
	Femur	# femur
	Knee	Dislocated or # patella, # of knee itself
	Tibia and fibula	# tibia or fibula
	Ankle	# medial or lateral malleolus, or distal tibia
	Foot	All bones of foot, except calcaneum
	Calcaneum	Calcaneum
Spine	Peg view	Odontoid peg and C1
	Lateral C spine	C1–T1
	Anteroposterior C spine	C1–T1
	Thoracic spine	T1–T12
	Lumbar spine	L1–L5

GENERAL PRINCIPLES OF MANAGEMENT

Fractures and dislocations are painful so ensure the child has adequate analgesia as soon as they reach you (see Chapter 3). You should immobilize the injury from the outset, whether with a splint, plaster cast or sling, because this will help a great deal with pain. Pain management is also very important for discharge.

Most injuries will require immobilization to heal, and for ongoing pain relief. Simple fractures, with no axial rotation and only minor degrees of angulation and displacement, will simply require a plaster cast and orthopaedic clinic follow-up.

Others will require either manipulation under general anaesthesia (an MUA) or some structural support from pins or screws such as K wires, or an open reduction with internal fixation (an ORIF).

These include fractures with:

- significant clinical deformity
- axial rotation
- significant angulation (usually >20°, but the upper limit is age dependent)
- significant displacement
- growth plate fractures.

There may be other reasons for immediate referral and hospital admission. One of these is simply for pain control. Another is if there is a risk of or evidence of:

- compartment syndrome (see Chapter 4)
- neurological or vascular compromise
- severe swelling needing elevation (e.g. hand injuries).

Open fractures
Open fractures need to be thoroughly cleaned under operating theatre conditions as soon as possible after injury.

Warning: Suspect an open fracture if there is any kind of wound overlying, or near to, the fracture. Refer to orthopaedics immediately!

If you suspect an open fracture, dress the wound with an antiseptic-soaked dressing, and give parenteral anti-staphylococcal antibiotics. Prevent other people from continually disturbing the wound – a digital camera image can be invaluable in this situation.

PLASTER CASTS

In the first 24 hours after injury the area is likely to swell, so a full plaster is not usually applied. The plaster should surround about 75 per cent of the limb, allowing a gap for swelling to occur. This is called a 'backslab'.

Plasters can be made out of plaster of Paris (POP). This is cheap and fairly easy to learn how to apply. Synthetic polymer materials are lighter in weight, and can be purchased in attractive colours! Because they are more expensive and are difficult to make into a backslab, most departments apply a POP backslab initially, then offer an appointment a day or two later for conversion to a full plaster.

If a plaster cast has been applied, ensure that the family knows it should not get wet. They must also understand to return if the plaster is uncomfortable or painful, if the limb becomes swollen, or if there is coldness, tingling or numbness distally, or if the cast is rubbing the skin.

If these symptoms occur, the plaster should be removed in order to inspect the underlying limb. If there has been a MUA or ORIF, orthopaedic advice should be obtained before moving the plaster.

CHAPTER 8

INJURIES OF THE SHOULDER TO WRIST

Introduction	69	The elbow	75
The shoulder	69	The forearm	87
The upper arm	73	The wrist	90

INTRODUCTION

For general principles of assessment, investigation and management of fractures and dislocations in children, see Chapter 7. Hand injuries are covered in Chapter 9.

Fractures of the upper limb are much more common than in the lower limb. The most common fractures are of the distal radius and clavicle. The commonest mechanism of injury in all age groups is a 'fall onto the outstretched hand' (FOOSH), in other words the protective reflex we all have to break a fall. In children the exact mechanism of injury is often less clear than when taking a history from an adult.

THE SHOULDER

Clavicle fracture

Assessment

Fracture of the clavicle (Figure 8.1) usually occurs following a fall. It is common throughout childhood. Birth injuries can occur, and may not present for a few weeks – often when a lump (callus) appears. Toddlers may not be brought to medical attention for a day or two after injury, as they tend to only have mild symptoms. Although delay in presentation should normally ring 'alarm bells' (see Chapter 15), it is quite common with clavicular fractures. In young children focal tenderness may not be clear, and reasonable arm function may be preserved; however, abduction of the arm is usually painful. If the child can abduct beyond 90° fracture is unlikely and X-rays are not needed. Occasionally, tenting of the skin over a displaced fracture occurs. This looks dramatic but does not need same-day referral.

Imaging

Most fractures are fairly obvious. The middle portion of the clavicle is most commonly broken. Distal clavicular fractures are covered in acromio-clavicular injury (below).

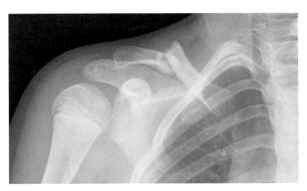

Figure 8.1 Displaced fracture of the clavicle.

Young children may have a greenstick fracture (Figure 8.2), which may be difficult to see because the clavicle curves.

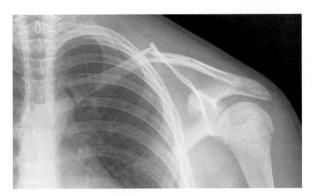

Figure 8.2 Greenstick fracture of the clavicle.

Management

Apply a broad arm sling (see Chapter 16), and arrange orthopaedic clinic follow-up. If a toddler will not keep a sling on do not worry, simply reassure the parents that the bone will heal well. Advise all parents that a lump may be present after healing, which will reduce in size over 6 months or so.

Shoulder dislocation

Glenohumeral dislocation is uncommon in children, and outside of the teenage age group tends only to occur with severe force, during fits or in those with connective tissue disorders.

Assessment

The deformity is usually obvious, and pain is severe. There is a palpable step below the acromion. Do not attempt to move the arm. There may be associated sensory loss over the deltoid area due to compression of the axillary nerve, which usually resolves once the joint is relocated.

Imaging

There are two types of dislocation – anterior (more than 90 per cent in children) (Figure 8.3) and posterior (more likely during a seizure because of strong muscle spasm).

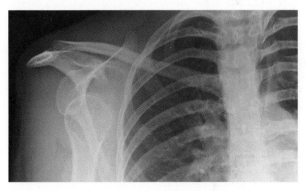

Figure 8.3 Anterior dislocation of the shoulder.

Here you can see that the humeral head is displaced inferior and anterior to the glenoid. There are no associated fractures. In a posterior dislocation the humeral head can appear to be in joint, as it is behind and in line with the glenoid. A 'light-bulb' appearance is the clue.

Management

Analgesia is the priority (see Chapter 3). However, the best analgesia is reduction of the dislocation. An X-ray should be performed first, though, to see if it is an anterior (>90 per cent) or posterior dislocation, and whether there is an associated fracture (in which case orthopaedic referral is recommended).

Reduction of the dislocation depends on adequate muscle relaxation. Much of this can be achieved through psychological measures (Chapter 3) so sedation is not always necessary. Self-reduction is possible after analgesia, sometimes during movements such as positioning for an X-ray, or if lying prone with the arm dangling down; this can work for recurrent dislocations. There is no place for brute force.

Relatively painless joint reduction can be achieved with nitrous oxide (Entonox), an intra-articular injection of lidocaine (see Chapter 16) and the slow external rotation method. Ideally the intra-articular block should be performed on arrival, pre-X-ray.

Slow external rotation is the gentlest method of reduction. Stand, or preferably sit, next to the child with them sitting up and relaxing back. Take their elbow and support it gently on one hand and use your other hand to hold the child's hand. Spend plenty of time gaining the child's trust and getting them to relax their shoulder muscles. Very slowly start external rotation. Over 5–10 minutes you are aiming for 90° of external rotation. At around this point the shoulder will slip back into joint, usually with a palpable clunk. There are many other methods of reduction so if this does not work, seek senior advice.

After reduction, place the arm in a broad arm sling (see Chapter 16), and X-ray again to check the shoulder is fully reduced. Arrange orthopaedic follow-up within a few days.

Acromio-clavicular joint injury

Assessment
This injury usually occurs in teenagers, following a fall directly onto the shoulder (Figure 8.4). After puberty there is true rupture of the ligaments, but before that age the apparent A–C dislocation is caused by a fracture through the epiphysis. Tenderness with or without swelling is usually localized to the point where the acromion meets the clavicle. Deformity may be seen and can initially be confused with glenohumeral dislocation.

Imaging
X-rays are necessary only if deformity is seen.

Management
Symptomatic management in a broad arm sling (see Chapter 16) for a week or two is usually sufficient. Arrange follow-up in an orthopaedic clinic for those with deformity.

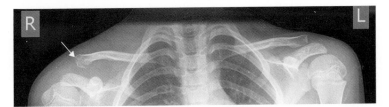

Figure 8.4 Right acromio-clavicular joint disruption with associated fracture of the distal clavicle.

THE UPPER ARM

Proximal humerus fracture

Assessment

Fracture of the neck of the humerus (Figure 8.5) can occur by falling onto the shoulder itself, or onto the outstretched hand. Ability to abduct the arm beyond 90° makes a fracture unlikely.

Imaging

X-ray findings may be subtle. Look for growth plate fractures or a buckle of the metaphysis.

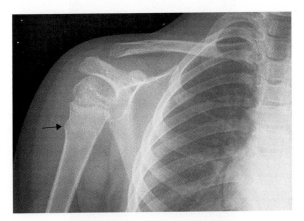

Figure 8.5 Buckle fracture of the proximal humerus.

Management

Refer displaced growth plate fractures or angulation greater than 20° for an immediate orthopaedic opinion. Otherwise, apply a collar and cuff (see Chapter 16) and arrange orthopaedic clinic follow-up.

Humeral shaft fracture

Assessment

Fracture of the humeral shaft is uncommon. Clinical diagnosis is usually straightforward.

Stop: A spiral fracture of the humerus (Figure 8.6) is highly likely to indicate non-accidental injury! See Chapter 15 and consult your child protection policy.

Assess for radial nerve injury, looking for signs of wrist drop or sensory loss in the thumb web-space on the dorsum of the hand.

Imaging

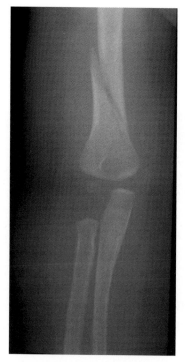

Figure 8.6 Spiral fracture of the humerus due to non-accidental injury.

Management

For spiral fractures, fractures with neurological deficit or displacement refer for an immediate orthopaedic opinion.

Place the remainder in a collar and cuff (see Chapter 16) and arrange orthopaedic clinic follow-up.

THE ELBOW

Normal or abnormal?

The many different ossification centres appearing at different ages around the elbow make interpretation of children's X-rays particularly difficult. It is helpful to have a working knowledge of these ossification centres.

The acronym CRITOE is often used to remember the order in which the centres appear (Table 8.1). As a broad rule of thumb, centres appear about every two years. Figure 8.7 shows where these are in the elbow. If in doubt, check a radiology textbook, or consult a senior.

Table 8.1 The CRITOE acronym for order of appearance of elbow ossification centres

Ossification centre	Age
C: Capitellum	1
R: Radial head	3
I: Internal (medial) epicondyle	5
T: Trochlea	7
O: Olecranon	9
E: External (lateral) epicondyle	11

The presence of a joint effusion makes a fracture much more likely. On examination swelling may be seen, but this can be quite subtle. Position both the child's elbows symmetrically (ideally at 90°) and compare the dimples on each side. On X-ray an effusion is detected by a positive 'fat pad sign' (Figure 8.8) on the lateral view.

In a normal joint, fat lines the outer surface of the joint capsule and is visible anterior to the humerus on the lateral view, because flexion makes it more prominent. It is seen as a small dark area.

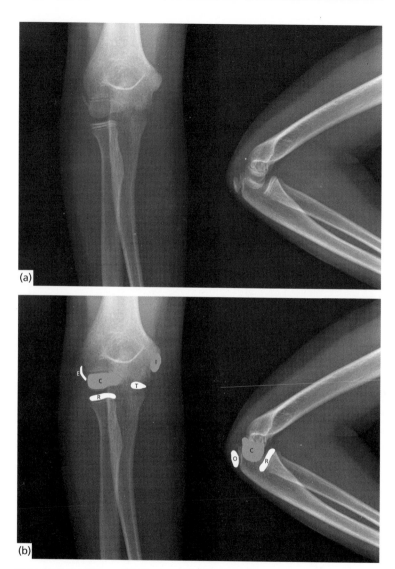

Figure 8.7 (a) Elbow of a 12-year-old with all ossification centres present. (b) Ossification centres of the elbow (see Table 8.1).

When there is a joint effusion the anterior fat pad becomes elevated away from the humerus, and the normally flat (stretched) posterior fat pad becomes visible (Figure 8.9).

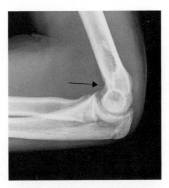

Figure 8.8 Normal anterior fat pad seen as a small lucency.

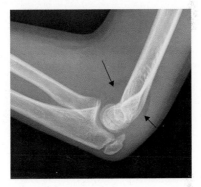

Figure 8.9 Abnormal fat pads implying joint effusion.

The fat pad sign is strongly suggestive of an intra-articular fracture. However, the absence of a fat pad does not rule out a fracture. Use your clinical examination to guide your management.

Supracondylar humeral fracture

Assessment

This is a common fracture in children, with a peak age at about 7 years old. It represents about 80 per cent of elbow fractures. It is generally caused by a fall. There is usually swelling (see above for detection), which may be mild or severe with deformity. It can be difficult to distinguish the more severe cases from a dislocated elbow (see below), although the management is similar.

It is extremely important to examine and record the distal neurological and vascular status of the arm. This fracture is associated with vascular and neurological injury and can lead to compartment syndrome (see Chapter 4).

The fracture can impinge on the brachial artery, the anterior interosseous branch of the median nerve, the radial or the ulnar nerve.

Examine the radial pulse volume and the capillary refill and compare with the opposite side. Ask the child if they have pins and needles, or any numbness anywhere. Test for motor or sensory deficit in the hand (see Chapter 9). If you find any abnormality, refer immediately to orthopaedics.

Warning: Check circulation and neurological function!

Moving the elbow can make these injuries worse.

Warning: Do not test range of movement in a clinically fractured elbow!

Imaging

There is a range of possible X-ray findings. There may be a simple greenstick fracture that is difficult to detect, although a joint effusion is usually present. At the opposite extreme, there may be significant displacement of the distal fragment posteriorly. In displaced fractures (Figure 8.10), the distal fragment is displaced posteriorly over 90 per cent of the time, and anteriorly in less than 10 per cent of fractures.

To detect subtle fractures (Figure 8.11) it is worth knowing about the *anterior humeral line*. This is a line drawn along the anterior surface of the distal humerus on a true lateral view. Normally this intersects the middle third of the capitellum. If the distal humerus is displaced backwards, it will intersect more anteriorly, or not at all.

Top-tip: In Figure 8.11 the anterior humeral line intersects the capitellum just anterior to its middle third, indicating slight angulation; we can see the fracture on the AP view.

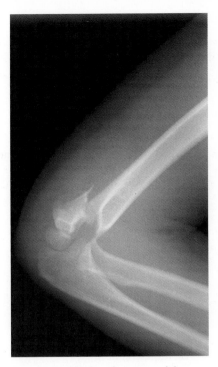

Figure 8.10 Displaced supracondylar fracture.

Management

If there are signs of ischaemia, fracture reduction by gentle traction and extension after appropriate analgesia (see Chapter 3) will often restore some circulation. This is best done by an orthopaedic surgeon. Displaced fractures are likely to need MUA or ORIF (see Chapter 7).

In the absence of displacement or neurovascular signs treatment of the child is with an above-elbow plaster backslab. Refer to the orthopaedic clinic for follow-up.

Dislocation of the elbow

Assessment

Dislocation of the elbow (Figure 8.12 on page 81) is uncommon in children and usually affects those over 11 years. On examination the deformity is obvious, with substantial swelling and severe pain. Assess for neurovascular deficit in the same way as supracondylar fractures (above).

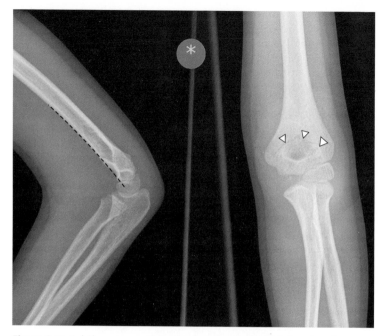

Figure 8.11 Subtle supracondylar fracture (arrow heads) showing the anterior humeral line on the lateral view.

Imaging

X-ray will typically show a posterolateral dislocation. Associated fractures may occur, typically in the medial epicondyle.

Management

The elbow joint will require reduction as soon as possible, usually under general anaesthesia. If the circulation is affected get senior help immediately.

Medial epicondyle injury

Assessment

This fracture constitutes around 10 per cent of elbow fractures and is often associated with a dislocated elbow (see above). There is a variety of mechanisms of injury. On examination, there will be tenderness over the prominence of the medial (ulnar side) epicondyle and likely swelling (see 'Normal or abnormal?' on page 75). In particular, assess ulnar nerve function.

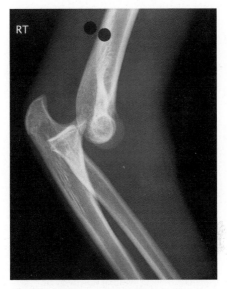

Figure 8.12 Elbow dislocation.

Imaging

There may be minimal or moderate displacement of the medial epicondylar epiphysis (Figure 8.13). In severe injury, the medial epicondyle may become trapped in the elbow joint. It is easy to mistake the medial epiphysis, within the joint, for the capitellum.

 Top-tip: If the child is over 6 years old and the medial epicondylar epiphysis cannot be seen on the AP view (see CRITOE on page 75), assume that it has been displaced and lies within the joint.

Management

Refer to orthopaedics if the medial epiphysis is displaced or there is evidence of ulnar nerve damage.

For undisplaced fractures, place in a collar and cuff (see Chapter 16) and arrange orthopaedic clinic follow-up.

Lateral condyle injury

Assessment

This constitutes around 15 per cent of elbow fractures, and is caused by a fall. On examination there will be tenderness on the prominence

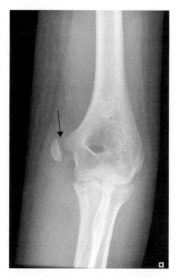

Figure 8.13 Medial epicondylar fracture.

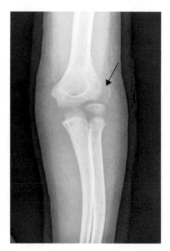

Figure 8.14 Lateral condyle fracture.

of the lateral (radial side) condyle (Figure 8.14). Unlike the other elbow injuries we have discussed, this is not usually associated with neurovascular problems, but it can be associated with growth problems.

Imaging

Although the fracture often includes a large chunk of unossified cartilage, X-rays can however appear innocent with just a sliver of bone broken from the lateral humeral metaphysis just above the capitellum ossification centre.

 Top-tip: Look for subtle slivers or pieces of bone – they are significant.

Management

Displaced fractures should be referred immediately to orthopaedics. Undisplaced fractures can be placed in an above-elbow backslab and referred to an orthopaedic clinic.

Olecranon fracture

Assessment

These rare fractures are usually due to direct trauma, usually in teenagers. Following a direct blow to the elbow, children are often tender over this area since there is little cushioning; however, if the olecranon is fractured (Figure 8.15), a large amount of generalized elbow swelling is present.

Imaging

It is easy to confuse the normal epiphysis with a fracture. The normal olecranon epiphysis appears between the ages of 8 and 11 and fuses by the age of 14. Seek senior advice if unsure.

 Top-tip: Most of the time you are just seeing a normal epiphysis!

Management

A truly fractured olecranon fracture may well need internal fixation, so get immediate orthopaedic advice.

Radial head/neck fractures

Assessment

Radial neck fractures are relatively common in children, and are caused by a fall. Radial head fractures are more common in adults. Most fractures in children are Salter–Harris II (see page 61). Greenstick fractures may also occur (Figure 8.16).

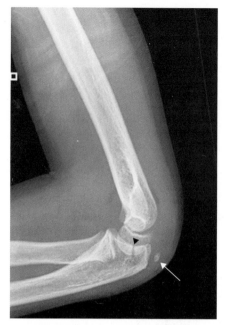

Figure 8.15 Olecranon fracture (arrow head). The olecranon ossification centre is arrowed.

Pain is often vague and referred to the wrist. Localizing the injury can be tricky, but the clues are pain on supination and pronation of the forearm, difficulty in fully extending the elbow and tenderness at a point between the lateral epicondyle and the point of the olecranon, 1 cm distally. You can feel the radial head at this point – it moves during pronation and supination.

There may or may not be mild swelling (this may be subtle, see 'Normal or abnormal?' on page 75).

Imaging

These fractures may be difficult to detect on X-ray. The presence of a joint effusion, as indicated by a positive fat pad sign (see 'Normal or abnormal?' on page 75) should give you a clue.

Similarly once you are thinking of it, you will notice the abnormality of the radial neck. The image in Figure 8.16 is fairly classical.

Radial head fractures (Figure 8.17) can occur in teenagers.

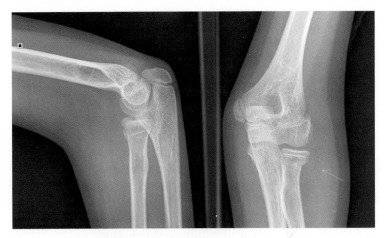

Figure 8.16 Radial neck greenstick fracture.

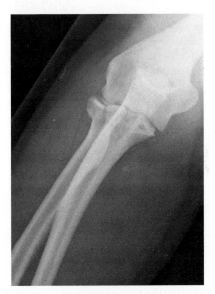

Figure 8.17 Radial head fracture.

Management

Place in a collar and cuff (see Chapter 16) and arrange orthopaedic clinic follow-up. Only displaced radial head fractures need immediate referral, and these are rare.

The 'pulled' elbow

Assessment

This injury is commonest in children between the ages of one and three following a sudden longitudinal pull on the arm. This mechanism of injury causes a small tear in the distal insertion of the annular ligament, and the periosteum at the head of the radius becomes entrapped in the joint. Some children are especially prone to this, so there may be previous episodes of the same injury. The ligament tightens as the child gets older.

Typical mechanisms would include the hand being grabbed as the child is pulling away, or a jerk while holding hands. As the injury is 'inflicted' by a third party, the history may not be forthcoming or may change, and is often ascribed to a fall initially. Although a changing history should normally ring 'alarm bells' (see Chapter 15) this is understandably guilt-driven and in fact this injury can occur very easily, without excessive force being applied. Reassurance should be given to those present, since feelings are often running high!

The arm usually lies limp and partially flexed by the child's side. The child will preferentially use the other arm, but may be playing happily. On examination, tenderness to palpation is often not elicited. Check the clavicle and the distal radius (without moving the elbow) to exclude these other common injuries. If elbow movement causes pain then a pulled elbow is the likely diagnosis in this age group. If *both* the history and the age group are completely classical, no X-ray is required, and you can go ahead and manipulate the elbow. However, if there is any uncertainty, X-ray first to exclude a fracture.

Management

Manipulating the elbow (see Chapter 16) is a simple procedure that usually gives satisfyingly rapid resolution of symptoms. Review the child after 10 minutes in your play area. Most will be using the arm happily and can go home.

See Video 20. Pulled elbow

If the child is still not using the arm (which is more common in older toddlers and repeat dislocators) you can have one more attempt, but if this does not seem to work it may be because the child is still sore, or has memory of the pain and is avoiding using the arm, or it is not yet reduced. Advise the parents that spontaneous reduction will usually take place and place the arm in a broad arm sling (see Chapter 16). If they are still not using the arm in 48 hours' time they should return for review.

Advise the parents in future to avoid games that involve pulling (e.g. swinging between two adults). A pull may however be unavoidable, for example if the child starts to run across a road. Some children present with repeated dislocations as it is not always possible to avoid a pull injury. Parents of repeat dislocators may be happy to be taught the reduction technique. This kind of 'recurrent injury' is not a child protection issue. You may have to explain the condition to colleagues such as social workers.

THE FOREARM

Mid-shaft fractures of the radius and/or ulna

Usually both bones of the forearm fracture during a fall, or less commonly one bone fractures with a dislocation of the other (see below, 'Fracture dislocations of the forearm'). With direct trauma, for example landing on a sharp edge or struck in self-defence, it is possible to fracture the mid-shaft of the ulna in isolation (Figure 8.18). However, these injuries are relatively uncommon.

Assessment

Fractures of the forearm bones are commonly associated with significant angulation and displacement.

Management

For greenstick fractures, up to 30° of angulation will remodel in a toddler. In teenagers, more than 10° is unacceptable. If the angulation is acceptable, place the arm in an above-elbow backslab and refer to an orthopaedic clinic within a day or two. Refer all other fractures for immediate orthopaedic advice.

Fracture dislocations of the forearm

The radius and ulna form a circle, in a sense. Therefore, if one breaks, it is possible for the other to dislocate. There are two patterns of fracture/dislocation: the Monteggia (Figure 8.19) and the Galeazzi.

A Monteggia injury

There is a fracture of the ulna, with an associated dislocation of the radial head.

In a normal child the radial head points to the capitellum in all views of the elbow. Therefore if the *radiocapitellar line* (a line drawn along the central axis of the radius on the lateral view) does not transect the middle of the capitellum, there is a radial head dislocation. Monteggia fractures with radial head subluxation are commonly overlooked.

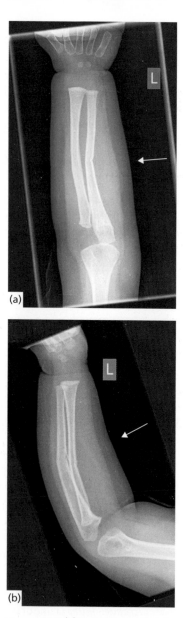

Figure 8.18 (a) Anteroposterior view of mid-shaft greenstick fractures of the radius and ulna. (b) Lateral view of mid-shaft greenstick fractures of the radius and ulna.

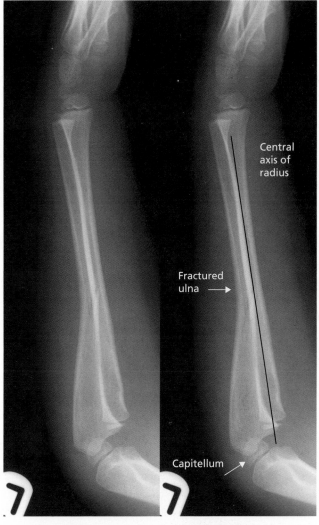

Figure 8.19 A Monteggia injury with a disrupted radiocapitellar line.

 Top-tip: Always check the radiocapitallar line if you see an ulnar fracture.

A Galeazzi injury

This occurs in teenagers and is rare. There is a fracture of the shaft of radius, associated with a dislocation of the distal ulna.

 Top-tip: If you see a shaft of radius fracture, always look to see if the gap between the distal ulna and the carpal bones looks normal.

Management

Refer all fracture dislocations of the radius and ulna for an immediate orthopaedic opinion.

THE WRIST

Distal radius fracture

Assessment

Fracture of the distal radius (Figure 8.20) is one of the commonest injuries in all age groups, usually occurring after a fall on the outstretched hand. Signs may be subtle. There may be slight local tenderness, particularly in a young child, and a fairly good range of movement. At the opposite extreme, there may be obvious deformity, swelling and tenderness over the distal radius. Essentially, if any child points to the distal radius when asked where it hurts, an X-ray will be worthwhile in the majority of cases!

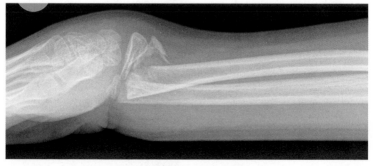

Figure 8.20 Displaced fracture of distal radius and ulna.

Imaging

Findings on X-ray vary from a simple undisplaced greenstick or torus fracture (Figure 8.21), or growth plate fracture (see Chapter 7), to severe angulated, displaced fractures of both distal radius and ulna.

Management

Refer immediately to orthopaedics if the fracture is angulated or displaced. Up to 25° of angulation will remodel in a toddler. In teenagers, more than 10° is unacceptable. For simple, undisplaced fractures, place in a forearm plaster of Paris backslab, or just a splint, and arrange orthopaedic clinic follow-up.

 See Video 3. Futura splint

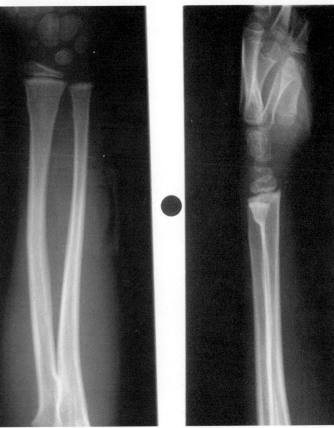

Figure 8.21 Torus fracture of the distal radius.

Scaphoid fracture

Scaphoid fractures can only occur once the scaphoid bone has calcified (Figure 8.22), at around 9 years old. Although uncommon, a missed scaphoid fracture may result in very significant disability of the wrist in future years due to non-union or avascular necrosis.

Assessment

Scaphoid injuries are usually caused by a fall on the outstretched hand. There is usually mild swelling on the radial side of the wrist if you look carefully.

The signs you should specifically examine for are:

- tenderness in the 'anatomical snuff-box' (Figure 8.22, arrow 1) to gentle pressure (firm pressure will always elicit tenderness in the normal wrist as the superficial branch of the radial nerve traverses this area)
- tenderness over the dorsal aspect of the scaphoid (Figure 8.22, arrow 2)
- tenderness over the palmar aspect of the scaphoid (Figure 8.22, arrow 3)
- pain at the wrist when compressing the thumb longitudinally (Figure 8.23)
- pain during passive radial and ulnar deviation of the wrist (Figure 8.24).

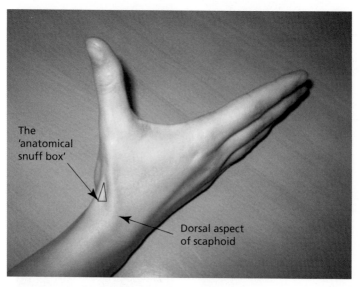

The 'anatomical snuff box'

Dorsal aspect of scaphoid

Figure 8.22 Surface anatomy of the scaphoid.

See Video 4. Scaphoid examination

Imaging

Ensure you request the appropriate view (see Table 7.1 on page 66). Four views are usually provided: anteroposterior, lateral, and left and right obliques. In about 10 per cent of cases the scaphoid fracture may not be visible on initial films, and review at 10–14 days with a view to further imaging is needed if you think there is a scaphoid fracture clinically (Figure 8.25).

Management

If you suspect a scaphoid fracture, you must treat the child as if they have one, even when no fracture has been seen on initial images. Place the wrist in a scaphoid plaster cast or a rigid splint with a thumb extension. Arrange orthopaedic clinic follow-up at 10–14 days.

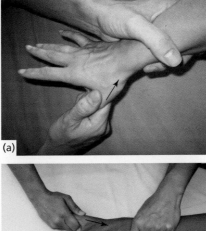

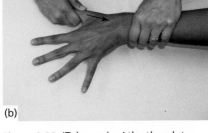

Figure 8.23 'Telescoping' the thumb to elicit pain (a) distraction (b) compression.

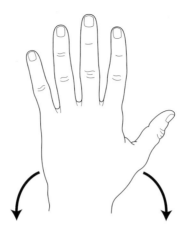

Figure 8.24 Radial and ulnar deviation to elicit pain (pressing on the volar aspect of the scaphoid while you do this will also elicit tenderness).

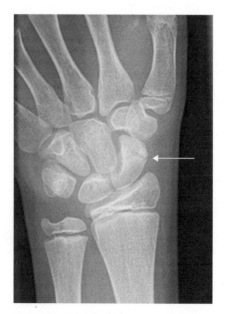

Figure 8.25 Scaphoid fracture.

CHAPTER 9

THE HAND

Introduction	95	Infections	115
Clinical examination	96	Cut wrists in deliberate	
Fractures of the hand	103	self-harm	117
Fingertip soft tissue injuries	110	Reflex sympathetic	
Tendon and nerve injuries	114	dystrophy/regional	
Finger: other soft tissue injuries	115	complex pain syndrome	117

INTRODUCTION

Hand injuries are common. Young children sustain crush injuries and burns while exploring their environment, and older children are prone to sports injuries. Most injuries are minor. However, the complexity and density of important structures in the hand make it vulnerable to serious, permanent injury. If a significant injury is missed, there may be enormous long-term consequences for their future training or occupation in terms of loss of function. Luckily long-term problems due to stiffness are very unlikely, since young children will continue to use their hands despite injury. This is different for adults.

Warning: If in doubt about the extent of a hand injury, always seek expert advice!

Consult your local policy for referral procedures, since hand specialists may be part of the orthopaedic or plastic surgery services, and referral may depend on the exact nature of the injury.

Hand injuries frequently swell. Swelling causes pain and stiffness. This may be prevented by elevation to shoulder level in a 'high arm sling' (see Chapter 16), if the child will cooperate. This helps to alleviate pain, and is necessary for a day or two if swelling is present or predictable.

See Video 13. High arm sling

Warning: Rings should always be removed on arrival to prevent swelling and ischaemia of a digit!

CLINICAL EXAMINATION

A methodical, slick system for examining hands is essential, albeit with modifications for young children. The hand is one area where you really do need to understand the underlying anatomy. Sometimes exploration under general anaesthetic is needed if a wound is deep to check for injury to tendons or nerves. Also, important fractures can be quite subtle.

 Warning: Have a low threshold for X-rays! Clinical examination is not that reliable for determining the probability of a fracture, and the radiation dose is very low.

The infant or pre-school child

Small children are unable to obey the simple commands needed to test hand function. You are therefore dependent on observation of function, posture and some limited tests. Look for the 'cascade' of normal finger posture (Figure 9.1), disrupted when flexor tendons are severed.

Fortunately in this age group, most structures are flexible so that fractures are less likely. The biggest challenge is when there is a wound. There is a

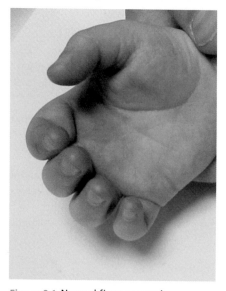

Figure 9.1 **Normal finger cascade.**

useful test of nerve function, which involves immersing the fingers until the skin goes crinkly. If a nerve is severed, the area of skin supplied by that nerve will not crinkle. However children who are small enough to need this test will often not stay in the water, and if the injury is a wound (most likely) you may still need to explore the wound because you cannot be confident you have excluded a tendon injury.

Older children

First, *ask*

- which hand do you use to write with?
- if laceration present: does your hand or your fingers feel funny or numb anywhere?

Look for:

- deformity
- swelling
- distribution of lacerations.

Test for:

- range of movement of affected joints
- localized tenderness (children can be remarkably specific if you test and retest, and get them to concentrate)
- function of individual tendons
- function of specific nerves
- sensation.

 Top-tip: Draw diagrams! It is much easier to interpret written notes if diagrams are used. Most Emergency Departments have ink pads and stamps.

Use the right terminology when writing notes.

- Avoid 'medial' and 'lateral' – use 'radial' and 'ulnar'.
- Avoid 'back' or 'front' or 'anterior' or 'posterior' – use 'dorsal' (Figure 9.2) and 'volar' or 'palmar' (Figure 9.3).
- Do not number fingers (second, third etc.): the fingers are thumb/ index/middle/ring/little.

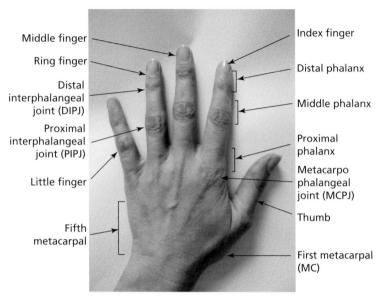

Middle finger

Ring finger

Distal
interphalangeal
joint (DIPJ)

Proximal
interphalangeal
joint (PIPJ)

Little finger

Fifth
metacarpal

Index finger

Distal phalanx

Middle phalanx

Proximal
phalanx

Metacarpo
phalangeal
joint (MCPJ)

Thumb

First metacarpal
(MC)

Figure 9.2 Dorsum of hand – description and abbreviations.

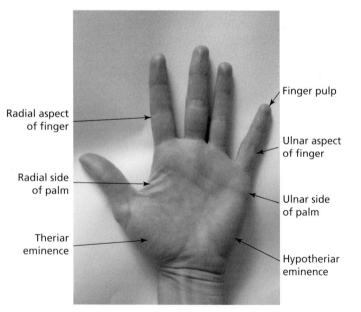

Radial aspect
of finger

Radial side
of palm

Theriar
eminence

Finger pulp

Ulnar aspect
of finger

Ulnar side
of palm

Hypotheriar
eminence

Figure 9.3 Volar or palmar aspect of hand.

Tendon examination

Remember that tendons also need testing in forearm wounds.

Extensor tendons

Ask the child to bring their fingers out straight, and watch closely to make sure they can fully extend the finger without any lag at any of the joints: metacarpophalangeal joint (MCPJ), proximal interphalangeal joint (PIPJ) and distal interphalangeal joint (DIPJ). Remember that swelling or pain may sometimes prevent full extension. Next ask them to keep their fingers straight and not to let you bend the finger as you test each one's strength against resistance. Make this into a game, competing for strength. A finger with a partially severed tendon may look fully extended but there will be weakness and pain when resisting flexion.

 See Video 5. Flexor and extensor tendon examination

Flexor tendons

There are two sets of flexor tendons. You need to understand the relationship of the two layers of tendons in order to understand the examination (Figure 9.4).

To test the *superficial tendons*, evaluate each individual finger in turn. Ask the child to place the hand, palm side up, on a flat surface. Then ask them to bend each finger, in turn, as you hold all the others down. The finger should flex at the MCPJ and PIPJ. Just like with extensor tendons, ask them to keep the finger there and not to let you straighten it, so you are also testing against resistance; if this is difficult there may be a partial tear.

To test the *profundus tendons*, again evaluate each individual finger in turn. Immobilize each finger against the flat surface, palm side up, by pressing down on the middle phalanx. Ask the child to bend the tip of the

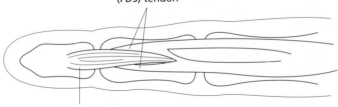

Figure 9.4 **Relationship of flexor tendons.**

finger. The finger should flex at the DIPJ. Again test against resistance as described above.

 See Video 5. Flexor and extensor tendon examination

Nerve examination

Sensory function

Test for sensation by asking if light touch feels 'normal or funny'. Do not ask the child simply if they can feel it, as sensation is rarely completely absent, and proprioception and some feeling will be present. If you think the child is not clear what you mean, use words such as 'strong' or 'fuzzy' and ask if it feels the same as uninjured areas. If they say no, and it fits a nerve distribution pattern, you will need to refer to a hand specialist. Sometimes they say it is not normal, because it is swollen or painful. If this area is close to the injury and does not fit an anatomical pattern of a nerve, you can ignore it.

The distribution of the sensory territories of the three major nerves may be quite variable. Damage to these large trunks occurs proximal to the wrist, so you need to check this with forearm or wrist wounds, and with fractures such as elbow fractures. For injuries of the hand itself, you will be testing the digital nerves.

For the three main nerves (Figures 9.5 and 9.6), the most reliable places to test are the first web space for the radial nerve, the index fingertip for the median nerve, and the little fingertip for the ulnar nerve.

Far more commonly, the digital nerves are damaged. There are two main trunks for each digit, which run along the ulnar and radial sides dorsally, with equivalent palmar branches (Figure 9.7). As above, absence of sensation is relative, not absolute.

Motor function

If you are not sure if you are detecting weakness, compare strength with the opposite hand. Weakness may also be caused by pain inhibiting the movement. This is where you need to be clear about your anatomy and risk of true weakness.

The radial nerve

The radial nerve supplies the wrist and finger extensors, which should be able to strongly resist flexion.

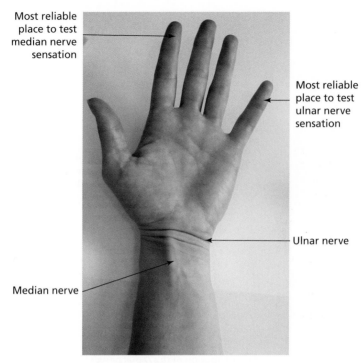

Most reliable place to test median nerve sensation

Most reliable place to test ulnar nerve sensation

Ulnar nerve

Median nerve

Figure 9.5 Path and distribution of the median and ulnar nerves.

The median nerve

The median nerve is best assessed by testing opposition. Ask the child to touch the tip of the thumb to the tip of the little finger, and to stop you 'breaking the ring'.

The ulnar nerve

The ulnar nerve operates most of the intrinsic muscles of the hand.
A simple test is to put your pen between child's little and ring fingers, and ask them to stop you pulling it out.

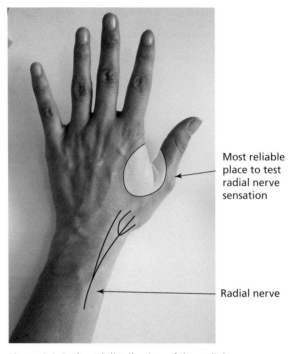

Most reliable place to test radial nerve sensation

Radial nerve

Figure 9.6 Path and distribution of the radial nerve.

 See Video 6. Radial, median and ulnar nerve examination

Wound exploration

Having reassured yourself that there is no damage to underlying structures by clinical examination, you should always confirm this by exploring any deep wound under local anaesthetic. Anything which glistens or looks white may be a tendon. Examine through the full range of movement as severed tendons may retract and hide.

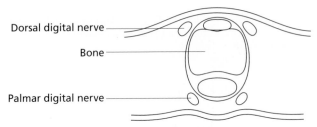

Figure 9.7 Distribution of the digital nerves.

Warning: Do not extend a wound in order to explore it!

Sometimes it can be difficult to assess a wound because of bleeding, and a tourniquet is required to create a bloodless field. In such cases, referral to a specialist is advised.

Warning: Seek advice if ever in doubt when exploring a wound!

FRACTURES OF THE HAND

There are some general rules that can be followed for phalangeal and metacarpal fractures.

- There should be a low threshold for ordering X-rays in hand injuries.
- Most injuries will cause swelling so the hand should be elevated in a high arm sling for a couple of days (see Chapter 16).
- Encourage exercises of the fingers.
- The best form of immobilization is 'neighbour' or 'buddy' strapping (see Chapter 16). This allows movement in the IPJs.
- If the neck or shaft of a metacarpal or phalanx is fractured examine for finger rotation (Figure 9.8).

First ask the child to lift the hand up to your eye level and check the nails look reasonably aligned, and that the affected finger is not rotated (Figure 9.8a). Then ask them to drop their hand down, turn it the other way around and slowly open and close their fist (Figure 9.8b).

See Video 7. Examining for finger rotation

Warning: Rotation of the little finger (clinodactyly) is fairly common in normal people but is bilateral – compare the degree of rotation with the uninjured hand

Lastly, ensure you request the correct X-ray view (see Table 7.1 on page 66). To see a finger clearly you need an anteroposterior and lateral view of the finger itself.

Metacarpal fractures

Assessment

The three main mechanisms are a punch (usually teenagers) or a fall onto the hand (less common). A glancing blow against an object does not

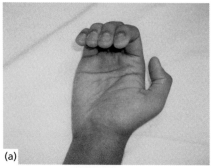

(a)

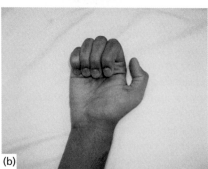

(b)

Figure 9.8 (a) Assessment of finger rotation looking at nail alignment (normal).
(b) Assessment of finger rotation looking at closure to fist (normal).

See Video 7. Examining for finger rotation

generally cause a fracture. Examine carefully for rotational deformity (see above). A fracture of the neck of the 5th metacarpal is often called a 'boxer's fracture'.

Check for a wound near the knuckles. You cannot tell if a wound communicates with the metacarpo-phalangeal joint, but it may, and will require a joint wash-out. Teenagers who punch inanimate objects are at low risk of infection, whereas if the wound has been caused by contact with another person's teeth there is a high risk of infection. Check the circumstances of the punch, and whether there are safeguarding or bullying issues.

Imaging
Both greenstick and growth plate injuries may occur. You will have requested a 'hand' view. Note that the views taken are usually an anteroposterior and an oblique view (Figure 9.9). If a displaced fracture is found, you may require a true lateral view to adequately assess displacement.

Management
Refer to the hand surgery service if there is rotational deformity, angulation greater than 20° in the metaphysis, angulation greater than 45° at the neck of the 5th metacarpal (Figure 9.9), more than 50 per cent displacement of the bone ends, a potential open fracture or non-greenstick fractures in three adjacent metacarpals.

For straightforward metacarpal fractures, apply neighbour strapping to the appropriate digit and elevate the hand in a high arm sling (see Chapter 16). Arrange hand specialist follow-up.

Fractures of the proximal and middle phalanges

Assessment
These fractures are commonly caused in ball games, but can be caused by a fall. Fracture patterns include transverse, spiral, epiphyseal and greenstick fractures. These can occur in the head, neck, shaft or base of the phalanx, or at the interphalangeal joints.

Clinical discrimination between minor soft tissue injury and fractures is poor, and although only a small minority of fractures need operative intervention, these are important to detect in order to prevent long-term disability, so have a low threshold for X-ray.

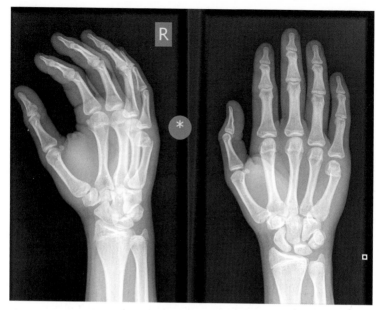

Figure 9.9 Fractured neck of fifth metacarpal.

Imaging

Phalangeal fractures can be obvious or subtle. Fractures such as that in Figure 9.10 would have obvious clinical deformity.

Management

Refer to your hand surgery specialist if there is finger rotation, angulation greater than 20°, displacement of the bone ends or an intra-articular fracture.

For uncomplicated fractures, neighbour strap the affected digit, place in a high arm sling (see Chapter 16) and arrange hand specialist follow-up.

Dislocations of the proximal and distal interphalangeal joints

Assessment

The PIPJ and the DIPJ can dislocate, either in a volar or a dorsal (more likely) direction, following hyper-flexion or hyper-extension injuries, usually in sports but sometimes a fall. Actual rupture of the collateral ligaments is rare compared with adults.

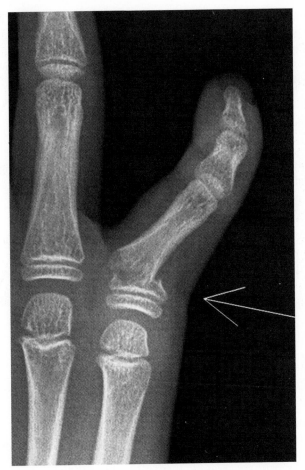

Figure 9.10 Displaced fracture base of proximal phalanx.

Imaging

Do not be fooled by the AP view, which may look normal, or you may spot a loss of joint space. However, the lateral view is obvious. There may be an associated fracture.

Management

The joint needs to be reduced urgently. Assess for neurovascular damage distal to the dislocation both before and after reduction. Reduction usually requires a digital block (see Chapter 16) and you will get better grip if you wrap the distal finger in gauze. Holding the proximal bone tight, simply push the distal bone into position. If this does not work use a little traction but be careful in children, as compared with adults it is possible to overdo it and superimpose soft tissues into the joint.

See Video 8. Dislocated finger reduction

Following reduction take another X-ray to confirm position then neighbour strap and elevate the finger and refer the child to your hand clinic.

Volar plate injury

This is an injury of the PIPJ on the volar side. It is caused by hyperextension, with the child often saying that the finger was 'bent back', usually in ball games. The complex 'volar plate' of the joint capsule pulls away from the volar surface of the base of the middle phalanx or it can pull off a fragment of bone of variable size.

Imaging

The X-ray findings are subtle, and easily missed unless a true lateral view of the finger is obtained and you look closely (Figure 9.11).

Top-tip: You need a 'finger' view with a true lateral to diagnose this injury; a 'hand' view does not give you the detail or the right view.

Management

If the fragment is large and contains a significant part of the articular surface it may need fixation. Fortunately the fragment is usually small, especially in younger patients, and rarely needs surgical treatment – but opinion differs regarding immobilization.

Arrange hand clinic follow-up, to avoid a fixed flexion deformity of the PIPJ in the future.

Fractures of the distal phalanx

Assessment

These are usually sustained by crush injuries, particularly doors being closed, and may involve more than one finger. Fractures of the terminal tuft, neck and base of the distal phalanx are relatively unimportant injuries in themselves. Often there is an associated soft tissue fingertip, nailbed or tendon injury (this is covered in 'Fingertip soft tissue injuries', below).

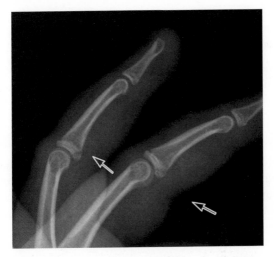

Figure 9.11 Avulsion fractures of the volar plate at the proximal interphalangeal joint.

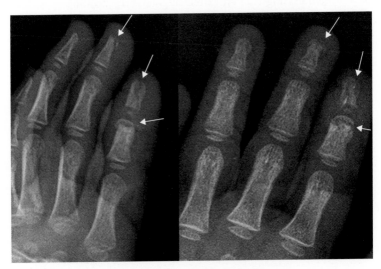

Figure 9.12 Crush fractures of distal and middle phalanges.

Imaging

A crush fracture of distal phalanges (Figure 9.12) is also called a 'tuft' fracture, or a fracture of the 'terminal' phalanx.

Management

If there is no associated soft tissue injury as described below, then neighbour strap the finger and arrange hand clinic follow-up.

FINGERTIP SOFT TISSUE INJURIES

Fingertips are complex anatomical structures that are frequently injured (most often shut in doors). These crush injuries are very stressful to children and their families. Consider intranasal diamorphine or oral morphine, for both pain and anxiety (see Chapter 3). Confusingly, these injuries evoke widely differing opinions in their management. Unfortunately, robust, long-term outcome studies do not exist to assist you in your decisions.

General principles

The main principles of management are as follows.

- Children's fingertips are extremely good at regenerating themselves, thus conservative management is possible in most cases, with a good cosmetic outcome.
- Restoration of normal anatomy is the aim. Much can be achieved with adhesive strips, tissue glue and dressings; sutures are not usually needed.
- Long-term problems may occur at the base of the nail if the skin of the nailfold is allowed to adhere onto the germinal matrix, resulting in abnormal growth of the new nail into the nailbed; this must be prevented (see below).
- Try to determine the presence or absence of a nailbed laceration. In many cases this is an educated guess. A practical approach to whether or not to repair needs to be taken because of the lack of evidence base for the necessity of repair, and the fact that proper repair in children often requires a general anaesthetic in an operating theatre, by a hand surgeon.
- The presence of a subungual haematoma larger than 50 per cent of the nail, or an underlying fracture, makes a nailbed laceration more likely.

Assessment

It helps to think methodically about the different components of the fingertip.

- Is the injury still bleeding?
- Is it a dirty injury?
- Is it a nail or a pulp injury, or both?
- Is there any bone exposed?
- If proximal to the DIPJ, what is the level of the amputation?
- How damaged is the skin and is there skin missing?
- Is the nail avulsed from its germinal matrix under the cuticle?
- Is there anatomical stability or will you need sutures to reoppose wound edges?
- Is there a subungual haematoma? If so is it able to ooze or is it contained?

X-ray

See Figure 9.12 for an example of crush fractures to the distal phalanges.

 Warning: Most crush injuries require an X-ray!

Management

This depends on findings on examination, as above. Be methodical in your assessment; do not let the surrounding anxiety of the family (and sometimes staff) distract you. Consider putting in a digital block (see Chapter 16) for analgesia and to allow you to properly examine the damage.

Since the exact injuries are highly variable, the principles outlined below will guide you. If there is an associated fracture, prescribe an antibiotic such as flucloxacillin and ensure follow-up is early (3–4 days). Always use non-adherent dressings, e.g. paraffin-impregnated gauze (such as Jelonet) or a silicon-based dressing (such as Mepitel).

Persistent bleeding

Apply a non-adhesive dressing such as Kaltostat, bandage tightly, elevate in a high arm sling (see Chapter 16) and leave well alone for at least 20 minutes.

Tissue loss

If bone is exposed, or the skin is very contused, contaminated or non-viable, refer to a specialist. The exception is the pulp itself, which has excellent powers of regeneration even if there is a considerable amount missing.

For injuries proximal to the DIPJ every attempt should be made to preserve the amputated part. It should be covered with sterile, soaked dressings, sealed in a plastic bag and placed within another bag containing ice. The remaining finger should be covered with a non-adherent dressing, and elevated in a high arm sling.

If referral is not needed, use non-adhesive dressings (e.g. Mepitel or Jelonet), bandage the area safe from dirt and fiddling children (see Chapter 16), and advise the family to try to keep it dry. Ideally, it should be left in peace for 5 days before review, as constant disturbance slows healing.

Nail and nailbed injuries

This is a controversial area and there is no good evidence that a perfectionist approach is needed in children.

Nails grow from the base (Figure 9.13). If the base has popped out from under the cuticle, the underlying germinal matrix and nailbed are likely to be disrupted, and if the gap is allowed to close, normal longitudinal growth of the new nail may not occur. Similarly, a large nailbed laceration will affect the growth of the new nail. Not only will the defect be cosmetic, but it may be painful.

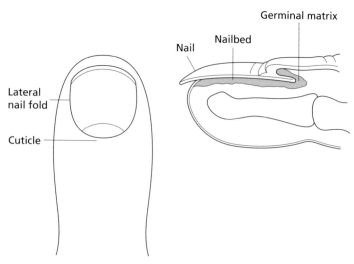

Figure 9.13 The nail and nailbed.

If the nail is very loose, remove the nail and inspect the nailbed; repair with fine sutures if needed. If the nail is quite firmly adherent, attempts should not be made to remove it as this causes further damage. Seek advice.

If the nail has already been avulsed or you have had to remove it, it must be replaced back in the nailfold. Various techniques can be employed. First clean the nail and trim any attached skin. If the nail is lost, a substitute splint must be inserted. This may be custom made using the wax paper backing of Jelonet dressings. Once in position, a combination of tissue glue across the nailfold with adhesive strips over the fingertip is usually sufficient to keep it in place for a week or two (Figure 9.14). Sometimes a suture either side ('stay' sutures) may be needed.

If the insertion of the nail under the cuticle is intact, the nail is best left alone even if there is a deep laceration through it. To repair an underlying nailbed injury would require removal of the nail, risking further harm, and these distal nail injuries do well with conservative management.

Anatomically unstable injuries

Large burst-type lacerations (Figure 9.15) or those involving more than 50 per cent of the digital circumference are likely to be anatomically unstable and require sutures. More minor lacerations can usually be maintained with adhesive strips and a supportive dressing. Just use common sense – bring the tissues back into normal alignment and judge if it will hold without sutures or not. If the wound edges are ragged and do not oppose well, do not worry – children heal well and the gaps will fill in quickly.

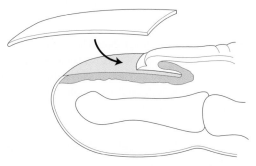

Figure 9.14 Nail being reinserted into nailfold.

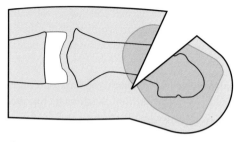

Figure 9.15 A burst-type laceration.

If suturing through nail is required, this can be quite difficult. One suture each side can be taken first through the nail, then through the skin separately. Each can then be pulled tight, bringing the nail into position, as a second stage. The same can be done if the nail is completely avulsed.

Subungual haematoma

Crush injuries to fingertips may cause a subungual haematoma. This is a collection of blood underneath the nail because the nailbed has torn but the overlying nail has remained intact. The blood under the nail may escape out of the side of the nail, but often becomes trapped underneath, causing pressure to build up in this very sensitive area. Trephining the nail releases the blood and is a very satisfying procedure because of the instant relief of symptoms. (see Chapter 16).

See Video 21. Trephining nail

It is not uncommon for this to present 24 hours or so after injury. If the haematoma is large enough to be causing pain, it is worth trephining – the central area is often liquid and you will achieve symptomatic relief.

Underlying fracture

For all except minor injuries, an X-ray should be performed. If a fracture is present, but confined to the shaft of the distal phalanx and undisplaced, a simple dressing may be applied and oral flucloxacillin prescribed if the skin is broken. If the fracture is through the epiphyseal plate, or the base of the distal phalanx is displaced, refer to a specialist.

TENDON AND NERVE INJURIES

See 'Clinical examination' at the start of the chapter for assessment.

Management

All suspected injuries should be referred immediately to your hand service.

FINGER: OTHER SOFT TISSUE INJURIES

Ulnar collateral ligament injury

This is an unusual injury that affects the base of the thumb at the first metacarpo-phalyngeal joint. In adults a true rupture of the ulnar collateral ligament (UCL) occurs, but in children it is associated with a Salter–Harris III fracture of the base of the proximal phalanx and the UCL itself is intact (see page 61). It happens with forced abduction of the thumb.

Management

All suspected injuries should be referred immediately to your hand service.

Mallet finger

This too is an unusual injury. A true mallet finger is the rupture of the extensor tendon as it inserts onto the distal phalanx. This is fairly common in adults, and can occur in teenagers. In younger children, analagous to the UCL injury pattern, it is more likely to be associated with an avulsion fracture of the physis and the actual tendon is intact. There is obvious droop of the distal phalanx when you look at it side-on.

Management

Immobilize with the digit in slight hyperextension in a splint and refer to a hand clinic. The splint must not be removed until review. At that point the hand specialists may allow removal to clean the finger and let the skin 'breathe' but it is crucial that the joint is not flexed while free. This is best demonstrated in the non-acute environment.

Mallet splints are available, made out of plastic, but the skin sweats and becomes a little macerated under these. Zimmer splint (aluminium with foam backing) is preferable, and can be custom made to cover the dorsum of the digit, curving round to incorporate the DIPJ, keeping the DIPJ in slight extension. Zimmer splints are less robust, so possibly more suitable for adults than children. There are pros and cons to both – follow your local policy.

 See Video 9. Mallet splint and 17. Zimmer splint

INFECTIONS

Paronychia

This is a localized infection, usually around the cuticle. It is usually caused by nail-biting. Once the infection has progressed from the reddened stage to develop a collection of pus, antibiotics are useless and drainage is required.

Management

Incision and drainage is required. A digital block may be needed (see Chapter 16). If a large collection of pus is visible, this may not be necessary as the overlying skin is dead. Insert a scalpel blade directly into the pus, making a decent sized hole, then 'milk' the finger to extrude all pus. Cover with a non-adherent dressing, and advise the family to soak the finger in warm water twice over the next 24 hours, milking any remaining pus out themselves.

If a paronychia is persistent more than 10 days, consider the presence of underlying osteomyelitis and request an X-ray.

Tendon infection

Any wound infection may cause tendon infection. Flexor tendons are contained within synovial sheaths, and infection can spread rapidly and be extremely destructive. The signs of this are pain, especially on finger extension, erythema and generalized (fusiform) swelling. The child will be holding the finger in a slightly flexed position. This condition requires urgent referral.

Warning: Refer immediately to a hand specialist if you have any suspicion of flexor tendon infection!

Pulp and palmar space infections

A collection of pus in the pulp space of the fingertip is called a felon. The finger pulp is hot, red, swollen, fluctuant and extremely painful. Refer to a hand specialist for surgical treatment.

The palm contains soft tissue spaces, confined by fascial compartments. If infection occurs, signs may be subtle because it is deep seated. Look for the loss of the normal dip between the metacarpals, and test for pain on compression.

Warning: Refer immediately to a hand specialist if you have any suspicion of a palmar space infection!

CUT WRISTS IN DELIBERATE SELF-HARM

Unfortunately deliberate self-harm (DSH) involving forearm or wrist cutting has become fairly common in teenagers in the UK and other similar countries. It is a sign of psychological distress, which may run quite deep. The child may or may not be forthcoming about DSH.

 Warning: Suspect deliberate self-harm if you see superficial lacerations on the insides of the wrists

DSH of any kind in children under 16 years should be taken seriously, and a full psychosocial assessment performed by an experienced multidisciplinary team.

REFLEX SYMPATHETIC DYSTROPHY/REGIONAL COMPLEX PAIN SYNDROME

This is a dysautonomia, which occurs from the age of 8 or so. It usually follows injury, and can cause chronic debilitating wasting of the arm or leg. Emergency physicians tend to see milder versions soon after injury, and in fact there can be dysautonomia immediately after injury. It can present quite dramatically with pallor, coldness, hyperaesthesia, swelling or stiffness of a limb, commonly the forearm and hand. Milder autonomic nervous system symptoms occur temporarily quite frequently in teenage girls with hand or ankle injuries and can be mistaken for fractures or dislocations with vascular injury. There may be a very abnormal posture, but the overriding feature is severe pain, even to light touch.

Without early intervention (see below) symptoms tend to worsen. Delay in diagnosis is common, and frequently follows multiple radiological imaging and prolonged immobilization, which usually make things worse.

Management
Reassure the patient and parent that there is no severe injury. Be sympathetic and patient but try to get the affected part to move to demonstrate that there is not a major mechanical issue. This may need passive demonstration of movements, or getting the child to take just two steps, etc.

Avoid immobilizing the affected part (e.g. splints, plaster, crutches). Give the patient and parents a goal-orientated, staged physiotherapy programme, involving increasing mobilization each day for the next 7–14 days. Very small goals each day that increase the mobility must be set. Encourage a positive outlook and convey the idea that the child should be back to normal by that stage. Do not discharge without arranging follow-up by someone experienced in these problems. If things are not improving at 14 days, formal physiotherapy, possibly with psychological input, is needed. In most cases, particularly if the parent understands the exercise programme, things will be fine.

CHAPTER 10

THE LOWER LIMB

The limping child   119   Injuries   126

THE LIMPING CHILD

Limping in children is a common presentation. In some cases there is a clear history of trauma and a specific injury can be identified, but many children attend without a clear history of injury and present a diagnostic challenge.

Hip joint pathology is a frequent source of non-traumatic limp, but may present with knee pain. Clinical examination of the hip joint is therefore mandatory in all limping children. Subtle restriction of hip internal rotation is the most sensitive clinical sign of hip joint pathology and should always be evaluated.

The differential diagnosis is wide and includes septic arthritis, transient synovitis, Perthes' disease, slipped upper femoral epiphysis (SUFE), inflammatory arthritides such as juvenile idiopathic arthritis, idiopathic chondrolysis, fractures, sprains and malignancies. SUFE and septic arthritis deserve special mention because diagnosis is often delayed or overlooked, and this can lead to serious long term consequences for the patient.

The age of the child helps to determine the most likely diagnosis:

- 0–5: septic arthritis, transient synovitis, Perthes' disease
- 5–10: transient synovitis, septic arthritis, Perthes' disease, SUFE
- 10–15: SUFE, transient synovitis, Perthes' disease, septic arthritis.

Investigation depends on your local policy, and depends on the severity of symptoms and risk of other pathology. Investigations may include X-ray, ultrasound, white count, C-reactive protein and erythrocyte sedimentation rate.

Warning: Knee pain is often a sign of hip pathology.

Transient synovitis

This is a harmless temporary inflammation of the synovium of the hip joint, which may cause an effusion. The cause is unknown but it may be a reaction to a viral illness.

The term 'irritable hip' is often used, but in fact this means any hip which is painful when examined, so this is just one cause. It is a diagnosis of exclusion, so you need to be sure you have considered the other conditions listed above, in particular septic arthritis. The most common age group is toddlers and early school age children.

Assessment

The child is most likely to present with a limp but otherwise be perfectly well. This is usually mild (intermittent, slight limp) but can be more severe (non-weight-bearing and marked decrease in range of movement).

Management

See 'Distinguishing between septic arthritis and transient synovitis' below. Transient synovitis is a benign condition and does not usually recur. It lasts 3–10 days. Since it is a diagnosis of exclusion, all cases should be followed up in an appropriate clinic to ensure return to normal within 2 weeks and lack of development of any new symptoms.

Septic arthritis

Assessment

Septic arthritis (bacterial infection within a joint) can develop rapidly over a couple of days. It is usually a result of haematogenous spread from a focus of infection elsewhere, such as throat, ear or skin infection. This sometimes follows secondary infection of vascular access sites or other skin problems but more often the primary source of the infection is never found. It can affect any large or medium size joint, e.g. shoulder, knee.

The most common symptom is the child not using the joint. The hip joint in a non-mobile infant will present with reduced movement rather than limp, and pain on changing the nappy. Overlying redness or warmth are not common, so you need to keep a high index of suspicion.

Management

See 'Distinguishing between septic arthritis and transient synovitis' below. Septic arthritis requires prompt drainage in an operating theatre and IV antibiotic therapy, if long-term complications are to be avoided.

Warning: Children under 3 years are especially vulnerable to septic arthritis!

Distinguishing between septic arthritis and transient synovitis

Transient synovitis is by far the commonest explanation for the 'irritable hip' and can occur at any age, although most frequently between 4 and 8 years. Septic arthritis can also occur at any age, but children under 3 years are especially vulnerable. Distinction between these two potential diagnoses is imperative.

Four findings are considered to be important and the more that are present the more likely the chance of septic arthritis:

- a history of fever
- inability to weight-bear
- an erythrocyte sedimentation rate >40 mm/hour
- a serum white blood cell count of >12 000 cells/mm^3.

Early in the disease process, symptoms and signs of the two conditions will be hard to discriminate, and blood markers, especially C-reactive protein, may not have risen.

X-rays are normal in both conditions. Ultrasound will identify an effusion in both conditions, confirming that the pathology is within the hip joint.

If in doubt, the child should be kept under close monitoring for the next 48 hours.

Slipped upper femoral epiphysis

This condition presents with thigh or knee pain. It occurs when the unfused epiphysis of the femoral head slips position. It happens around 8–15 years (earlier in girls because puberty is earlier). It is more common in boys than girls and both sides can be affected. Two body types are classically, though not necessarily, associated with this condition:

- obese
- tall and thin.

The actual slipping of the femoral epiphysis may occur gradually or suddenly. There may be a history of a few weeks of more minor symptoms preceding the acute event.

Warning: There may, or may not, be a history of trauma!

Trauma can precipitate a slip, but many parents try to associate limping with recent trauma, which is often a 'red herring'.

Assessment
Remember that the child will commonly complain of thigh or knee pain rather than of hip or groin pain. This is a well-known pitfall but if overlooked will lead to missed or late diagnosis, long-term complications and litigation. The child may be limping or non-weight-bearing. On examination hip movements, particularly internal rotation, may be restricted. Watch the child's face to detect pain, and watch to see if they are tilting their pelvis to compensate.

 Warning: SUFE may present with isolated thigh or knee pain!

X-ray
You should request a pelvis view to help you to compare with the opposite side, but beware of bilateral disease. Subtle slips will be missed on an

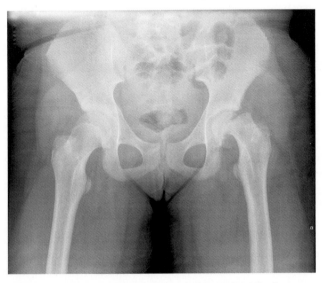

Figure 10.1 Obvious left slipped upper femoral epiphysis.

anteroposterior (AP) view; they are better seen on a true lateral. However, in practice to reduce the amount of radiation, a 'frog leg' lateral view is usually performed, which also allows comparison with the other hip.

A line drawn along the superior border of the femoral neck on the AP view (Klein's line) should normally cut through the top of the epiphysis. In a slipped upper femoral epiphysis, the whole of the epiphysis may lie below this line (Figures 10.1 and 10.2).

On the AP view the earliest signs are widening and irregularity of the physis.

If in doubt, seek a radiologist's advice.

Top-tip: Radiological diagnosis can be tricky; further imaging, such as a radio-isotope bone scan or computed tomography (CT), may be needed.

Management
If you suspect a slipped upper femoral epiphysis, seek immediate orthopaedic advice. The patient should avoid further weight-bearing.

Perthes' avascular necrosis of the femoral head
This is caused by avascular necrosis of the femoral head and presents with hip, thigh or knee pain. It usually affects children in the 5–9 age group, but can happen from 2 to 16 years. It occurs in boys more frequently than girls, particularly slim, active boys. Anything which affects the vasculature of the small vessels that supply the femoral head, via the capsule, can cause Perthes' disease; this includes haematological conditions like sickle cell disease, abnormal anatomy or steroid treatment. Usually no cause is found. The condition may be bilateral but rarely affects both hips at the same time.

Warning: There may or may not be a history of trauma!

It is not clear if trauma can precipitate Perthes' disease, but many parents try to associate limping with recent trauma, which is a 'red herring'. Many cases are labelled as an 'irritable hip' (e.g. transient synovitis) but the symptoms fail to settle as expected and Perthes' disease is eventually diagnosed.

Assessment
Remember that the child will more likely complain of thigh or knee pain than hip or groin pain. The child may be limping or non-weight-bearing.

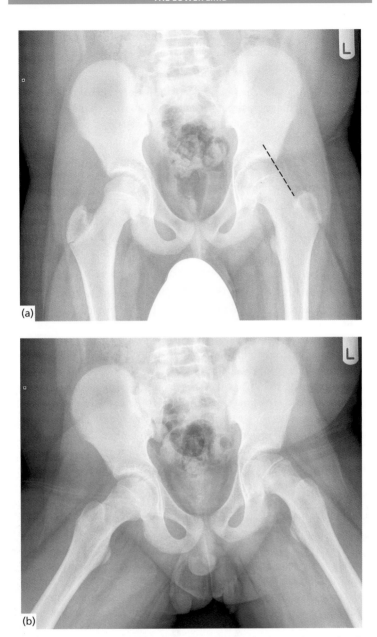

Figure 10.2 Subtle left slipped upper femoral epiphysis. On the AP view in (a), Klein's line does not intersect the epiphysis. On the frog lateral view in (b), the slip is slightly more obvious.

On examination hip movements, particularly internal rotation, may be limited by pain. Watch the child's face to detect pain, and watch to see if they are tilting their pelvis to compensate.

 Warning: Perthes' disease may present with isolated thigh or knee pain!

X-ray

X-ray the pelvis to help you to compare with the opposite side. In the initial stages little may be seen on X-ray. Later the femoral head epiphysis shows patchy sclerosis and fragmentation giving a 'moth-eaten' appearance and can eventually become flattened.

If in doubt, seek senior advice. Further imaging, such as magnetic resonance imaging, may be needed for diagnosis.

Management

If you diagnose Perthes' disease (Figure 10.3), the condition does not need urgent attention but orthopaedic referral is required.

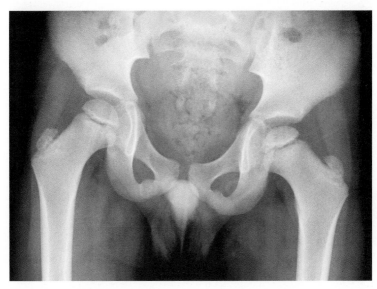

Figure 10.3 **Left Perthes' disease.**

INJURIES

Avulsion fractures around the hip

Children may sustain avulsion fractures following sudden movements, usually during sport. The five places this can occur are the ischial tuberosity, the greater and lesser trochanters of the femur, and the anterior superior and anterior inferior iliac spines (Figures 10.4–10.6). The clue is in the history. The child may or may not be able to weight-bear. X-ray if you get the right history and the child can localize the pain. Although most are managed conservatively unless significant displacement is present, a diagnosis helps you to give sensible discharge advice such as staying off sports for 6 weeks. Refer to orthopaedics for follow-up.

The same five apophyses can become inflamed with repetitive sports use, rather than fracture acutely. Other traction apophysitis conditions include Osgood–Schlatter's disease of the knee and Sever's disease of the heel (see below for both).

Femoral shaft fractures

Considerable force is usually required to fracture the femur. There is often a history of a fall with the leg twisted awkwardly under the child.

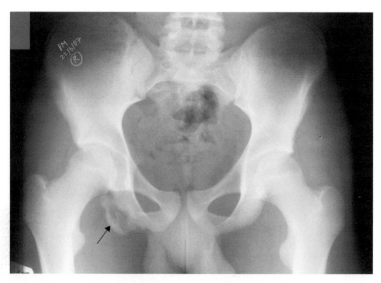

Figure 10.4 Avulsion fracture of the right ischial tuberosity.

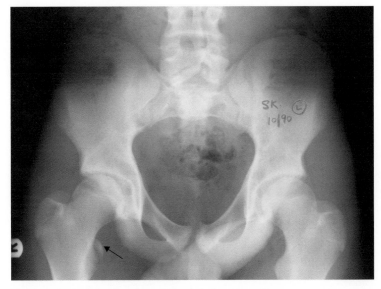

Figure 10.5 Avulsion fracture of the right lesser trochanter.

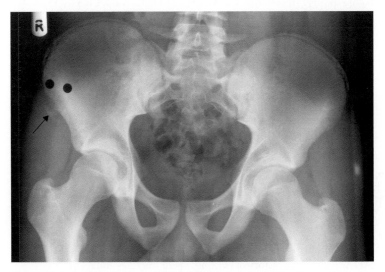

Figure 10.6 Avulsion fracture of the right anterior superior iliac spine.

Stop: Assess A B C and check for other injuries! Does the history fit? Non-accidental injury?

Femoral shaft fractures alone can be responsible for significant bleeding, although in isolation will not cause clinical signs of shock.

Assessment

Diagnosis is usually obvious. There is often significant swelling of the affected thigh, with associated tenderness. The child will be unable to weight-bear or lift the limb off the bed, and will be in considerable pain. However, in infants and toddlers with chubby thighs, signs are more subtle.

Imaging

Fractures may be transverse, spiral (Figure 10.7) or supracondylar. Seventy per cent occur in the middle third of the femur. You must be able to see the joint above and below the fracture on the image, to screen for associated injuries.

Management

Support the leg with the hip and knee slightly flexed. The child will require intranasal or intravenous opiate analgesia and a femoral nerve block, ideally before splintage then moving to X-ray (see Chapter 3 and Chapter 16).

Following radiographic confirmation refer to an orthopaedic surgeon for admission to hospital. Younger children will be placed in traction (gallows for infants, skin traction for older children), and the over-fives may be considered for an intramedullary nail.

Injuries of the knee

It is important to reiterate that knee pain is sometimes the result of hip joint pathology and clinical examination of the hip should always be undertaken.

Warning: SUFE may present with isolated thigh or knee pain!

Most acute knee injuries are sprains, sustained during sport or while falling over, usually with a history of twisting. Major fractures and meniscal or ligamentous tears are uncommon in children under 12 years; meniscal injury is rare in small children but increases in frequency towards late

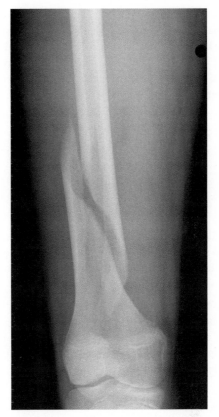

Figure 10.7 Spiral fracture of the femur.

adolescence. Avulsion fractures of the tibial plateau and tibial spine occur in younger children and teenagers, and can be quite subtle; they are the equivalent of an anterior cruciate ligament injury in adults – as we saw in the ulnar collateral ligament of the thumb or the avulsion injuries of the pelvis and hips, the ligament is stretchy, but at its attachment the bone avulses.

Assessment
Accurate assessment of acute knee injuries can be difficult because of pain. Your notes should record if the patient is fully, partially or non-weight-bearing, and the range of movement of the joint (from 0 to 120°).

After injury, the knee is often held flexed and will not extend. This is referred to as a 'locked' knee; in adults, locking is suggestive of a meniscal injury or a loose fragment of bone within the joint, but in children hamstring spasm is often the primary cause of the inability to extend the knee. It can usually be overcome with gentle persuasion by putting your hand under the knee, on the couch, and asking the child just to touch it with the back of their knee, if only for a second, just to prove they can do it. You may need Entonox analgesia to relax the child. Persistent hamstring spasm precludes any reliable examination.

Examination should include assessment of the joint, the ligaments and the extensor mechanism.

 See Video 10. Knee examination

The joint

An effusion is the cardinal sign of an injury within the joint. It is most easily identified with the knee extended. Like with the elbow, compare with the opposite side to detect a subtle effusion. By and large if there is no effusion, serious injury is unlikely.

A large effusion that develops within an hour of the injury usually consists of blood (a haemarthrosis) and indicates significant intra-articular injury – usually a fracture, or significant ligament or joint capsule tears; small osteochondral fractures from the surface of the joint are sometimes responsible and are easily overlooked.

The ligaments

Ligament injury is best assessed with the knee in a slightly flexed position. This relaxes the posterior capsule of the joint which might otherwise mask some ligament injuries. Place your own bent thigh underneath the child's knee so the quadriceps muscles can relax; this may take a little encouragement.

First palpate to see if there is focal tenderness and then check that the ligaments are intact. When assessing if a ligament is intact remember that children are stretchy. Assess the normal side first to see how stretchy it is, and to gain the child's confidence.

The medial collateral runs from the medial femoral condyle to the medial aspect of the tibia; the lateral collateral runs from the lateral femoral condyle to the fibula. After palpation, gently stress the ligaments by resting one of your hands on the thigh to check it is relaxed (see above), then take the child's lower leg in your other hand, and exert a valgus and varus strain.

To assess the cruciate ligaments, flex the knee to 90° and gently sit yourself on the child's toes. Grasp the upper tibia with both hands and push and pull it back and forth to test for laxity. You may need to compare with their unaffected side.

The extensor mechanism

The extensor mechanism consists of the quadriceps muscle, the patella, the patella tendon and the tibial tuberosity (Figure 10.8). Injury can disrupt these components at their junctions with each other. You should therefore palpate along this mechanism to identify any localized tenderness or any obvious gap or boggy swelling which might indicate injury.

Now see if the child can actively extend their knee by getting them to do a 'straight leg raise'. This means raising the whole leg up, with the knee in full extension so that the heel lifts off the examination couch.

Imaging

X-ray if completely non-weight-bearing, if there is a large effusion or if the mechanism of injury is significant. The Ottawa knee rules can apply from puberty.

If you cannot see a fracture, check you are not missing one by checking for radiographic signs of an effusion, as described for the fat pads in the elbow (see Chapter 8). An effusion, haemarthrosis or lipohaemarthrosis (Figure 10.9) can be seen on the lateral view and are clues that you should ensure orthopaedic follow-up for your patient.

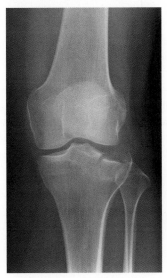

Figure 10.8 Fracture of the tibial plateau.

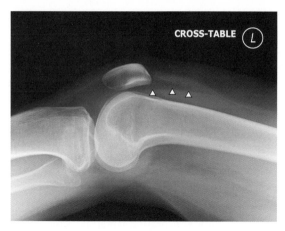

Figure 10.9 Horizontal-beam lateral view of a lipohaemarthrosis of the knee of the same patient.

 Top-tip: You can see in Figure 10.9 that behind the patella there is a black, lucent shadow which contains a fluid level (remember that the leg has been placed horizontally).

Management

If you see a fracture, it is best to refer for same-day orthopaedic consultation. Otherwise, all the other injuries can be reviewed in an orthopaedic clinic, ideally a week or so later, when the pain and swelling are settling. There is little evidence for compression bandages, which soon loosen beyond usefulness, but a splint such as a detachable 'cricket pad splint' can be very useful when used with crutches. Advise elevation when not walking around, and encourage quadriceps exercises to prevent muscle wasting; this is simply repetitive straight-leg raises (see above), aiming for 50 a day!

Patellar fracture

Fractures of the patella can be caused by a direct trauma but are rare in childhood. Children can sustain a so-called 'sleeve' fracture, which occurs on sudden quadriceps contraction, such as jumping. The inferior pole of the patella is avulsed. The bony fragment sometimes looks trivial on X-rays but there is often a large chunk of articular cartilage attached to it and the injury is significant.

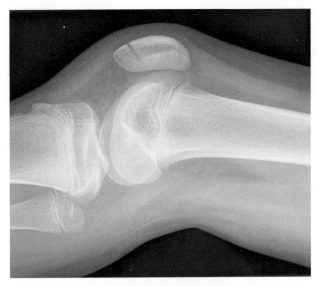

Figure 10.10 Fracture of body of patella.

Assessment

There will be pain and swelling around the patella and difficulty extending the knee or performing a straight leg raise (see 'Assessment' under 'Injuries of the knee' above).

Imaging

There are four types of image you may see. First is a true fracture of the body of the patella (Figure 10.10); second is a congenital bipartite patella, which may be mistaken for a fracture; third is the patellar sleeve fracture, which is the most difficult to spot; lastly, a patellar dislocation can cause a small fracture (see 'Patellar dislocation', below).

Top-tip: A patellar sleeve fracture may look small and innocent on the X-ray but there will be significant disruption to the articular cartilage, so seek advice.

A congenital bipartite patella occurs when there is an accessory bone found in the upper, outer quadrant of the patella. The edges are rounded, and there are no matching clinical signs.

Management

Refer immediately to orthopaedics if you suspect a fracture.

Patellar dislocation

Assessment

This often follows a direct blow to the medial side of the knee, but may happen spontaneously, for example twisting while running. It is most frequently seen in adolescent girls and is often recurrent. On examination, the patient usually holds the knee in flexion, with obvious lateral displacement of the patella.

Imaging

Following reduction, X-rays are mandatory to check for a small osteo-chondral fracture of the articular surface, either at the back of the patella or over the lateral femoral condyle, sustained either during dislocation or reduction.

A 'skyline' view may be needed but may be impossible at this stage as it requires the knee to be flexed and at this stage there is often a haemarthrosis and too much pain; it can be done at follow-up instead.

Management

Do not obtain an X-ray to confirm dislocation – this is very obvious clinically. Go straight to reduction.

Reduction of a dislocated patella can often be achieved using Entonox for analgesic and sedative effect. Ensure the child is able to use the breath-activated mechanism. Entonox should be inhaled for 2–3 minutes prior to attempting reduction of the dislocation. Reduce the patella by firm pressure over the lateral aspect, with both thumbs, while an assistant gently extends the leg at the heel. After the patella is reduced, apply a full-length cylinder plaster or splint ('cricket' splint), and arrange orthopaedic clinic follow-up.

Osgood–Schlatter's disease and Sinding–Larsen–Johansson syndrome

Assessment

Osgood–Schlatter's disease (Figure 10.11) is a traction apophysitis of the patellar tendon as it inserts into the tibial tuberosity, particularly common in sporty children during late childhood and early adolescence. It is bilateral in about a quarter of cases and often takes up to 18 months to resolve. Localized pain is felt at the tibial tuberosity, and symptoms are worse following activity and improve with rest.

On examination a lump is seen or felt around the tibial tuberosity due to microfractures and subsequent callus formation. The lump may be tender.

Sinding–Larsen–Johansson syndrome is less common but gives rise to similar symptoms at the other end of the patella tendon where it joins the lower pole of the patella.

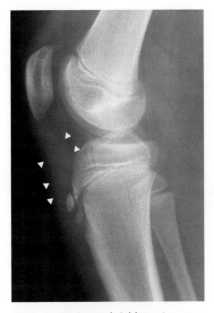

Figure 10.11 Osgood–Schlatter's disease: note swelling of the patellar tendon (between arrow heads).

 Top-tip: This is primarily a clinical diagnosis. Fragmentation of the tibial tuberosity is common in normal teenagers but swelling of the patellar tendon and blurring of the fat planes does suggest local inflammation.

Imaging

X-rays are not necessary if the clinical picture is characteristic, but do screen for other more serious explanations for symptoms if they have been prolonged or do not fit the clinical picture

Management

The child should be advised to reduce their level of activity according to the pain. This is a difficult trade-off and some will continue normal sports. This is not harmful. Reassurance that this is a common condition is often sufficient. Persistent difficulties in doing sports may respond to physiotherapy for quadriceps and hamstring stretching, and rarely a plaster cast may be needed.

Fractures of the tibia and fibula

Assessment

Fractures of the shaft of either the tibia or fibula usually require significant trauma, either direct or by twisting. Greenstick-type fractures occur.

The exception to this, and the commonest fracture, is called a 'toddler's fracture' seen in 1–3 year olds, when minor twisting trauma can result in spiral fracture. It may even occur on suddenly standing up. Unlike other spiral fractures, toddler's fractures are not usually suspicious of non-accidental injury.

On examination, there may be little to find, except a limping child. There is no swelling, and direct pressure often does not elicit tenderness. The clue is in twisting the foot with dorsiflexion, to cause torsion of tibia, which moves the fracture and causes pain.

Imaging

The diagnosis may be obvious, but subtle greenstick fractures (Figure 10.12) and toddler's fractures (Figures 10.13 and 10.14) can be tricky.

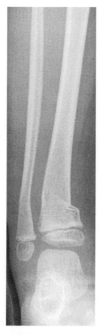

Figure 10.12
Greenstick fracture
of the distal tibia.

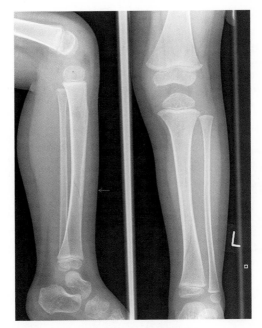

Figure 10.13 Spiral fracture of the tibia ('toddler's fracture').

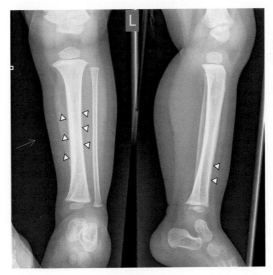

Figure 10.14 Healing toddler's fracture.

In a toddler's fracture the periosteum can hold the bone so tightly that displacement does not occur, and there may be no visible X-ray changes. However, around 10 days later, reabsorption along the fracture line and callus at the outer cortex are visible.

In Figure 10.13 the fracture is visible in both views, if you look carefully.

Figure 10.14 shows a fracture in the healing phase. The periosteal reaction is seen as another line outlining the cortex on both sides.

Management
Undisplaced greenstick fractures and toddler's fractures may be immobilized in an above-knee plaster cast.

Warning: If you suspect a toddler's fracture and the X-ray appears normal, immobilize the leg in a plaster and X-ray again after 10 days!

For all other fractures obtain an orthopaedic opinion.

Ankle injuries

Assessment
Ankle fractures are less common in children than adults, and, if present, tend to be greenstick or epiphyseal fractures. As with other parts of the body in children, an avulsion fracture is more likely than a ligament tear or sprain.

Teenagers also present with a special category of fracture called 'transitional fractures' because they are in transition from adolescence to maturity. They sometimes appear innocuous but often involve the articular surface and require CT evaluation and surgical treatment. There are two common patterns: the Tilleaux fracture and the triplane fracture. Use the Salter–Harris classification to alert you (see page 61).

The well-known 'Ottowa ankle rules' for imaging in adult injuries apply to children aged 8 years and older. For younger children, bony tenderness or inability to weight-bear are indications for X-ray. The Ottowa rules are more specific (Figure 10.15). An X-ray is needed if

- the child is/was unable to weight-bear two steps on the affected side both at the time of injury and now – this may need a little coaxing in order to prevent unnecessary X-rays
- there is tenderness at the tip or the posterior half of the lateral or medial malleolus (up to 6 cm from the tip).

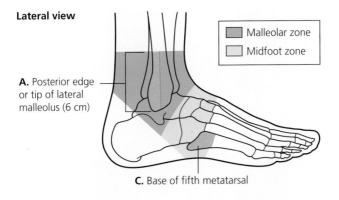

Lateral view

Malleolar zone
Midfoot zone

A. Posterior edge or tip of lateral malleolus (6 cm)

C. Base of fifth metatarsal

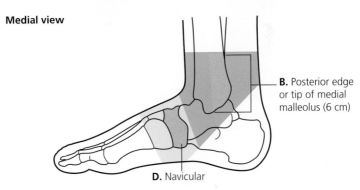

Medial view

B. Posterior edge or tip of medial malleolus (6 cm)

D. Navicular

Figure 10.15 Ottowa ankle rules illustration.

When you examine, and record your findings, you must be clear if there is medial and/or lateral tenderness, and whether each of these is bony or over the medial ligament complex (deltoid) or lateral ligament complex (usually the anterior talo-fibular ligament). Bilateral tenderness may imply an unstable ankle.

Imaging

Look for small avulsion fractures of the lateral malleolus (Figure 10.16), which are the commonest fracture pattern. In larger fractures it is important to check that the joint is stable, by checking that the gap between the talus and tibia and fibula is parallel, as it is when normal. In the X-ray see that the gap between the talus and the articular surfaces of the tibia and fibula measures the same all the way around. This view is called a mortise view, and is a modified AP view to help you assess the joint congruity. Disruption of the articular surfaces or ligaments will result in movement called 'talar shift'.

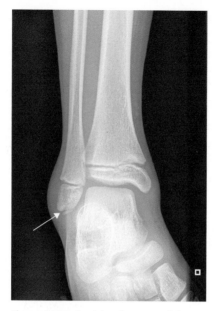

Figure 10.16 Avulsion fracture of the lateral malleolus with normal joint congruity.

Medial malleolus fractures (Figure 10.17) are less common and tend to be bigger.

Watch out for growth plate fractures involving the distal tibia. Fractures that extend into the articular surface can be easily overlooked on plain films and often need CT evaluation. This is especially true in the teenager who is vulnerable to transitional fractures (see above).

Management

Sprains can be treated in the usual way (see Chapter 4). Most children do not want or need to rest the ankle, but elevation to help swelling can be useful. The important thing about ligamentous injuries in the ankle is the loss of proprioception (balance). This is subtle but if not recognized, and the child returns to sports as soon as the bruising and swelling settles, the proprioception problem can make them re-injure the ankle easily.

Get the child to stand on one leg and they will see how wobbly the affected side is compared with the other leg. They should practise balancing on one foot several times a day, for example when brushing teeth, practising on

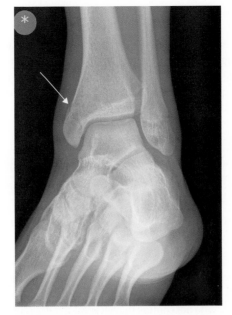

Figure 10.17 Medial malleolus fracture.

the bottom stair, and, when more confident, standing on their bed or a football.

Children recover from sprains quickly and the use of crutches should be discouraged. If sporty, referral for physiotherapy is beneficial so that the child may return to normal activities as soon as possible. The ankle can be regarded as healed once the proprioception and gait are normal.

Teenagers may take up to 6 weeks to recover, and should be followed up in an appropriate clinic to encourage normal gait, if you sense that they will not achieve normal function without encouragement.

If you see a fracture, refer immediately to orthopaedics if there is any talar shift or a displaced fragment. Fractures that involve the articular surface, such as transitional fractures, should also be referred. They require internal fixation.

For simple, undisplaced fractures apply a below-knee backslab and arrange orthopaedic clinic follow-up. Small avulsion fractures can be treated as a sprain.

Calcaneum fracture

Assessment

The commonest cause of a calcaneal fracture is a fall from a height at or above head height, landing on the heels. This is more common in adults: in children mostly teenagers are affected. There is swelling and weight-bearing is very painful. The axial load exerted can also cause lumbar spine and pelvic fractures.

 Stop: Always assess the spine and pelvis for associated injury!

Stress fractures of the calcaneum can also occur (see 'Other heel problems', below).

Imaging

It is important to specifically request calcaneal views (Figures 10.18 and 10.19), as a normal AP and lateral of the foot may not reveal a calcaneal fracture. On the lateral view, do not confuse the calcaneal apophysis with a fracture.

The fracture can be difficult to spot on the lateral view, but is crucial not to miss.

In Figure 10.20 the angle measures 26° and you can see a subtle fracture dividing the calcaneum in two.

 Top-tip: Bohler's angle will help you spot a fracture. Draw a line from the highest point of the anterior process to the highest point of the middle section near the back of the talus. Draw a second line from here to the highest point of the posterior tuberosity at the back. This angle normally should measure more than 30°.

Management

Refer immediately to orthopaedics in case further imaging (CT) or admission for analgesia and elevation is needed.

 Warning: Double check there are not bilateral calcaneal fractures; this is common and the pain from the worse side distracts patients and clinicians!

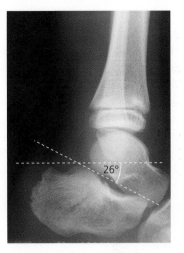

Figure 10.19 Calcaneal fracture, lateral view, demonstrating reduction in Bohler's angle.

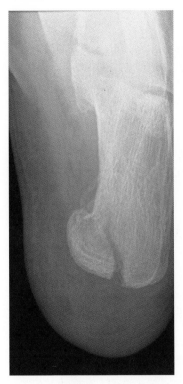

Figure 10.18 Calcaneal fracture, axial view.

Other heel problems

Children may also get Achilles tendinitis, retrocalcaneal and Achilles bursitis, plantar fasciitis, calcaneal bursitis, calcaneal stress fractures and Sever's disease. Sever's disease is a traction apophysitis of the Achilles tendon where it inserts onto the calcaneum, similar to Osgood–Schlatter's disease. It does not produce a lump like Osgood–Schlatter's disease, affects a younger age group (8–13 years) and X-rays are normal.

Treatment of all of these disorders is largely conservative. Do not worry if you cannot make a precise diagnosis – recommend non-steroidal anti-inflammatory medication and arrange orthopaedic follow-up (www.childrensmemorial.org/depts/sportsmedicine/healthtopics.aspx).

Fracture of the proximal fifth metatarsal

Assessment

These are usually caused by an inversion injury, causing peroneus brevis to avulse its bony attachment. On examination there is usually localized tenderness.

Imaging

Do not mistake the apophysis, which lies parallel to the shaft of the fifth metatarsal (Figure 10.20), for a fracture. Having said that, the apophysis itself may be avulsed or fractured. If in doubt, the exact site of tenderness should answer your question.

 Top-tip: Most fractures are transverse, not longitudinal.

Management

For undisplaced fractures, arrange either a below-knee backslab or simply crutches, depending on ability to weight-bear and patient preference. Arrange orthopaedic clinic follow-up.

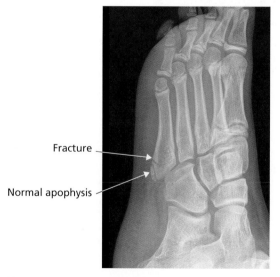

Figure 10.20 Fracture of fifth metatarsal with normal apophysis.

Other metatarsal injuries

Greenstick fractures of one or more metatarsals occur in small children when jumping from a height, e.g. bed. Older children may sustain greenstick, epiphyseal, transverse neck fractures or spiral shaft fractures. Stress fractures may occur in athletic children.

For multiple or displaced fractures apply a below-knee plaster cast. Otherwise apply a crêpe bandage and supply crutches. Arrange orthopaedic clinic follow-up.

Toe injuries

Assessment

Stubbed and crushed toes are common. Dislocations are unusual in children.

Imaging

Management is the same whether bruised or fractured so X-rays are unnecessary unless involvement of the metatarsal is suspected.

Management

Treatment of crush and nail injuries is similar to fingertip injuries (see Chapter 9), although usually less aggressive. Dislocations can be reduced under a digital block (see Chapter 16).

Otherwise, management is tricky because of pain and footwear issues. It consists of common-sense measures such as elevation, crutches and wide-fitting shoes. Neighbour strapping (see Chapter 16) may be of benefit after the initial swelling subsides. Show the family how to do it and allow them the gauze and tape to take some home to trial.

CHAPTER 11

BURNS, SCALDS, CHEMICAL AND ELECTRICAL INJURIES

Introduction	146	Complications	151
History	146	Chemical injuries	152
Examination	147	Electrical injuries	153
Management	150	Heat illness and hypothermia	154

INTRODUCTION

Major burns are an important cause of death in children in the UK. Many of these deaths are due to inhalation injury with only minor skin burns. Death is more common in areas of socioeconomic deprivation, and unfortunately neglect and arson are major factors.

Stop: Check – is there possible smoke inhalation?

Most minor burn injuries occur in the home in children under the age of 3 years and are due to hot liquids or contact with everyday objects – often an iron. Sunburn can occur due to lack of protection in hot weather or because of misuse of sunbeds.

Many such injuries are preventable. They are not life threatening but they may leave permanent scars or abnormal pigmentation.

In terms of terminology, a burn is the response of the skin and subcutaneous tissues to thermal energy generated by heat, chemicals, electricity, radiation, etc. A scald is a burn produced by a hot liquid or vapour.

HISTORY

Your history needs to take the following factors into account:

- Risk of inhalational injury: possible exposure to smoke or hot gases if in an enclosed space.

- The risk of associated injuries, for example injuries sustained while trying to escape.
- The context of the burn – was there an element of neglect?
- A delay in presentation or lack of detail in the explanation for the burn, which may imply neglect or non-accidental injury (see Chapter 15).
- The likely depth of the burn: this depends on the temperature and the duration of contact. Burns from hot fat or oil, or contact with very hot surfaces, e.g. an exhaust pipe, may be full thickness; surfaces with much lower temperature, e.g. a warm radiator can also cause full-thickness burns if the duration is long (such as a post-ictal contact).
- Whether the patient is at risk of deeper than expected burn, such as patients with poor reflexes (e.g. severe learning difficulties) or poor mobility (physical disability).
- Factors which will confound your examination, e.g. toothpaste put on the burn by the family as a misguided first aid measure.

 Warning: If you have any 'alarm bells' which imply safeguarding issues, seek senior advice!

Remember to check the tetanus immunization state of the child (see Chapter 4).

EXAMINATION

General

Exclude potentially major injuries before concentrating on the burn.

- **A**irway – are there burns or swelling around the mouth and/or nose?
- Cervical spine – were other injuries sustained? Do you need to immobilize the spine?
- **B**reathing – is there smoke inhalation? If so is your patient wheezing? What are the oxygen saturations?
- **C**irculation – in the first couple of hours this is only relevant to alert you to other injuries: burns do not cause early shock.

 Stop: If you find any of these issues, call for senior help and refer to see advanced trauma or paediatric life support guidelines!

Warning: Do not forget to check for carbon monoxide poisoning if there was a fire within an enclosed space!

The more detailed management of these injuries is outside the remit of this book.

After this initial ABC assessment, concentrate on alleviating pain (see Chapter 3) before continuing with your examination. Once this has been dealt with, you next need to assess burn depth and size, and check that the child has not got cold (either in the pre-hospital environment or due to cold first aid measures that have been left on for too long).

 Warning: Wet dressings frequently cause hypothermia and peripheral shutdown!

Depth of burn

The depth of burn injury is classified in many ways. Americans use the terms first, second and third degree burns. In the UK we use the following classification:

(I) 'Superficial': simply erythema, which fades quickly
(IIa) 'Superficial dermal': blistered areas with a healthy pink base; this is a partial thickness burn
(IIb) 'Deep dermal': blistered areas with a mottled, pale base; this is also a partial thickness burn
(III) 'Full thickness': the burn appears white, brown or charred, and lacks sensation.

In practice, burn depth is difficult to assess in the acute situation and many burns are of mixed depth; if you are unsure seek advice. At 24–48 hours it is usually much easier to estimate burn severity.

 See Video 11. Burns

Size of burn

The area of skin that has been injured is expressed as a percentage of the body surface area (BSA). Areas of simple erythema (red skin without blistering) are not included in the calculation but are a common cause of overestimation of the size of the burn.

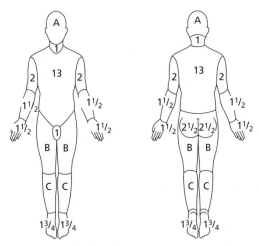

Percentage of body surface area

Area	Age 1	5	10
A=$\frac{1}{2}$ of head	$9\frac{1}{2}$	$8\frac{1}{2}$	$6\frac{1}{2}$	$5\frac{1}{2}$
B=$\frac{1}{2}$ of one thigh	$2\frac{3}{4}$	$3\frac{1}{4}$	4	$4\frac{1}{2}$
C=$\frac{1}{2}$ of one leg	$2\frac{1}{2}$	$2\frac{1}{2}$	$2\frac{3}{4}$	3

Figure 11.1 Lund and Browder charts for assessment of burn area in children.

For small areas of burn the simplest method is to calculate 1 per cent as the area of the child's hand (including the fingers, not just the palm, as is commonly misunderstood).

For BSA over 5 per cent use a burns chart (Figure 11.1). The burns chart for children under 5 years is different from older children and adults because of their different head and body proportions.

It is useful to use a burns chart not only to assess BSA but also to draw the burn, which makes your notes easier to understand.

Pattern of the burn

Look to see if the burn involves important areas like the eyes, genitalia or nipples. Check that the pattern matches the history exactly – are there splash marks in the right places for the scald as described to you? If there was a contact burn does the shape match what you would expect? Are there any older or non-burn injuries?

Warning: Are your examination findings compatible with the history given? Could there be possible non-accidental injury or neglect? See Chapter 15.

MANAGEMENT

First aid treatment

If the burn has not already been cooled, run cold water over the burn for 5 minutes or immerse in cold water. Then cover the wound with a clean, non-fluffy covering or cling wrap.

 Warning: Do not leave wet cloths on the burned areas as this can cause hypothermia!

Initially creams or ointments should not be put on the burned areas. Parents may apply these or other inappropriate substances such as toothpaste or butter to the burn. This should be gently discouraged for potential future accidents, and the correct first aid advice given.

Medical treatment

 Warning: Treat pain before making a detailed assessment of the burn itself!

Pain is always present in minor burn injury because nerve endings in the skin have been damaged and are exposed. Therefore, covering the burn is the best way of soothing pain. Calm the carer and the child and use distraction if necessary. Intranasal opiate can be useful in calming the child (and therefore everyone else; see Chapter 3). Supplement this with oral analgesia and keep the burn covered until the analgesia is working.

Cover the injuries with cling wrap, or proper dressings if you have time to examine quickly and properly (see above) and the dressings are 'ready to go'. If specialist advice is required, temporary dressings such as cling wrap are perfectly acceptable.

For definitive burn dressing the wounds should gently be cleaned with water first. Initially the wounds should be dressed with a non-adherent dressing such as paraffin gauze. Some departments advocate the use of silver sulphadiazine (Flamazine), which is soothing but distorts the appearance of the burn. To apply effective dressings see Chapter 16. Facial wounds are very difficult to dress so can be left exposed and Vaseline ointment applied regularly.

At discharge, it is worth mentioning to the carers that some analgesia before the planned dressing change is a good idea.

Referral and follow-up

Burns which should be referred for same-day specialist advice are those involving more than 10 per cent BSA, any with full thickness areas and those in special areas, e.g. around the eyes, mouth, perineum or nappy area, nipple.

For the remainder, the location of follow-up will depend on local guidelines, ranging from burns clinics run by plastic surgeons, to Emergency Department (ED) clinics, through to nurse-led clinics at the family doctor's practice.

As we mentioned above, non-stick dressings such as paraffin gauze (Jelonet) are best for the early days when serous fluid will still ooze out. After that, drier non-stick dressings such as silicon-based dressings (Mepitel) are useful. After the first day or two dressing changes should be minimized to avoid disturbing healing tissues.

If you are planning primary care follow-up it is important to give some prophylactic advice at this point. Remember these four points. It is important to tell the parents to look out for the signs of toxic shock syndrome (see below) over the next 5 days. After that, in the healing stages the burn will go through an itchy phase, and emollient creams such as Diprobase help the itch. The burn should be protected from sunshine for the next 12 months, as it will burn easily. Finally, the parents should not worry about the colour of the scar until the second year, as it is usually more obvious in the first year.

COMPLICATIONS

Localized infection

This is rare in the first 48 hours. Infection prevents wound healing, but can be difficult to diagnose. Erythema around burns is common, and does not need to be treated with systemic antibiotics. You should suspect infection if the burn is painful, the erythema is spreading, the wound has an offensive smell, there is excessive oozing or if the child is systemically unwell (beware toxic shock syndrome, below).

Mild local infection may clear with daily dressings. If you choose to prescribe antibiotics, ensure senior review within 48 hours. Infection should be treated with an anti-streptococcal and anti-staphylococcal antibiotic such as flucloxacillin or erythromycin. Swabs should be taken but the results must be interpreted with caution since many burns have organisms in the healing tissues.

Toxic shock syndrome

This is much more common in children than adults and can occur in a child with a very minor burn. It is caused by toxin-secreting bacteria, usually staphylococci or streptococci. It usually presents at 2–5 days post burn. Prognosis is related to time to diagnosis, with delay actually leading to death in some cases.

The presenting symptoms are fever, rash and watery diarrhoea. Clinically the child is shocked and may progress to need intensive care.

Stop: Take suspected toxic shock syndrome seriously! Give anti-staphylococcal IV antibiotics as soon as possible, consider IV fluids, and involve senior help and the intensive care team early.

CHEMICAL INJURIES

General information

Chemical injuries most commonly occur due to accidents in schools, or with cleaning agents in the home. The affected area should be rinsed with running water until further facts are established. For chemical injuries to the eyes, see Chapter 5.

Specific antidotes are rarely necessary but advice should be sought from the National Poisons Information Service (Toxbase website www.toxbase. org or the National Poisons Information Service 0844 892 0111).

If the chemical has been brought in by the family, find out whether it is acid or alkali by dipping litmus paper into it.

Acids

Acid substances usually cause immediate pain, but most burns are superficial because acids cause coagulation of the surface tissues, forming a protective barrier to further damage. Treat by irrigation using 500 ml of saline via an IV giving set. Repeat if pain is still present.

Alkalis

Alkalis are found in household cleaning products and may be highly concentrated in substances such as oven cleaner or dishwasher tablets.

Wet concrete is also alkaline and, while uncommon as a childhood injury, is very serious.

 Warning: Alkaline injuries are much more serious than acid injuries!

Alkalis permeate between cell membranes, causing deep-seated damage. Deceptively, they may be less painful than acids initially.

Treat in the same way initially as acids, by irrigation (as above), but it may take several hours and many litres for the burn to become pain-free.

 Warning: Litmus paper is not useful for monitoring response to irrigation: it is just used to see if the injury is acid or alkaline. Response to treatment is judged by symptoms.

The subsequent management of any chemical burn is the same as for a thermal burn (see above).

ELECTRICAL INJURIES

Electrical injuries may cause cardiac dysrhythmias, deep burns and deep soft tissue damage.

History

Was this a domestic voltage supply or something much higher? Young children sustain electrical burns in the home when they poke metal objects into live sockets or they touch live wires. This type of electrical injury is low voltage. Much more serious injuries occur with high voltage supplies like a telegraph wire or an electricity substation or railway track.

 Stop: Patients who have injuries due to high voltage electricity may have severe injuries in addition to a major burn!

In any electrical accident check for a cardiac dysrhythmia in the history if the child is old enough to describe feeling faint or having palpitations.

Examination

Check for cardiac dysrhythmia by putting the child on a heart monitor and checking that you have sinus rhythm over a minute or so, with no ectopic beats. If the child is in sinus rhythm when first monitored, there is no need for further monitoring.

Now look at where the skin touched the electricity supply to examine the 'entry point'. Assess in the same way as a non-electrical burn (see above). Next look for an 'exit point' – this is where the current can leave the skin as it exits the body – e.g. a finger on the opposite hand or through a foot. These two things will give you a picture of the trajectory of the current and therefore where to look for underlying damage. Often there is no exit point, so rely on symptoms to see where the affected areas may be.

Damage to deeper structures between entry and exit points can result in a compartment syndrome developing (see Chapter 4). Make sure you palpate the muscles for tenderness and test the full range of movement of neighbouring joints.

Warning: Ask for senior advice if you suspect a dysrhythmia or deep-seated injury!

Lightning can kill, but survivors are more common. Dysrhythmias and respiratory arrest may occur on scene. The skin may have a pathognomonic fern or feather-like pattern, and deep-seated soft tissue injury is common.

Management

Seek senior advice for high voltage injuries. Otherwise, if there is no evidence of dysrhythmia or compartment syndrome you can discharge the child but give the parents advice about the symptoms and signs of compartment syndrome (see Chapter 4).

HEAT ILLNESS AND HYPOTHERMIA

Heat illness

In prolonged exposure to heat from external sources or prolonged exercise, children may develop:

- heat cramps
- heat exhaustion – irritability, dizziness, headache, nausea
- heat stroke – temperature over 41°C, shock, coma, convulsions.

These may be associated with sunburn. The cause is fluid loss from sweating, with inadequate replacement of water and salt. Children with cystic fibrosis are at greater risk.

Standard oral rehydration solutions are usually adequate in the early stages. In heat exhaustion and heat stroke, intravenous replacement is needed.

When the core temperature is over 39.5°C clothes should be removed and the child should be sponged with tepid water. A fan of cold air can be used with caution – if the skin is cooled too rapidly then capillary vasoconstriction occurs and the core temperature rises further.

Stop: This is a rare and serious condition! Seek senior help.

Hypothermia

Children have larger body surface areas than adults, and can therefore lose heat easily. After road traffic accidents, burns where cold dressings have been left on for too long, or children immersed in water or found wandering, hypothermia can occur.

Mild hypothermia (above 33°C) will respond to warm blankets, warming mattresses (such as the chemical activated type Transwarmer) and warmed drinks or warmed IV fluids.

At 32°C or below more aggressive measures are needed, which are outside the scope of this book.

CHAPTER 12

BITES, STINGS AND ALLERGIC REACTIONS

| Bites in general | 156 | Stings | 159 |
| Specific bites | 157 | Allergic reactions | 160 |

BITES IN GENERAL

History

Bites from various animals are quite common in children. Although there are more and more exotic pets being kept in UK households in the last few years, the general principles of wound management mainly apply (see Chapter 4). Bites are usually heavily contaminated with bacteria, and the wound edges are often irregular or crushed. Depending on the size of the animal, there may be quite a significant crush component, including an underlying fracture (e.g. a large dog). Check the child's tetanus immunization status.

Ask about the circumstances of the bite to ensure there was no irresponsible behaviour or neglect, or that the animal may pose a risk to others, in which case you may have to contact the police if the family has not already done so. In the UK some breeds of dog are covered by the Dangerous Dogs Act.

 Warning: Consider if there were issues of child safety in the incident, and if the animal still poses a threat to others!

Examination

Assess the wound for the extent of crush injury, the state of the wound edges, damage to deep structures such as nerves, vessels, tendons, bones and any possibility of joint penetration.

Consider whether this is a puncture wound, a small open wound or a large wound likely to need cleaning and repair under general anaesthesia.

Management

Manage all bites as a contaminated wound (see Chapter 4), and do not be falsely reassured by small wounds.

Warning: The risk of infection is increased in puncture versus open wounds!

Consider X-rays if you suspect a fracture or foreign body (for example of a broken tooth if bitten by an older dog).

Explore and irrigate the wound thoroughly (see Chapter 16). Avoid closure with sutures if possible – you can draw the wound edges a little closer together to aid healing but avoid closing the skin, so that infection can easily drain from the wound. If the cosmetic effect of allowing healing by secondary intention is too great, get advice from a plastic or maxillofacial surgeon.

Give antibiotic prophylaxis:

- if the wound is >24 hours old
- for puncture wounds
- if there is extensive tissue damage
- for wounds to the hands
- if the wound has needed to be closed
- for reptilian or human bites.

For advice on tetanus immunoglobulin see Chapter 4. Consider rabies prophylaxis if the child was bitten in an area where rabies is present.

SPECIFIC BITES

Human bites

History

The human mouth carries large numbers of aerobic and anaerobic bacteria, which means that bites have a high risk of infection. If the person who bit the patient is known to have, or is at risk of, hepatitis or HIV infection, consider whether there may be transmission of the virus. Follow your local guidelines if you think the child is at risk.

Warning: Remember the history of a bite may not be clear, for example a wound from a punch type injury or in child maltreatment!

Examination

See 'Bites in general', above.

Management

See 'Bites in general', above. Prophylactic antibiotics are required to cover both aerobic and anaerobic bacteria, e.g. co-amoxiclavulinic acid. If allergic to penicillin prescribe erythromycin and metronidazole. Consider hepatitis B and/or HIV prophylaxis (see above).

Dog bites

History

The child may have been very frightened by the event, and bites from aggressive dogs may involve the police and the Dangerous Dogs Act. The size of dog is important, as a bite from a large dog is associated with significant soft tissue and bone injury.

Examination

See 'Bites in general', above.

Management

See 'Bites in general', above.

Cat bites

History

See 'Bites in general', above.

Examination

See 'Bites in general', above.

Management

See 'Bites in general', above. The most common organism to cause infection is *Pasteurella multocida*, which is found as a commensal in the mouths of cats. This can lead to severe wound sepsis with associated septicaemia.

Penicillin is the antibiotic of choice for *Pasteurella*. If allergic to penicillin prescribe erythromycin, although this is less effective.

Snake bites

History

Try to identify the snake. The only poisonous snake native to the British Isles is the adder (*Vipera berus*). Adder bites generally only lead to local symptoms. More serious bites from imported snakes (envenomation) are occasionally seen. Systemic symptoms include respiratory distress, vomiting, abdominal pain or diarrhoea.

Examination

Local effects include pain, swelling, bruising and enlargement of regional lymph nodes. Systemic signs of envenoming are hypotension, angioedema, depressed level of consciousness, electrocardiogram abnormalities, spontaneous bleeding, coagulopathy, respiratory distress and acute renal failure.

Management

If the bite is on a limb, the whole limb should be bandaged with a compression bandage and immobilized to reduce systemic effects. Do not apply a tourniquet.

For specific treatments, follow local guidelines or use a toxicology reference source such as (in the UK) the National Poisons Information Service, (Toxbase website www.toxbase.org or the National Poisons Information Service 0844 892 0111).

Stop: If any signs of envenomation: assess and treat A, B, C, before focussing on specific treatments!

Insect bites

Bites may occur without a clear history. Symptoms within the first 48 hours are caused by a localized allergic response causing itching, erythema and swelling. After this time, erythema and swelling may indicate secondary bacterial infection.

Management

Ice packs, elevation and analgesia can give symptomatic relief. If further treatment is needed, advise topical and/or oral antihistamines. If secondary bacterial infection is suspected then give oral antibiotic, e.g. flucloxacillin.

STINGS

Bee and wasp stings

Rarely a sting may lead to a generalized severe anaphylactic response in a susceptible individual (see below). If the sting is still present remove it.

Bee and wasp stings more usually present as localized pain and swelling. Treat as for insect bites.

Jellyfish stings

Stings from jellyfish in the waters around the British Isles lead to local irritation only. Treat as for insect bites. Other countries tend to have local guidelines.

ALLERGIC REACTIONS

History

Allergic reactions vary from mild to severe. The speed of progression of symptoms is a guide to severity. Severe reactions usually occur within 2–20 minutes of exposure. Peanut and latex allergies are becoming more common. In the context of injuries, allergy to dressings, tetanus immunization and antibiotics must be asked about.

Symptoms and signs can be localized or systemic. They can be mild, moderate or severe, and may affect:

- the airway and mouth – lip, tongue and mouth swelling, difficulty swallowing or speaking, stridor
- breathing – difficulty in breathing, wheezing
- circulation – flushing, peripheral vasodilation, hypotension
- skin – flushing, urticaria, sweating
- gastrointestinal tract – nausea, diarrhoea, abdominal pain.

To remember all the right questions, structure your history in the order of A, B, C, skin and gastrointestinal symptoms. Pay particular attention to what part of the airway is affected – is it just the lips, or does it involve the mouth, or is there throat discomfort?

Skin reactions are characterized by flushing and urticaria (raised, blotchy, itchy areas).

Examination

Again, structure your approach as A (looking in the mouth and listening for stridor), B (respiratory rate, oxygen saturations, presence of wheeze, difficulty in completing sentences), C (heart rate, blood pressure, flushing).

Management

In a moderate or severe reaction, have a low threshold for administration of intramuscular (IM) adrenaline. Do not give intravenous adrenaline as this can cause arrhythmias and does not work any faster or better than IM adrenaline.

Stop: If symptoms are severe, administer IM adrenaline and get help!

After giving the adrenaline, consider if you have an A, B or C problem and treat accordingly. Airway swelling responds well to nebulized adrenaline (5 ml of 1:10 000, neat). Wheezing responds to bronchodilators. Hypotension will be due to vasodilation, so give IV fluids.

Figure 12.1 on the next page shows the European Resuscitation Council guidelines for anaphylaxis in children.

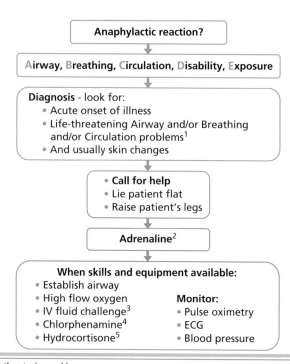

Anaphylactic reaction?

↓

Airway, **B**reathing, **C**irculation, **D**isability, **E**xposure

↓

Diagnosis - look for:
- Acute onset of illness
- Life-threatening Airway and/or Breathing and/or Circulation problems[1]
- And usually skin changes

↓

- **Call for help**
- Lie patient flat
- Raise patient's legs

↓

Adrenaline[2]

↓

When skills and equipment available:
- Establish airway
- High flow oxygen
- IV fluid challenge[3]
- Chlorphenamine[4]
- Hydrocortisone[5]

Monitor:
- Pulse oximetry
- ECG
- Blood pressure

---

1 Life-threatening problems:

Airway:	swelling, hoarseness, stridor
Breathing:	rapid breathing, wheeze, fatigue, cyanosis, $SpO_2 < 92\%$, confusion
Circulation:	pale, clammy, low blood pressure, faintness, drowsy/coma

---

2 Adrenaline *(give IM unless experienced with IV adrenaline)*
IM doses of 1:1000 adrenaline (repeat after 5 min if no better)

- Adult   500 micrograms IM (0.5 mL)
- Child more than 12 years: 500 micrograms IM (0.5 mL)
- Child 6 – 12 years: 300 micrograms IM (0.3 mL)
- Child less than 6 years: 150 micrograms IM (0.15 mL)

Adrenaline IV to be given **only by experienced specialists**
Titrate: Adults 50 micrograms; Children 1 microgram/kg

3 IV fluid challenge:
Adult - 500 – 1000 mL
Child - crystalloid 20 mL/kg

Stop IV colloid
if this might be the cause
of anaphylaxis

---

	4 Chlorphenamine (IM or slow IV)	5 Hydrocortisone (IM or slow IV)
Adult or child more than 12 years	10 mg	200 mg
Child 6 – 12 years	5 mg	100 mg
Child 6 months to 6 years	2.5 mg	50 mg
Child less than 6 months	250 micrograms/kg	25 mg

Figure 12.1 European Resuscitation Council algorithm for treatment of anaphylaxis in children, reproduced with permission.

CHAPTER 13

FOREIGN BODIES

Soft tissues	163	Inhaled foreign bodies	168
The eye	166	Swallowed foreign bodies	173
The ear	166	Vaginal and rectal	
The nose	167	foreign bodies	177
The throat	167		

SOFT TISSUES

Presentation to the Emergency Department with a foreign body (FB) is very common, occurring either through injury, or deliberately (usually in young children). Your management will depend upon

- the site
- the size
- the presence or absence of infection
- the length of time the FB has been there
- the nature of the FB.

Stop: It is important to do no further harm when trying to remove a FB!

Some FBs are better left *in situ*, until/unless they are causing a problem. The sections below will help you balance this judgement call.

Nature of the FB

Organic FBs are more likely to cause infections and other complications, whereas some inorganic FBs such as small pieces of glass or airgun pellets can remain *in situ* for life, or at least many years, before causing problems.

Site

Think before you try to remove a FB. For instance, are you in dangerous territory, such as near vessels or important nerves? Might you have to extend the wound to get it out? If so, could you be running into joints, nerves or tendons? If there is a risk of this, you need a surgeon to remove the FB.

Warning: If in doubt, refer to a surgeon!

Size

If the FB requires a large anaesthetic field for its removal, calculate the maximum safe dose of anaesthetic you may use, for the size of the child. If you are likely to exceed this dose, refer for general anaesthesia.

If the FB itself is large, do not underestimate where it could be penetrating. FBs can be like icebergs: innocent-looking amounts that are visible may only be a small part of the FB. In particular, beware of the trunk or the axillae or inguinal areas.

 Warning: Do not remove truncal, axillary or inguinal FBs unless you are certain they are very superficial!

Infection

If infection is present (cellulitis or abscess), the FB needs to be removed, regardless of its nature or site. This situation is more complex and you should ask for senior advice.

Duration

If the wound has closed (24–48 hours), even a FB that looks superficial on X-ray may be very difficult to remove. Unless it is easily palpable under the skin, refer to a surgeon.

Splinters

These are commonly found in hands or under nails. Splinters should be removed using 'splinter forceps'. These are a special kind of forceps with a very fine point – always use them as they make removal much easier.

Small pieces of splinter or dirt remaining far under the nail after the main splinter has been removed should be left alone – most wood softens to a pulp in a few days and will come out with a bead of pus.

If splinters are small and break off, leave them for a few days. They generally work their way out.

Fish hooks

These are usually embedded in fingers. There are three methods of removal, depending on the size of the barb. Small barbs may simply be pulled out, although an incision may be necessary to enlarge the wound.

Those with a single barb close to the shaft may be pulled out with an 18- or 16-gauge needle inserted onto the tip of the barb, to 'cover' it and stop it sticking on the way out.

Larger barbs may have to be 'pushed through'. The shaft is fed in to the finger until the barb starts to cause bulging of the overlying skin. A scalpel is then used to create an exit point for the barb, then the whole thing is fed through this new incision.

Glass

Glass can be very difficult to spot in a wound (Figure 13.1). Most glass is radio-opaque. Once the FB has been removed, a confirmatory X-ray is imperative.

 Warning: Always request a soft tissue X-ray for wounds caused by glass!

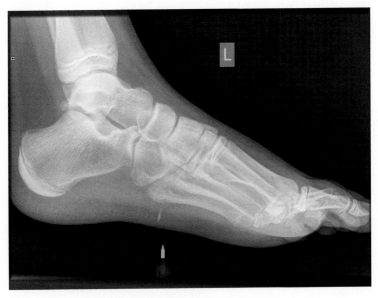

Figure 13.1 **Glass foreign body in foot.**

Role of ultrasound

Soft tissue ultrasound is a good method of identifying the presence of a FB. The accuracy of ultrasound depends on operator experience, and should be discussed with a radiologist.

THE EYE

See Chapter 5 for general information and Chapter 16 for removal.

 See Video 19. Foreign body removal in an eye

THE EAR

External auditory canal

Assessment

This is very common in young children. The child may have told someone what they did, or may have been witnessed inserting a FB or suspected that they did. In others, there is no clear history of a FB, and the child presents with pain or discharge from the ear. Occasionally live insects can enter the ear.

A FB in the ear canal can be quite painful, and to permit examination or removal the child may need strong analgesia, for example intranasal diamorphine, which is useful for both analgesia and anxiolysis (see Chapter 3).

The FB is usually clearly seen with an auriscope. Occasionally wax can be mistaken for a FB. Sometimes the discharge is too thick to allow the FB to be noticed. Such cases are usually diagnosed after referral to an ear, nose and throat (ENT) clinic.

Management

See Chapter 16.

Embedded earrings

Assessment

Stud-type earrings can become embedded within the pinna. Most commonly, the back or 'butterfly' becomes embedded, with inflammation and sometimes infection. If swelling is severe, the front of the earring may also become embedded.

Management

The earring is usually easily removed with an inferior auricular nerve block, which is invaluable (see Chapter 16). Once pain-free apply gentle pressure to the front of the earring to release the butterfly at the back.

Occasionally, a small skin incision over the butterfly is required; remove the whole earring. If the pinna is infected antibiotics may be required, although simply removing the earring is often sufficient.

THE NOSE

Assessment
This is very common in young children. The child may present with a history of inserting a FB into their nose or may have been witnessed inserting a FB. In others there is no clear history of a FB, and the child presents with a unilateral, offensive discharge or bleeding from the nose.

Lay the child back with their head extended and use the light of an auriscope to look up the nostril. The FB is usually obvious.

Management
Before resorting to pinning the child down and using instruments to extract the FB, try the 'kissing' technique (see Chapter 16).

 See Video 18. Kissing technique

THE THROAT

Assessment
Usually the child will have ingested something sharp, such as a bone, and have felt it get 'stuck'. Another common situation is if a child has tried to swallow a coin.

 Warning: If there is any history of choking consider inhalation (see 'Upper airway', below)!

The majority of children are able to describe their symptoms. Quite often, the FB has descended into the stomach and it is the scratch that is still felt.

 Stop: If the child is distressed, call for senior help! Do not upset the child further, or send them for an X-ray.

If the child is cooperative examine the throat (see Chapter 16) and if the FB cannot be seen, it may be behind the fauces, on the tonsil. If the child will cooperate, spray the throat with lidocaine anaesthetic, use a tongue depressor spatula to push the anterior fauces to one side, and the FB may come into view.

Imaging

If examination of the mouth does not reveal a FB, consider whether it is radio-opaque, and will therefore be seen on a soft tissue lateral neck X-ray.

Fish bones may or may not show up, depending on the size and type of bone; ask your radiographer.

 Warning: Do not send a child for an X-ray if there is any suspicion that the FB is in the upper airway!

Management

If the foreign body is visualized, remove it with forceps if the child is cooperative.

If the FB is visible in the hypopharynx or oesophagus on X-ray, refer to the ENT (or otolaryngology) specialists.

If the FB has not shown up on X-ray or is not radio-opaque, your management depends on the degree of distress. If distressed refer to the ENT specialists. However, the majority of children can go home with simple analgesia, and should be encouraged to drink and eat soft foods, and attend an outpatient clinic 24 hours later if symptoms persist – symptoms of a scratch will be improving at this stage.

INHALED FOREIGN BODIES

Inhaled foreign bodies occur most commonly in pre-school children. Almost anything can be inhaled, and foods such as peanuts or sweets and beads are the commonest culprits. Sadly, inhaled FBs causing severe airway obstruction often result in death at home or en route to hospital.

The history of inhaled FB is usually clear, but not always. Always suspect a FB if there is a sudden onset of choking or stridor.

Sometimes it may present several weeks or months later, and can be mistaken for asthma or a recurrent chest infection.

Upper airway

Children with complete airway obstruction rarely survive to hospital. In those who reach hospital there is most likely to be stridor, gagging, choking or drooling, but sometimes the child may just be very quiet and apprehensive and sitting with an upright posture, in which they are most comfortable.

If this is the case, it is imperative not to upset the child further. Crying and struggling may convert a partially obstructed airway into a completely obstructed one.

 Stop: If there are signs of airway obstruction, proceed to a resuscitation area but keep the child as calm as possible! Call for senior help.

Encourage and reassure the child while awaiting senior help. Use the time to prepare equipment such as Magill's forceps, equipment for intubation and needle cricothyroidotomy, and call an operating department technician to help you. Sevoflurane for gaseous induction can be useful.

An algorithm for upper airway obstruction is presented in Figure 13.2. The method you use depends on symptoms and the age of the child.

The Heimlich manoeuvre (Figure 13.3) can be used in children aged 4 years and above.

Back blows (Figure 13.4) can be used in all age groups.

In younger children there is a risk of injury to abdominal organs, so chest thrusts (Figure 13.5) are recommended instead.

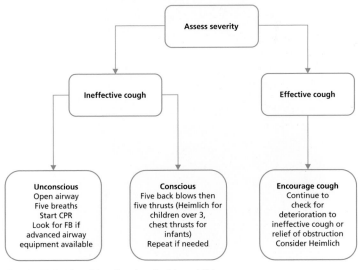

Figure 13.2 Algorithm for the choking child.

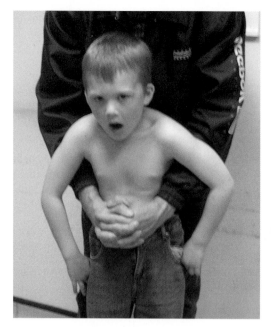

Figure 13.3 The Heimlich manoeuvre.

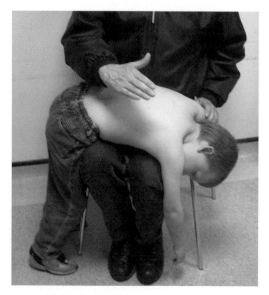

Figure 13.4 Back blows.

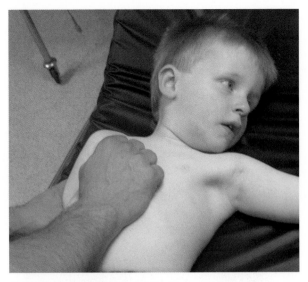

Figure 13.5 **Chest thrusts in infants.**

Lower airway

Assessment

If a FB passes through the main bronchus to the lower airways, a child will present with persistent cough or wheeze or recurrent chest infection. This may be hours to months after the event. On examination there may be localized wheezing or absent breath sounds. However, examination may be normal. Children can present with signs of wheezing, a pneumonia or empyema with no clue to an inhaled FB. The FB is often discovered at bronchoscopy.

 Warning: Beware delayed presentation!

Imaging

A chest X-ray should be performed for an acute inhalation of a FB, or in the chronic situation, for atypical wheezing or recurrent chest infections.

The FB is often not radio-opaque. In 90 per cent of acute cases there is hyperinflation of the lung distal to the FB which can act as a ball-valve,

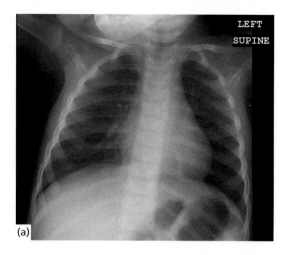

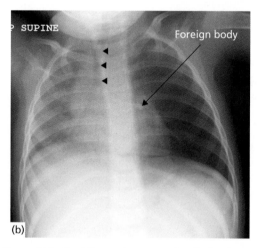

Figure 13.6 Chest X-rays demonstrating 'ball-valve effect': (a) normal inspiratory view, and (b) expiratory view with relative hyperinflation of left lung. Note the tracheal shift to the right (arrowheads).

 Top-tip: The inspiratory film was virtually normal. In a child who is too young to cooperate with expiratory views, lateral decubitus views may be used. Discuss this with your radiographer.

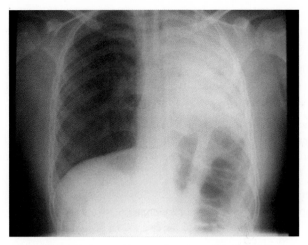

Figure 13.7 Left lung collapse a few days after inhaled foreign body.

allowing air to enter but not be expelled from the obstructed segment. This is best seen in an expiratory film.

In Figure 13.6 you can also see tracheal shift to the right.

In the remainder (particularly with a delay in presentation or diagnosis) there are signs of collapse of the obstructed segment of lung (Figure 13.7).

Management
Refer for removal of FB by bronchoscopy under general anaesthesia.

SWALLOWED FOREIGN BODIES

Assessment
Ingestion of a FB is common in children. The child may give a history of ingestion or be witnessed swallowing a FB. The parent or carer may give a history of items last seen with the child that are now missing or alternatively the child may be found retching or choking.

Coughing is a good clue that the FB may actually be in the airway (see 'Inhaled foreign bodies', above).

Warning: In a child with a 'swallowed' FB, check specifically for coughing!

Common places for the FB to lodge are at the cricopharyngeus level or the oesophagogastric junction, although the vast majority pass easily through to the stomach and beyond.

Imaging

X-rays are useful in a stable situation. A lateral neck X-ray can help confirm that the FB is behind the airway, i.e. in the oesophagus (Figure 13.8).

Request an 'AP neck and chest' X-ray if you are searching for an asymptomatic FB, which will avoid irradiating the gonads. This will capture the position of the FB, unless it has passed beyond the pylorus, which is all you need to know (Figure 13.9).

Management

For foreign bodies in the mouth and upper throat, see above.

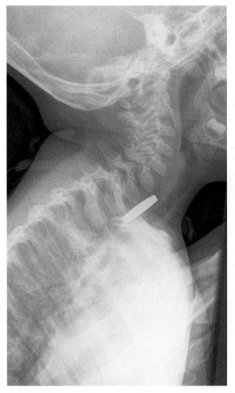

Figure 13.8 Coin stuck at cricopharyngeus muscle in oesophagus, clearly visible behind airway.

Once a FB reaches the stomach, most will pass through the gastrointestinal tract uneventfully. Figure 13.10 provides an algorithm for a swallowed FB.

'Button' batteries (the rounded ones used for electronic gadgets) can be very toxic and have a slow but deep action due to alkalinization of the surrounding tissues. All such ingestions should be referred to a surgeon immediately.

 Warning: Beware 'button' batteries – they can be very harmful!

If discharging the child, advise the parents that complications are very unlikely, but that they should return if the child starts vomiting, refusing to eat, or complaining of abdominal pain. Searching the stools can be discouraged!

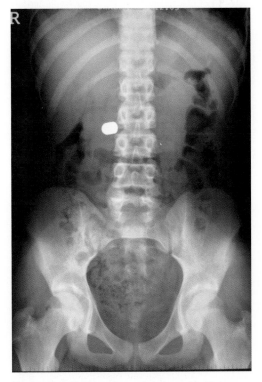

Figure 13.9 Battery through pylorus and into intestines.

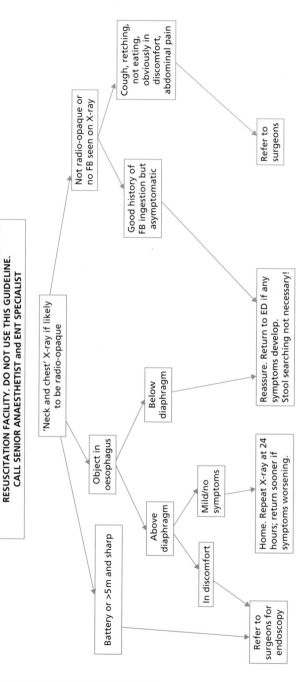

Figure 13.10 Management of a swallowed foreign body (except button batteries – see text).

IF DISTRESSED OR SIGNS OF AIRWAY OBSTRUCTION MOVE PATIENT TO RESUSCITATION FACILITY. DO NOT USE THIS GUIDELINE. CALL SENIOR ANAESTHETIST and ENT SPECIALIST

'Neck and chest' X-ray if likely to be radio-opaque

Not radio-opaque or no FB seen on X-ray

Battery or >5m and sharp

Object in oesophagus

Above diaphragm

Below diaphragm

In discomfort

Mild/no symptoms

Refer to surgeons for endoscopy

Home. Repeat X-ray at 24 hours; return sooner if symptoms worsening.

Reassure. Return to ED if any symptoms develop. Stool searching not necessary!

Good history of FB ingestion but asymptomatic

Cough, retching, not eating, obviously in discomfort, abdominal pain

Refer to surgeons

VAGINAL AND RECTAL FOREIGN BODIES

Assessment

A vaginal or rectal FB is rare in younger children and there is often no clear history. The child will usually present with discharge or pain. Although simple experimentation occurs, inappropriate sexualized behaviour should be considered.

 Stop: Consider sexual abuse and seek senior advice!

Adolescent girls may present with a history of a lost tampon, or a lost condom.

Management

All young children with suspected vaginal or rectal FB should be referred for further specialist assessment. It is not appropriate to perform a vaginal or rectal examination of a young child in the ED.

In adolescents, removal of a lost tampon or other vaginal FB is often simple. If the FB is a lost condom or other sexual item, remember to consider the maturity of the girl, the appropriateness or consensuality of the sexual liaison, and issues such as post-coital contraception and sexually transmitted diseases (refer if necessary to Chapters 15 and 17). Seek senior help if you are unsure.

CHAPTER 14

INJURIES OF THE EXTERNAL GENITALIA AND ANUS

Introduction	178	Anal injuries	182
Female external genital injuries	179	Associated pathology	182
Male external genital injuries	180	Self-inflicted injuries	182

INTRODUCTION

Injury to the genital area usually happens as a result of straddle injuries in girls and zip injuries in boys. Other injuries are uncommon. Staff can feel insecure in dealing with injuries in this area, as non-accidental injury has got to be borne in mind.

As always, non-accidental injury will be picked up by spotting a history that is flawed, lacks detail or lacks plausibility, in combination with an injury pattern which is either not typical of the mechanism stated, or is unusual.

Warning: Be systematic in just the same way as when you consider a non-accidental injury in any other area of the body (see Chapter 15). Most injuries in the UK are straightforward accidents.

Non-traumatic vaginal discharge and vaginal or rectal bleeding are not covered in this book.

There is obviously a great deal of psychological distress associated with injuries in this area. Many children presenting to the Emergency Department have bled immediately after the incident. This alarms parents, but fortunately most have stopped bleeding by the time they reach hospital.

Injuries in this area are painful, as the genital area has a rich nerve supply. Some children have discomfort on passing urine at presentation and blood in the urine may be described. This is rarely from the urethra, usually being contamination by blood from the injured genitalia.

From about 4 years old, children can be embarrassed or anxious about examination of the area. It is important to look calm, be reassuring and to examine children in privacy. It is wise to involve a chaperone (as experienced as possible), and to avoid repeated examination of the child by getting the right colleague for a second opinion if you need one.

FEMALE EXTERNAL GENITAL INJURIES

History

Blunt injury

A fall onto a hard object, particularly a straddle-type injury such as astride the bath or gym or play equipment, is the commonest cause of injury to female external genitalia. The direct force involved leads to compression of the soft tissues of the vulva between the object and the pelvis. A punch or kick to the genital area gives similar findings to a fall onto a hard object. This assault may be unintentional in rough play.

Stretch injury

When females accidentally do 'the splits' this can result in superficial lacerations of the skin of the perineum or posterior fourchette, especially if labial adhesions are present.

Accidental penetrating injury

This mechanism is less common but potentially more damaging than the others. Take a careful history and stop to consider if the story may be untrue. Listen to the detail and use accessory sources of information (see Chapter 15).

Examination

Blunt injury causes bruising, abrasions and/or lacerations, which are usually anterior and asymmetrical. Lacerations tend to usually be superficial and are most commonly found between the labia majora and labia minora. Bruising of the soft tissues may be severe but the hymen is not damaged.

In penetrating injuries make sure that the full depth of penetration can be visualized. If superficial, manage as above. If not, refer to an experienced surgeon.

 Stop: Some penetrating injuries are deceptively deep and require surgical exploration and repair!

When examining the female genitalia (Figure 14.1), be precise when describing the injured areas.

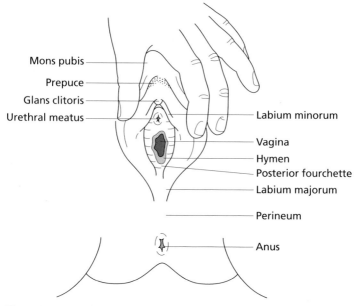

Figure 14.1 The female perineum.

Most accidental injuries involve the anterior area or the sides, and are fairly superficial. Be more suspicious about posterior injuries involving the vaginal orifice or deeper injuries, particularly involving the hymen.

 Warning: If in doubt, always seek a second opinion from a more experienced colleague!

Management

Clean all abrasions and superficial lacerations gently with normal saline. Advise frequent warm baths or very gentle showering of the affected area, avoiding soap. Most will heal within a week. Advise the parents to give frequent analgesia and plenty of oral fluids so that weak urine is passed frequently, so as to avoid urinary retention.

MALE EXTERNAL GENITAL INJURIES

Zip injury

The foreskin or shaft of the penis may get caught in a zipper, causing an abrasion or superficial laceration. The zip can be disengaged by cutting its distal end off and separating the two halves. A penile block may be needed and is relatively straightforward – ask for senior advice. A sedative analgesic such as intranasal diamorphine, or procedural sedation/general anaesthesia, may be necessary (see Chapter 3).

Penile blunt injury

Most penile injuries in childhood are due to a fall onto a hard surface (straddle injury) or an object falling onto the penis. These result in contusions and superficial lacerations.

 Warning: Beware of a large haematoma following minor trauma – this could be a ruptured corpus cavernosus which needs surgical exploration!

Clean all abrasions and superficial lacerations thoroughly with normal saline. Advise frequent baths or very gentle showering of the affected area, avoiding soap. Most will heal within a week. Advise the parents to give frequent analgesia and plenty of oral fluids so that weak urine is passed frequently to avoid urinary retention.

Penile strangulation injury

A variety of objects (e.g. hair, fibres from clothes, rubber bands) may be put accidentally or intentionally around the penis. The object acts as a tourniquet and the penis becomes swollen distal to the tight band. As the swelling increases the constricting band can become buried and invisible. Urgent release of the constriction is necessary. Try to remove the constricting object by unwinding it from the penis. If this is not possible then surgical exploration and removal under general anaesthesia will be needed.

 Warning: If the condition is not diagnosed promptly tissue loss may occur!

Injuries to the scrotum and testes

A punch or kick gives similar findings to a fall onto a hard object; this may be unintentional in rough play. The most likely injury is a contusion. The resultant swelling may make it difficult to decide whether this is a simple contusion or whether the testis has been damaged. Torsion of the testis, a hydrocele or rupture of the testis can all occur. An ultrasound examination may help. Discussion with a surgeon is advised for scrotal and testicular injuries. Penetrating injuries can occur, for example, while climbing over a gate or railing. These must all be referred to a surgeon.

ANAL INJURIES

Minor injury to the anus due to an accident in childhood is very uncommon. All patients with anal and peri-anal injuries should therefore be referred for senior advice.

ASSOCIATED PATHOLOGY

Sometimes minor trauma can cause more severe effects if the area was already inflamed. This will potentially confuse your examination. These conditions commonly occur under the age of 6 years. Examples of such conditions include vulvovaginitis, psoriasis, streptococcal infection, candidiasis, threadworms, lichen sclerosis et atrophicus, or inflammatory bowel disease.

SELF-INFLICTED INJURIES

Minor abrasions and bleeding can occur if children scratch themselves because of irritation due to vulvovaginitis or threadworms (see above). Foreign bodies can be inserted into an orifice during experimental play (see Chapter 13).

Other than that, self-inflicted injury is unlikely except in children with learning disabilities. If a parent alleges, or the child confesses, that an injury was self-inflicted, senior advice should be sought.

CHAPTER 15

NON-ACCIDENTAL INJURY

Introduction	183	Sources of information	186
The spectrum of child abuse	184	Good record keeping	186
Pointers to non-accidental injury	184	What do I do if I have some concern?	187

INTRODUCTION

Sadly, any clinician treating minor injuries in children has to be aware of the possibility of non-accidental injury (NAI). You could be forgiven for thinking that paediatricians are perhaps obsessed by the subject, but the reality is that delay in diagnosis is still common, the diagnosis itself can be extremely difficult to make and the repercussions of either a 'false negative' or 'false positive' diagnosis can be very damaging.

The problem is that although the deaths of the more publicized cases in the UK have occurred after systematic, sustained abuse, the more likely scenario is a one-off injury in a younger child which raises a degree of suspicion; then, as the pieces of the jigsaw are slotted in, concern escalates and the diagnosis of NAI is made some days (or weeks) later, with the input of a consultant paediatrician, social workers, imaging (skeletal survey) and so on. Non-expert, frontline professionals need to have 'radar' for signs of NAI, and know what to do next.

Nearly all hospitals or minor injury units have local policies for suspected NAI. 'Safeguarding' is the term used for child protection these days, and covers the range of issues from minor welfare concerns, through neglect, to actually inflicted injury.

Virtually all urgent and emergency care facilities have a safeguarding policy.

 Stop: Follow your local Child Protection Policy at all times!

Nationally, in the UK, there is a NICE (National Institute for Health and Clinical Excellence) guideline called 'When to suspect child maltreatment', published in 2009.

 Link: http://guidance.nice.org.uk/CG89

THE SPECTRUM OF CHILD ABUSE

Child abuse can take several different forms: physical abuse, neglect, emotional abuse and sexual abuse. Statistically, physical abuse is more common in the under 2-year-old age group, and is associated with social fragmentation. However, it occurs in all social classes and at all ages. Fatal physical abuse tends to affect infants aged 1–3 months.

Most of the time, things are not so graphic. Wherever you see children with minor injuries you will soon discover that neglect and poor supervision are much more common causes of welfare concerns than inflicted injury, and that it is not easy to be sure whether an injury was inflicted, accidental or whether there was an element of neglect. It is possible to be judgemental but a family may be living in overcrowded accommodation, or the child may be very active or difficult to control. If in doubt, ask experienced colleagues for their opinion.

POINTERS TO NON-ACCIDENTAL INJURY

 Warning: At any time in your consultation there may be a pointer to NAI!

General tips

Consider NAI in the following circumstances:

- the story of the 'accident' is vague and lacks detail
- the story is variable and changes with each telling, e.g. at triage, to doctor, in radiology
- there is delay in seeking medical help
- the history is not compatible with the injury observed
- the history is not compatible with the child's developmental stage (e.g. rolled off a bed, aged 3 months)
- the patient is a non-mobile infant (accidents are less easy to sustain and this age group is most at risk)

- there is an unusual number of previous attendances with injuries or minor medical conditions
- there is history of violence or neglect among the rest of the family
- the child discloses abuse (this is unusual)
- the appearance of the child and/or interaction with the carers appears abnormal.

 Warning: In an infant who is not fully mobile and has an injury, you must consider NAI as part of your initial differential diagnosis!

When you listen to the history it should flow, unless there is a language barrier or the adults who have brought the child were not there at the time of the accident. Most of us could ask our parents to recall an accident from our childhood and still receive a detailed, blow-by-blow account, many years later. Suspect NAI in a situation, for example, such as an infant not using its arm, with no explanation other than 'he must have done it ....'.

 Warning: Be highly suspicious of injury with absolutely no explanation!

Have a low threshold for X-ray in children under 4 years. Children of this age group rarely sustain true soft tissue injuries. The only common injury that may present with a vague history but is innocent, is a pulled elbow (see Chapter 8).

Specific injuries

Certain injuries are highly suspicious of NAI. These include:

- a subdural haemorrhage or skull fracture without a high impact head injury (e.g. fall from above head height)
- a spiral fracture of the humerus.

Other injuries may happen in NAI or accidents, so the detail of your mechanism of injury is crucial (see below), for example:

- torn frenulum (blow to the lip)
- fractured femur (usually an awkward landing or a twist)
- spiral fracture of the tibia (a twisting mechanism should be described)
- scalds and burns.

SOURCES OF INFORMATION

In the snapshot of your consultation, things are rarely clear-cut. You need your 'radar' to be primed for certain clues (as above), then you need to build up a picture of information or hand the case on to the right authorities, depending on your local policy, and how much information there is to hand.

Many urgent and emergency care settings will have virtually no prior information on the child, although previous attendances at the same facility is information that should be available and will be an important thing to alert you, if the pattern and frequency of attendances is cause for concern.

The general practitioner (family doctor) is ideally placed to have knowledge of both the child and also the family. For example, safeguarding issues with siblings, or mental health or drug abuse in the parents, is valuable information.

In the UK, pre-school children have a named Health Visitor, who often has quite a lot of information about the family's parenting skills and social situation.

After that the School Nurse has this responsibility, but will usually have a much higher caseload so may not know the child well.

If a child is of known concern, they may have a 'child protection plan'. This has superseded the Child Protection Register in the UK. In practice, this information may be hard to find out, as already mentioned, but asking the family if they have their own Social Worker is a good surrogate question (which will trigger you to find out more if there is one). This is a useful question to ask during the initial assessment/triage phase.

GOOD RECORD KEEPING

The history should always include a precise mechanism of injury.
For example:

- Falling over – how? Why? Onto what surface? Landing which way?

Then record what happened next:

- Who was there? Was the child obviously in pain? How long before medical help was sought?

Be clear in your record of your examination:

- Document shapes and sizes of marks on skin, the child's use of a limb in a limb injury, use diagrams when possible.

- Be specific about all conversations with other professionals: date and time of each conversation, with whom, and record your agreed outcome.

Ensure the child's notes have all relevant demographic information. This matters if things escalate in the future, or for example, if the parents abscond with the child. Details of siblings help the GP or social worker trace all relevant family information.

The minimum dataset your organisation should record is:

- the full name
- the child's up-to-date address
- any other names by which the child may be known
- the child's date of birth
- names of those with parental responsibility, and full names and ages of siblings (take this as a routine in your history)
- their contact telephone number
- the family doctor's and health visitor's details
- name of school.

WHAT DO I DO IF I HAVE SOME CONCERN?

Do not be afraid to voice concern – you have a duty to do so. There are robust arrangements for investigation, which will take the same approach of risk stratification, prior information and differential diagnosis that any other medical condition would.

In relaying your concern to the parents, the worst-case scenario is that they will disengage with the situation, cover up facts or even take their child away from your place of safety.

If you are a frontline professional, you can keep things calm by not stating an opinion, and simply saying that you are referring the child to a specialist (paediatrician) or to social care, as your role is only to make an initial assessment of the injury. Play down your role, as asking for senior or specialist advice is something the parents cannot reasonably be upset about.

If you are the receiving professional, be open and non-accusatory. Further advice is outside the remit of this book.

Some worked examples of real life cases are available at www.hodderplus. com/emergencycare/casevignettes

CHAPTER 16

PRACTICAL PROCEDURES

Introduction	188	Foreign bodies	195
Examination of ears,		Irrigation of eyes	197
nose and throat	188	Reduction of 'pulled elbow'	197
Slings	190	Trephining a nail	197
Neighbour strapping	193	Wound management	198
'Blanket wrap' for		Regional anaesthesia	
immobilization for		(nerve blocks)	204
procedures	194		

INTRODUCTION

There is a wide range of practical procedures needed for the management of minor injuries – many are not well described or taught in conventional education. Because young children do not understand the purpose of what you are doing, procedures such as suturing or foreign body removal are more likely to be performed under general anaesthesia than in adults, to prevent psychological traumatization.

To get procedures done smoothly, you need good communication skills with children, as well as good practical skills. Experienced staff, especially if aided by play therapists, can overcome most situations and get the child through the procedure without too much stress. See Chapter 3 for tips on psychological strategies.

EXAMINATION OF EARS, NOSE AND THROAT

Many children dislike examination of their ears, nose and throat (ENT). It is often best left until last. The following clinches are designed to prevent the strongest of children escaping! This is important, both to prevent the child being hurt by being poked by your equipment, and to make the examination as rapid as possible. If a parent loses their grip, it may be better to employ the skills of a strong nurse.

Ears

Before you start, show the child your auriscope and briefly shine its light at their eyes. This ensures they feel they are not being 'pounced upon' and

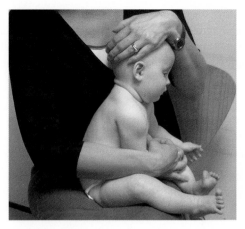

Figure 16.1 Ear examination.

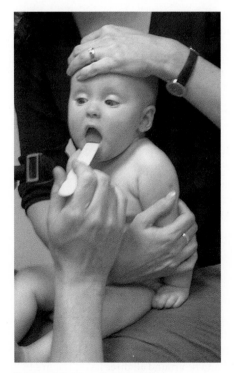

Figure 16.2 Throat examination.

the light can help engage them. Sit the child sideways on the adult's lap, asking them to 'cuddle' the child with one of their hands holding the child's arm, and their other hand over the child's head, as shown in Figure 16.1. The child faces the opposite way for examination of the other side.

Nose and throat

Make sure you are in good light or use the light of the auriscope or a pen torch. Sit the child on the adult's lap, facing you. The adult is asked to put one of their arms across both of the child's, and the other hand across its forehead, as shown in Figure 16.2, with the head tilted slightly backwards.

In order to get a view of the throat, try to get the tongue depressor between the teeth. If the jaw shuts, persistent firm pressure will result in the child eventually giving way. You can then advance the tongue depressor onto the tongue.

SLINGS

Broad arm sling

Using a triangular bandage, place it across the chest as shown in Figure 16.3. Take the bottom corner up to the shoulder on the affected side, and tie a knot at the side of the neck with the remaining corner (Figure 16.4). At the elbow, bring the free flap across and pin to the front of the sling (Figure 16.5).

See Video 12. Broad arm sling

High arm sling

Using a triangular bandage, place it across the chest, over the injured arm, as shown in Figure 16.6. Take the bottom corner under the arm, up to the shoulder on the affected side and tie a knot to the side of the neck (Figure 16.7). Tie and secure as for broad arm sling.

See Video 13. High arm sling

'Collar and cuff'

Place a foam (e.g. collar and cuff) or a long bandage around the neck, keeping one side long and the hand partially elevated. Wrap the short end around the wrist on the affected side. Bring the long end across, meeting above the wrist, and tie around all three layers (Figure 16.8). Then cut off any excess foam or bandage.

See Video 14. Collar and cuff

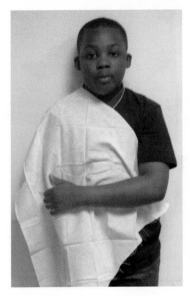

Figure 16.3 Application of a broad arm sling. Step 1.

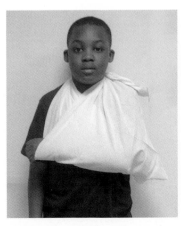

Figure 16.4 Application of a broad arm sling. Step 2.

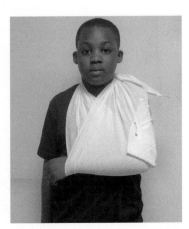

Figure 16.5 Application of a broad arm sling. Step 3.

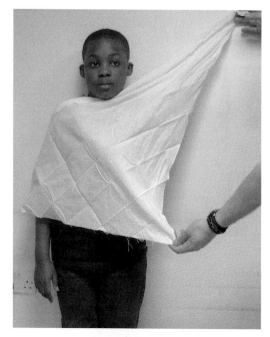

Figure 16.6 Application of a high arm sling. Step 1.

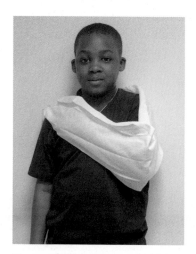

Figure 16.7 Application of a high arm sling. Step 2.

Figure 16.8 Application of a collar and cuff.

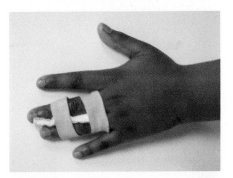

Figure 16.9 Application of neighbour strapping.

NEIGHBOUR STRAPPING

Place some folded gauze between the affected finger and a neighbouring finger to prevent the skin rubbing, then place tapes across the proximal and middle phalanges, avoiding the proximal interphalangeal joint and distal interphalangeal joint, to permit movement of the joints, as shown in Figure 16.9.

See Video 15. Neighbour strapping and 16. Bedford splint

'BLANKET WRAP' FOR IMMOBILIZATION FOR PROCEDURES ON THE HEAD OR FACE

It is sometimes easier to wrap the child up to get a very short procedure done quickly by stopping arm and leg movement. Most parents understand that for a quick procedure it is better to achieve what you want to do safely, and in the shortest time possible. Speed does not substitute for humanity though – if a child is really struggling and upset you need to change tactics.

Warning: If the procedure is going to take longer than a minute or so, consider procedural sedation (Chapter 3)!

First lay the child on a blanket. Then wrap one side of the blanket diagonally across the child, incorporating the body and one arm; then wrap the other side around to include the other arm, leaving only the head out (Figure 16.10).

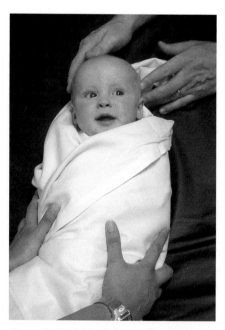

Figure 16.10 A blanket wrap for short procedures.

FOREIGN BODIES

Removal of nasal foreign body

'The kissing technique' is a humane little technique that unfortunately is not well known, but in the majority of cases means you do not need to progress to either instrumentation or general anaesthesia. The added bonus is that the parent does it all!

Tell the child that mummy/daddy is going to give him 'a big kiss'. Step 1: ask the parent to sit the child on their lap sideways on, cuddled up to their chest. It is worth having a tissue handy to catch the offending article! Step 2: the parent occludes the unaffected nostril with a finger. Step 3: they seal their mouth over the child's and deliver a short, sharp puff. If a parent is unable to understand this, a bag and mask device over the mouth can deliver the same effect.

The force of the air going up through the nasopharynx forces the foreign body down the nostril. Sometimes more than one puff is necessary to actually eject the foreign body. The child usually doesn't mind if you make a game out of it.

 See Video 18. Kissing technique

If this technique fails, then a blanket wrap (as above) may be necessary to remove the foreign body with some fine forceps. If it is difficult to retrieve, refer to ENT because you may hurt the child, and risk further damage or aspiration.

Removal of a foreign body in the ear

There are many techniques for removing a foreign body in the ear. Small right-angled forceps (Tilley's forceps or crocodile forceps) may be used for pieces of paper or cotton wool. Alternatively, suction may be applied by using a fine suction catheter. Also, irrigation using a syringe and warm water may be used for small objects (e.g. insects). For insects, ensure the insect is dead first, by dripping in a small amount of oil (e.g. olive oil, microscope oil).

For seeds and beans do not use irrigation, as the FB may swell.

A Jobson Horne's probe (straight with a loop at the end) is needed for rounded objects such as beads; if you do not have one of these you can straighten out a paper clip, leaving a bend in the middle. Make an angled 'hoop' at one end by bending it back on itself, taking care to ensure the sharp end does not protrude, as shown in Figure 16.11. This shape is ideal for manoeuvring behind the object, then scooping it out.

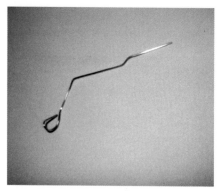

Figure 16.11 A paper clip bent into a scoop to retrieve rounded objects.

For embedded earrings, see 'Auricular nerve block' on page 207.

Removal of a foreign body in the eye

Particles in the wind, or on plants, can lodge in the eye. These may be seen in a good light on the surface of the cornea, or may require a slit lamp to magnify the cornea. Alternatively, the foreign body can be stuck under the upper or lower eyelid, or may have gone, leaving an allergic reaction or an abrasion.

Anaesthetic drops are usually needed. These sting, so the child will need a lot of reassurance; younger children will often need to be referred to an ophthalmologist.

Once the drops are in, hold the upper eyelid and get the child to look in all directions. If you cannot see anything, pull the lower eyelid down. If still nothing, get the child to look at the floor and using a cotton wool bud, evert the upper eyelid.

At any of these stages another cotton bud soaked in water can be dragged across the tissues to lift off the foreign body.

If this does not work, in a cooperative child the 'scoop' of the bevel of a standard IV needle can be used to dislodge it, keeping the needle sideways to the eye, ideally under the magnification of a slit lamp. This is best not attempted until you have been taught the technique.

 See Video 19. Foreign body removal in an eye

IRRIGATION OF EYES

Unlike commercially available 'eye baths', copious water is actually required to relieve symptoms from chemicals or dust. This requires a litre or more of normal saline IV solution, run through a giving set, and run as a steady stream over the affected eye(s), with the child lying on their back with their head over the side of the couch or ideally, backwards over a sink. Topical anaesthetic drops are needed before you start, to help keep the eye open. These sting, so the child will need a little cajoling.

REDUCTION OF A 'PULLED ELBOW'

This common injury is sustained when a toddler is pulled by the hand (see Chapter 8). If it is classical, you can proceed straight to manipulation.

 Warning: Make sure the mechanism of injury is classical, and the child is the right age group, before attempting reduction without an X-ray!

You must explain what you are about to do to the parent, in the most reassuring terms! It is important to warn them that the child will cry.

Step 1: sit the child on the parent's lap, sideways on. Step 2: put one thumb over the head of the radius and with your other hand, hold the child's hand.

Step 3: fully supinate and pronate the forearm. You may feel a click, either beneath your thumb or transmitted down to the hand. Step 4: if not, try bring the arm into full extension and supination (there may be resistance) then return the arm to its original position – sometimes the click is felt at this stage.

Step 5: whether or not a click was felt, leave the room at this stage to allow the child to settle down and play with some toys, to see if they start using the arm. Review the child after 10 minutes. See Chapter 8 for further management.

 See Video 20. Pulled elbow

TREPHINING A NAIL

Crush injuries to fingertips are common, and may cause a subungual haematoma (see Chapter 9). Trephining the nail releases the blood and is a satisfying procedure because of the instant relief of symptoms.

To do this, the nail is literally melted by a hot metal wire, to make a hole through which the blood drains (beware, it often spurts out like a fountain!). If performed quickly and efficiently there is only a second or so of pain at most; get a second member of staff to hold the child's hand down to prevent sudden withdrawal.

 See Video 21. Trephining nail

Your place of work should ideally have a purpose-made battery operated device in which a fine wire heats up, but if not, a paper clip can be used. A needle will do the job, but is at increased risk of penetrating the nailbed and causing further pain or harm. When the metal is red hot, puncture the nail with one firm, swift action, withdrawing quickly. Do not be put off by burning and hissing!

The paper clip technique involves straightening out one side of a paper clip and applying some elastoplast to the remaining clip to prevent you burning your fingers as it heats up. Heat the straight part in a flame (paraffin oil lamp or cigarette lighter) then proceed as above.

WOUND MANAGEMENT

Wound irrigation

See Chapter 4 for advice about wound management.

To clean a wound adequately, irrigation with copious quantities of water is the most important principle, to decrease the bacterial load. For example if you dilute a tenth of a tenth of a tenth (i.e. 10 mL three times over), the bacteria are diluted by 1000.

Infiltrate the wound with local anaesthetic if necessary. Place the affected part on a good thickness of absorbent towels. Use a 20-mL or 50-mL syringe and a large bowl of water or saline to repeatedly flush inside the wound, or use a litre of IV saline directing the flow through a standard intravenous giving set.

 See Video 22. Wound irrigation

Adhesive strips and glue

Adhesive strips such as Steristrips and tissue glue provide equal, if not better, cosmetic outcomes for many wounds than sutures do. It all depends on the tension across the wound, which is only partly related to its depth, but significantly related to wound length and the direction of the wound to Langer's lines (see Chapter 4).

Both adhesive strips and glue are probably of similar efficacy and both may be used together if a wound needs good support. Adhesive strips cannot be used on hairy areas; tissue glue cannot be used near the eyes.

Applying adhesive strips

These should be laid perpendicular to the wound, bringing a small amount of tension to the wound edges to ensure adequate opposition but not bunching up of the edges. For children it is worth laying extra strips at 90° over either end of the main strips. Tincture of benzoin can help stick them down, especially if the skin is sweaty or the wound moist, but make sure this does not go into the wound.

Circumferential strips should not be applied around fingertips, apply them longitudinally to allow for swelling.

See Video 23. Steristrips

Steristrips should remain in place for a day or so longer than sutures – i.e. 5 days if not under tension and a week if on a mobile part of the body.

Applying tissue glue

Tissue glue is not totally painless – there is burning during the exothermic reaction as it hardens. However, it is a concept which seems to appeal to children, thus overcoming their apprehension usually. Note sterile gloves stick easily to glue!

Take care only to place the glue as a seal over the top of the wound. If it drips between the wound edges, it will have the opposite effect of preventing healing.

See Video 24. Glue

Warning: Care must be taken to avoid the eyes!

If any glue is dropped near the eyes stop and wipe *immediately* with a wet swab. If this does not work, it will gradually come off over the coming days, but further attempts at removal before this time are likely to result in more damage. If any glue enters the eye, refer immediately to ophthalmology.

The glue will dissolve after several washes so advise the family to keep the wound dry for 5 days then treat as normal, and it will disappear over the next 2 weeks.

Local infiltration of anaesthesia

If there is no regional block for a particular area (see below), anaesthetic agents may be infiltrated locally. The choice of anaesthetic is explained in Table 16.1.

Infiltration of local anaesthesia is generally very safe, but overdose may result in facial tingling, cardiac arrhythmias and seizures.

STOP: If the toxic dose of local anaesthetic is likely to be exceeded, the child will need general anaesthesia for wound repair!

STOP: Will the child cooperate or will they need sedation or general anaesthesia? See Chapter 3.

After cleaning, inject anaesthetic into the wound edges using a blue (23 gauge), or orange (25 gauge) needle, passing the needle straight into the subcutaneous tissues through the wound edge rather than through the intact skin, which is more painful. Slow injection will decrease stinging. A dental needle is best, if available.

Table 16.1 Common choices of local anaesthetic agents and doses

Drug	Toxic dose	Indications
Lidocaine 1%	3 mg/kg (= 0.3 mL/kg)	Local wound infiltration. Onset 2–3 minutes Offset variable but usually < 1 hour
Lidocaine 2%	3 mg/kg (= 0.15 mL/kg)	More effective than 1% if able to stay within toxic dose
Lidocaine 1% with adrenaline (1:200 000)	6 mg/kg of lidocaine component (= 0.6 mL/kg)	Vascular areas, e.g. face, scalp. DO NOT use in end-organs, e.g. fingers, penis, pinna
Bupivacaine	2 mg/kg (0.4 mL/kg of 0.5% solution)	Longer acting than lidocaine. Onset 5 minutes. Offset 1 – 4 hours

Always inject further anaesthetic through the area you have just anaesthetized, waiting half a minute if there are few injections and the child is cooperative.

See Video 25. Injecting local anaesthetic

Suturing

For a full description of the indications for, and pitfalls regarding, suturing see Chapter 4.

When choosing suture material, bear in mind that absorbable sutures are useful for avoiding suture removal in children. Evidence is lacking for comparison with non-absorbable sutures, in terms of infection rates and long-term cosmesis. Find out what your local policy is.

The size of suture depends on the amount of tension or wear and tear over the area, but should be the smallest size possible, e.g. 3-0 or 4-0 for scalps, 4-0 or 5-0 for limbs, and 5-0 or 6-0 for faces.

Warning: Think twice before suturing a wound on the face – are you sufficiently skilled?

This is the technique for inserting interrupted sutures, the commonest approach for wound closure for traumatic wounds.

Step 1: pick up the needle with the suture holder, as shown in Figure 16.12. The needle holder should be placed about two thirds of the way back along the needle.

Step 2: introduce the needle to the skin at 90° and aim vertically down to include sufficient tissue to provide support for the suture, and avoid tension on the wound, as shown in Figure 16.13.

Hold the tissue with forceps, avoiding crushing the edge of the wound. Push the needle through, following the curve of the needle. Pull most of the thread through, allowing a small length to remain for tying. Pick this end up with your needle holder in your right hand.

Step 3: tie a triple knot to secure the suture. Now pick up the long needle end of the thread in your left hand and wrap it twice around the needle holder clockwise, as shown in Figure 16.14.

Without letting go, let the thread slide off the needle holder and pull it tight to form a knot, as shown in Figure 16.15.

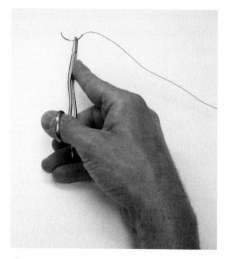

Figure 16.12 The correct position for holding a needle.

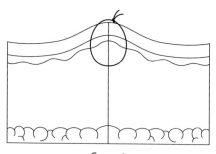

Correct

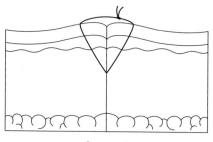

Incorrect

Figure 16.13 A cross-section of skin tissues demonstrating the correct and (incorrect) placement of a suture.

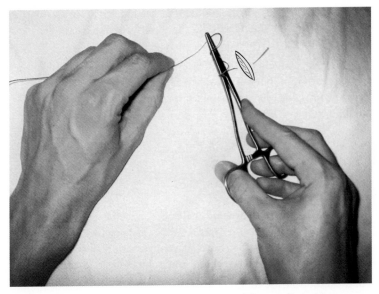

Figure 16.14 Wrapping the suture thread around the needle holder.

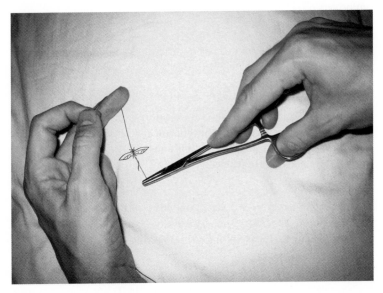

Figure 16.15 Tying a knot.

Do not leave the knot over the middle of the wound, but bring it to the side. Ensure that the wound edges are not inverted, everted or under tension. This leads to scarring.

Step 4: repeat, wrapping anticlockwise once around the needle holder and tie. Step 5: the same but wrap clockwise again. Cut the ends long enough to permit grasping when removing, particularly for scalp sutures in children with dark hair.

 See Video 26. Suturing

Applying dressings

Keeping dressings on children is a challenge! The actual wound dressing which you use can be whatever your unit's normal practice is, but keeping it in place for a few days, not to undo all your good work, is challenging. A 'belt and braces' approach for toddlers and some older children is worth it.

For the most part, use common sense, such as using the most adhesive dressings or tape that you have. There are certain areas of the body where little techniques handed down through generations of nurses are useful to know, such as the hand. These are difficult to describe in text but the online version of this book contains some videos to help you.

 See Video 27. Dressings of hand of toddler

REGIONAL ANAESTHESIA (NERVE BLOCKS)

Techniques of regional anaesthesia are usually easy to learn and, once mastered, can be very satisfying. Injection of anaesthetic away from the affected site is well tolerated by children, and the side-effects of intravenous analgesia are avoided.

Digital block

The four digital nerves are distributed around the phalanx as shown in Figure 16.16. Inject 1 mL of 2% lidocaine as close to the bone as possible, along two perpendicular sides, aspirating before injecting. Repeat on the other side.

 Warning: Do not use lidocaine combined with adrenaline to inject a digit!

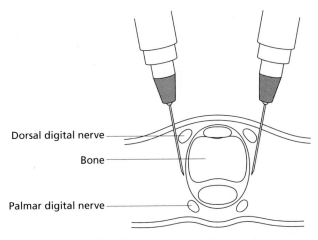

Dorsal digital nerve

Bone

Palmar digital nerve

Figure 16.16 The digital block technique.

After performing the block consider the use of a tourniquet to decrease bleeding and prolong duration of anaesthesia.

 Warning: A tourniquet should not be used for more than 20 minutes!

Make a glove tourniquet by placing the hand in a disposable glove after cutting the glove fingertip. Roll back the glove fingertip to the base.

Metacarpal block

An alternative to the digital block is a metacarpal block. This carries the advantage of a single, rather than two, injections, and possibly better anaesthesia of the dorsum of the finger. A 3-mL aliquot of 1% lidocaine is injected where the metacarpal neck becomes the head, in the palm. The dotted lines on Figure 16.17 show where to inject.

Auricular nerve block

This block is invaluable for procedures on the lower half of the pinna, in particular for removing embedded earrings.

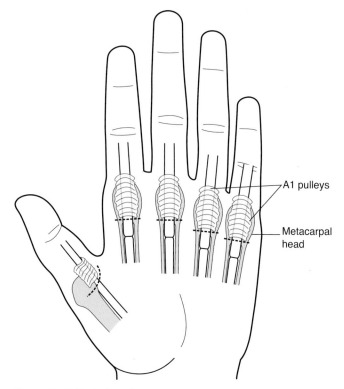

Figure 16.17 Technique for a metacarpal block.

The earlobe is often swollen and may be infected and extremely tender; injecting anaesthetic into the earlobe is very painful and difficult. However, injecting away from the ear is usually well tolerated.

The block works up to around halfway up the pinna. It blocks branches of the greater auricular and auriculotemporal nerves.

Using about 4 mL of 2% lidocaine, the needle enters the skin 1 cm below where the earlobe joins the face (near the angle of the jaw, as shown in Figure 16.18). Direct half the volume anteriorly towards the tragus, and half posteriorly, back towards the mastoid.

Femoral nerve and 'three in one' nerve blocks

Either of these blocks are used to provide analgesia for a fractured shaft of femur. The block should be performed before X-ray, or application of traction.

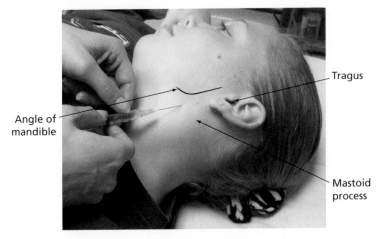

Figure 16.18 The inferior auricular block technique.

A femoral nerve block uses a syringe and needle directed vertically downwards. A 'three in one' block, via an intravenous cannula instead of a needle, uses the same initial anatomical landmarks, but is placed higher, before the trifurcation of the femoral, obturator and lateral cutaneous nerve of the thigh; it is a less painful technique, and avoids inadvertently hitting the nerve with a needle.

 Warning: These blocks take about 20 minutes to work, so IV morphine or intranasal diamorphine may be required in the interim!

The femoral nerve block

Use 0.5% bupivacaine to a maximum of 2 mg/kg (i.e. maximum volume 0.4 mL/kg). Draw up the anaesthetic in a syringe then attach a 21 Ch needle. Partially abduct the leg and locate the femoral pulse and the inguinal ligament. For a child under 8 years old, enter the skin 1 cm lateral to the pulse, just below the inguinal ligament, and for children over 8 years, enter 2 cm lateral to the pulse.

Aim directly downwards as far as you would for arterial or venous sampling, aspirating regularly. If there is no flushback, slowly inject the anaesthetic.

Modified femoral nerve block ('three in one' block)

Use the same volume of anaesthetic and landmarks as for the femoral block, but use a 20 Ch cannula.

Direct the cannula in line with the leg, at 45° to the skin, as shown in Figure 16.19. Once it is halfway in, try to advance the cannula over the needle. If you are in the right place (a potential space overlying the psoas fascia) it should advance freely.

Check there is no flushback, then attach your syringe and inject the anaesthetic. This should inject freely, as if into a vein.

Foot blocks

The nerve distribution to the foot is individually quite variable, but installation of a block is much easier than local infiltration into the sole of the foot.

Warning: These blocks take 10–15 minutes to work!

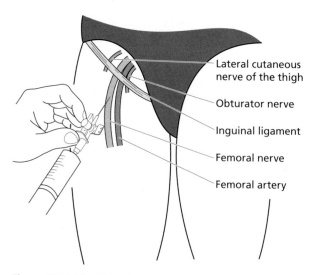

Lateral cutaneous nerve of the thigh

Obturator nerve

Inguinal ligament

Femoral nerve

Femoral artery

Figure 16.19 The 'three in one' block technique.

Dorsum of the foot

Infiltrate 1 mL of 2% lidocaine either side of the dorsalis pedis artery, as shown in Figure 16.20. This anaesthetizes the medial plantar nerve. Aim to puncture the skin only once, with repositioning of the needle by withdrawing slightly.

Medial border of the sole

Infiltrate 1 mL of 2% lidocaine either side of the posterior tibial artery, behind the medial malleolus, as shown in Figure 16.21, using the same technique as above. This anaesthetizes the posterior tibial nerve.

Lateral border of the sole

Infiltrate 3–5 mL of 1 per cent lidocaine between the lateral malleolus and the Achilles tendon, in a line, a few centimetres higher than the tip of the lateral malleolus (Figure 16.22). This anaesthetizes the sural nerve.

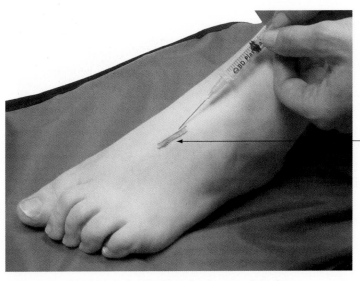

Figure 16.20 Landmarks for blocking the dorsum of the foot.

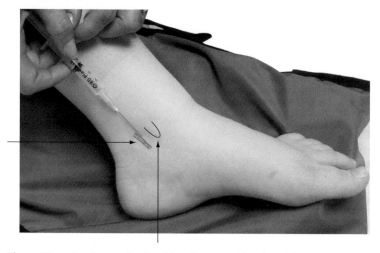

Figure 16.21 Landmarks for blocking the medial border of the sole.

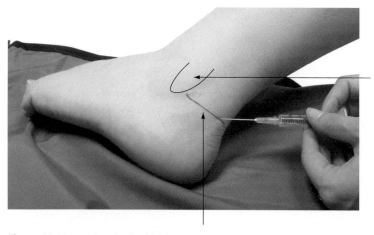

Figure 16.22 Landmarks for blocking the lateral border of the sole.

CHAPTER 17

MEDICO-LEGAL ISSUES

Introduction	211	Clinical documentation	213
Consent	211	Formal written reports	213
Parental responsibility	212	Confidentiality	214
The child's capacity to consent	212	What if I have made a mistake?	215

INTRODUCTION

This chapter is not an exhaustive text, but a guide for those practising in the Emergency Department (ED). If you practise outside England and Wales, please seek senior advice as there may be subtle differences in the law. The UK General Medical Council's guide '0–18 Years: Guidance for all Doctors', is very useful.

CONSENT

Doctors should rarely need to consult patients against their will. In general terms you need consent to examine a patient and perform any tests and procedures. Consent is implied if the patient communicates and fully cooperates with you. In paediatric practice, the most likely scenario you will face is a child objecting to examination or a procedure, which is most cases is easily overcome with experience.

Written consent is usually obtained for a procedure that requires sedation or general anaesthesia. For small procedures such as suturing written consent is not normally sought in the UK.

Common sense is essential and it stands to reason that certain sensitive procedures such as intimate examinations, particularly of a young girl by a male clinician, require another member of staff as a chaperone. On occasion, a working knowledge of the law is essential.

Parents can consent for children if they have 'parental responsibility'.

PARENTAL RESPONSIBILITY

In current UK law, the biological mother has parental responsibility (PR), so long as this has not been removed from her (e.g. court proceedings). Since December 2003, the law states that the biological father has PR, so long as this has not been removed from him, and he is named on the birth certificate. For children born before December 2003, the biological father also had to be married to the mother in order to have PR.

These are the most common scenarios. There are other possible situations, which are covered in the on-line version of this book.

Any parent can be stripped of PR by a court. Any adult can be granted PR by a court.

Other legal guardians are appointed by the court, and may be other family members, a foster parent, the police or a social worker.

In practice, it is important to clarify who is accompanying the child, and record this. If a parent is not present, it is best to check that they know the child is receiving medical attention. Formal consent from someone with PR is not usually sought for simple things like X-rays and wound/fracture treatments if the child has the capacity to consent (see below). Otherwise, you must do this, so in practice check the status of a male described as 'father'.

THE CHILD'S CAPACITY TO CONSENT

In English law, below the age of 16 a child or young person may give his/her own permission to receive treatment if they are sufficiently mature to be aware of the purposes of the examination, and to understand the treatment being recommended ('Gillick' or 'Fraser' competence).

This means that they must be able to

- understand the concept the doctor/nurse is explaining
- be able to balance the consequences of treatment versus non-treatment
- be able to remember this information.

If there is any doubt about the patient's ability to understand the nature of the examination or proposed procedures, consent should be obtained from the persons with parental responsibility (see above). If this is not possible, it is good practice to involve another family member although in legal terms they are unable to give consent.

If you are unable to obtain consent, for example an unconscious child or a child not mature enough to give their own consent (see above), it is wise to wait for their legal guardian, but you may, under common law, treat if it is an emergency. In practice, it is common for a child to be brought by another family member, or a teacher, and while caution should be exercised, clinical examination and X-rays are commonly performed in good faith.

If consent is refused but the child is competent, i.e. his/her opinion is contrary to what the treating clinicians consider to be in their best interests, the child's wishes may be overturned by someone with parental responsibility as defined above (except in Scotland) or a doctor. Preferably two doctors, of the most senior grade available, should assess the situation independently, then document their reasons why intervention is in the best interests of the child.

In situations where the legal guardian refuses, you must act in the best interests of the child. If the situation is an emergency, again it is good practice for two doctors to take this decision, as above, and treat under common law. If it is not an emergency, the case must be brought before a court.

CLINICAL DOCUMENTATION

Date and time every entry in the notes and be sure the patient's name is on every sheet. Be precise in your written notes. The details of the mechanism of injury may later become very important in child protection or assault cases.

Injuries are best recorded with diagrams and body maps.

Discharge advice is crucial because we cannot all get it right all of the time. We are typically very good at recording history, examination and differential diagnosis, but not so good at recording safety net information such as how long to expect recovery to take, what to do if it is taking longer or the condition is worsening, etc.

FORMAL WRITTEN REPORTS

You may be asked to provide a report on your medical consultation for the police, the coroner, or as part of a response to a complaint. In most cases, consent to disclose information is required (see 'Confidentiality', below).

If you do provide a written report for the police or coroner, social services or other non-medical personnel, be very conscientious in not medicalizing your language. You can avoid being called to court by explaining things clearly in non-medical terms!

Do not be drawn into giving opinions on causation unless you feel very competent to do so. For legal reports you will be a 'professional witness', which means that you are giving an opinion at the level of someone else of your level of training. Often the court will be wanting a broader experience of this situation, for which they need an 'expert witness'. Do not wander out of your depth!

CONFIDENTIALITY

Children are as entitled to confidentiality for their medical care as adults. It is particularly important to reassure teenagers of this if they are trying to share a problem with you.

Consent to divulge medical information to anyone who is not a clinician directly involved in the care of a child must be given by the child (if competent) or (more usually) the person with parental responsibility. The only exceptions to this rule are:

- if the protection of the child outweighs the need for consent (e.g. safeguarding issues, when the police or social services may be requesting information)
- if the issue is a matter of public safety (e.g. terrorism, violent crime)
- the case is a road traffic accident (usually simple information such as 'in a critical condition' is sufficient) or subject to high level criminal investigation (e.g. grievous bodily harm, manslaughter)
- if requested to do so by a judge
- for notifiable diseases.

In reality, most requests are very genuine, and if you can establish the authenticity and purpose of the request you will often decide that it is in the child's best interests to divulge the information asked. This may not mean divulging all the medical information, but only that which is relevant to the enquiry.

The same rules apply to telephone enquiries for information. Always establish the identity of the caller and ask them to send a brief request by fax or email.

When faxing or emailing information outside your area of work, ensure safety of data transfer (e.g. confirm receipt, use secure systems, etc.).

WHAT IF I HAVE MADE A MISTAKE?

 STOP: If you ever realize you have made a clinical mistake discuss this as soon as possible with your senior!

If the patient's family is still in the department a more senior member of staff can often give an explanation, apologize and determine whether the treatment needs to be changed. This rapid local resolution is the best option, and is usually accepted by the family. If the patient has gone home and the error is discovered, a senior member of staff can recall the patient by telephone and offer an explanation and apology as above.

If the mistake comes to light as a result of a complaint by the family, there is a systematic complaints process in the UK National Health Service. Your senior will discuss the case with you and request a written statement in most cases.

If you have made a serious error that has caused harm to the patient, inform your medical defence society as well as your senior.

But remember, we all make mistakes. So long as you are polite to all your patients, recognize your limitations and are humble enough to seek help whenever you need it, most problems will be resolved reasonably amicably and without significant harm.

INDEX

Page numbers in *italic* refer to figures; those in **bold type** refer to tables

abdominal pain 160
abrasions 21
abscesses 29
accident prevention, *see* prevention
　　of accidents/injury
acetaminophen 11
Achilles bursitis 143
Achilles tendinitis 143
Achilles tendon 143
acromio-clavicular joint injury
　　72, *73*
adder bites 158
adhesive strips 23–4, 198–9
adrenaline **200**
　　intramuscular *vs* intravenous
　　　160–1
agitation 15
airway obstruction
　　lower airway 171–3
　　upper airway 168–9, *169, 170–1*
allergic reactions 160–1
　　symptoms and signs 160
Ametop 12
anaesthesia
　　agents and doses *200*
　　local infiltration 13, 200–1
　　regional, *see* nerve blocks
　　topical 12–13
　　wounds 21, 22
analgesia
　　inhalational 12
　　intranasal 11–12, **12**
　　options 11
　　see also opiates
anal injuries 182
　　self-inflicted 182
anaphylaxis, European Resuscitation
　　Council guidelines *162*
ankle, radiographic studies **66**

ankle injuries 138–41
　　lateral malleolus fractures 139, *140*
　　medial malleolus fractures 140, *141*
　　Ottawa ankle rules 138–9, *139*
　　sprains 140–1
　　Tilleaux fracture 138
　　transitional fractures 138
　　triplane fracture 138
anterior humeral line 78, *80*
antibiotics
　　allergy to 160
　　broad spectrum 42
　　intravenous 25
　　prophylactic 24, 26
　　topical 37
arm, *see* forearm; upper arm injuries;
　　upper limb
arthritis
　　juvenile idiopathic 119
　　septic, *see* septic arthritis
auricular nerve block 166, 205–6, *207*
avulsion fractures
　　ankle transitional fractures 138
　　around hip 126, *126–7*
　　lateral malleolus 139, *140*
　　tibia 129, *131*

back
　　backache 56
　　injuries 46–57
　　pain 56
　　sprains 56
back blows 169, *170*
backslabs 68, 79, 87, 91, 141, 144
balance (proprioception), loss of 140
bandages 24
　　neighbour (buddy) strapping 103,
　　　106, 145, 193, *193*
batteries, swallowed 175, *175*

Battle's sign 33
bee stings 159
benoxinate 37
benzoin tincture 199
bites 156–7
    cat bites 158
    dog bites 156, 158
    examination 156
    history 156
    human bites 157–8
    infection 157
    insect bites 159
    management, general 157
    snake bites 158–9
bivalve (scoop) stretcher 50–1, *50*
black eyes 40
blanket wrap 194, *194*, 195
blepharospasm 37
blocks, *see* nerve blocks
body surface area (BSA) 148–9, *149*, 151
Bohler's angle 142, *143*
bones, child's *vs* adult's 58, *59*
'boxer's fracture' 105
'breath-holding attack' 31–2
breathing, difficulty in 160
buccal cavity wounds 41–2
'bucket-handle' fractures 60, *62*
buckle fractures 58, *59*
    proximal humerus *73*
bupivacaine **200**, 207
burns 146, 185
    burns chart 149
    complications 151–2
    depth 148
    examination 147–9
    first aid 150
    follow-up 151
    history 146–7
    inhalational injury 146
    management 150–1
    pain management **9**
    pattern 149
    referral 151
    size 148–9, *149*
    treatment 11, 150
bursitis
    Achilles 143
    retrocalcaneal 143
'butterfly stitches' 23

calcaneum
    bursitis 143
    fractures 142, *143*
    radiographic studies **66**
    stress fractures 143
candidiasis 182
carbon monoxide poisoning 148
cardiac dysrhythmia 153, 154
carers, role in prevention of
        accidents 4
cat bites 158
'cauliflower ears' 39
cervical spine 32, *55*
    fracture-dislocations *57*
    immobilization 47, *47*, *48*, *49*
    ligamentous injuries 46, 56
chaperones 211
chemical injuries 152–3
    acids/alkalis 39, 152–3
    eyes 39
chest infection 171
chest thrusts 169, *171*
child abuse 184
Child Accident Prevention Trust,
        leaflets 4
child-friendly environment 2
child protection 183, 186
children
    infants 96–7
    number attending Emergency
        Departments 1
    pre-school 17, 96–7
    role in prevention of accidents 4
    under 3 years 3
chin lacerations 43
chloramphenicol 37
choking 168, *169*
chondrolysis, idiopathic 119
ciprofloxacin 26
clavicle, radiographic studies **66**
clavicle fractures 69–70, *70*
    delay in presentation 69
    distal 70
    greenstick 70, *70*
cleaning fluids, household 39
clotting screen 27
co-amoxiclavulinic acid 42, 158
codeine 11
codeine phosphate *13*

College of Emergency Medicine (UK), guidelines 15
compartment syndrome 28, 78, 154
complaints procedure, NHS 215
computed tomography (CT)
    head injuries 30, 31, 33–4
    neck and back injuries 46, 56
concentration, poor 35
concussion 35
confidentiality 214–15
consent 211
    child's capacity to 212–13
contusions 27
cornea
    abrasions 37–8
    foreign bodies 38
coughing 171, 173
'cricket pad splint' 132, 134
CRITOE 75, **75**
crocodile forceps 195
crutches 141, 144, 145
cyclopentolate 37

Dangerous Dogs Act 156, 158
degloving injuries 29
dehiscence 25
deliberate self-harm (DSH)
    wrist and forearm cutting 117
    see also non-accidental injury
dental injuries 42–3
deprivation
    social 3
    socioeconomic 146
diamorphine 110, 166, 181
    intranasal **9**, 11–12, **12**, *13*
diarrhoea 160
diclofenac 11, *13*
    contraindications *13*
digital block 111, 116, 145, 204–5, *205*
discitis 56
dislocation, spine 56–7
dislocations 58
    assessment principles 63–5
    examination 63–5
    general approach 58–68
    history 63–5
    management principles 67–8
    X-rays 65–6

distal clavicular fractures 70
distraction, during treatment of pain 10
dizziness 35
documentation 213
dog bites 156, 158
dressings 24
    allergy to 160
    application of 204
    non-adherent (non-stick) 111, 112, 116, 151
    silicon-based 24
drooling 168
drowsiness 14
dysautonomia 117–18

ears
    embedded earrings 166–7
    examination 188–90, *189*
    foreign bodies 166–7, 195–6, *196*
    pinna injuries 39
    tympanic membrane injuries 39–40
    wax 166
Ehlers-Danlos syndrome 58
elbow
    dislocation 79–80, *81*
    lateral condyle injury 81–3, *82*
    medial epicondyle injury 80–1, *82*
    olecranon fractures 83, *84*
    ossification centres 75, **75**, *76*
    'pulled' 86–7, 185, 197
    radiographic studies **66**
    supracondylar humeral fractures 77–9, *79*, *80*
electrical injuries 153–4
    entry/exit points 154
EMLA 12
empyema 171
Entonox **9**, 12, *13*, 72, 130, 134
envenomation 158, 159
epiphyseal plate 60
epistaxis 40
errors, *see* mistakes
erythema, around burns 151
erythromycin 151, 158
European Resuscitation Council, anaphylaxis guidelines *162*
exercises, quadriceps 132
eyebrow wounds 36–7

eye injuries 37–9
  anaesthetic drops 37, 39
  chemical injuries 39
  corneal abrasions 37–8
  corneal foreign bodies 38
  foreign body removal 196
  hyphaema 38
  penetrating injuries of the globe 38
eyelid wounds 36
eyes
  black eyes 40
  irrigation 197
  mydriatic drops 37
  see also cornea; eye injuries

face
  blanket wrap for short
    procedures 194, *194*
  fractures 43–5, *43*, *44*, *45*
  lacerations 36–7
  wounds, pain management **9**
fall onto the outstretched hand
  (FOOSH) 69
fat pads 75, 76–7, *77*, 84
feet, plantar wounds 26
felon 116
femur
  fractured **9**, 185
  nerve blocks **9**, 206–7
  pain management **9**
  radiographic studies **66**
  shaft fractures 126–8, *129*
fentanyl 11, 14
fibula
  fractures 136–8
  radiographic studies **66**
finger nails
  injuries 112–13
  nail alignment *104*
  nailbed laceration 110
  nail biting 116
  nail and nailbed injuries 112–13, *112*, *113*
  subungual haematoma 110, 114
  trephining 197–8
fingers
  finger cascade *96*
  finger rotation 103, *104*, 106
  mallet fingers 115
  nails, *see* finger nails

neighbour (buddy) strapping 103,
  106, 145, 193, *193*
phalanges, *see under* hand fractures
rotational deformity 105
ulnar collateral ligament injury 115
fingertips
  anatomically unstable 113–14, *114*
  burst-type lacerations 113–14, *114*
  crush injuries 110–11, 114, 197–8
  felon 116
  pulp infection 116
  soft tissue injuries 110–14
  subungual haematoma 110, 114, 197
  underlying fractures 114
  see also finger nails
fish hooks 164–5
Flamazine 150
flucloxacillin 17, 24, 25, 111, 114, 151, 159
flushing 160
foot
  fifth metatarsal fracture 144, *144*
  metatarsal injuries 145
  plantar wounds 26
  radiographic studies **66**
foot blocks 208–9, *209–10*
forceps
  crocodile 195
  Tilley's 195
forearm
  deliberate self-harm (DSH) 117
  fracture/dislocations 87–90, *88*, *89*
  radiographic studies **66**
  see also radius; ulna
foreign bodies (FBs) 21
  ball-valve effect 171, *172*
  'button' batteries 175, *175*
  closed wound 164
  ear 166–7
  infection 164
  inhaled 168–73, *172*, *173*
  nature of 163
  nose 167
  rectal 177
  removal 195–6
  site 163–4
  size 164
  soft tissues 163–6
  swallowed 173–5, *174*, *176*
  throat 167–8

ultrasound 166
vaginal 177
fractures 58
  assessment principles 63–5
  base of skull 33
  'blow-out' 43, *43*
  'bucket-handle' 60, *62*
  'buckle' (torus) fractures 58, *59*
  examination 63–5
  general approach 58–68
  history 63–5
  lumbar 46
  management principles 67–8
  metaphyseal corners 60, *62*, 63
  open 67–8
  plaster casts 68
  thoracic 46
  Tilleaux fracture 138
  'toddler's fracture' 58, 63, 136–8,
    137
  torus ('buckle') fractures 58, *59*,
    91, *91*
  triplane fracture 138
  X-rays 65–6
  see also greenstick fractures;
    and specific fracture sites
Fraser competence 212
frenulum, torn 41, 185
fundoscopy 33

Galeazzi injury 87, 90
General Medical Council, guide on legal
    issues 211
genitalia, external injuries 178–9
  female 179–80, *180*
  non-accidental 178
  self-inflicted 182
Gillick competence 212
Glasgow Coma Scale (GCS) 30, 32–3, **32**
glass injuries 22, 165, *165*
glenohumeral dislocation 71
greenstick fractures 60, *61*
  clavicle 70, *70*
  metatarsal 145
  radial neck 83, *85*
  radius 88
  tibia and fibula 136, 138
  ulna *88*
growth plate (physis) injuries 60, 91

haemarthrosis 130, 131, 134
haematomas 27, 33, 34, 39
  septal 40
  subungual 110, 114, 197
haemorrhage, subdural 34, *35*
hair tourniquet syndrome 26–7
hallucinations 15
hand
  dorsum 98
  fractures, *see* hand fractures
  infections 116
  injuries, *see* hand injuries
  palmar aspect *98*
  palmar space infections 116
  radiographic studies **66**
  reflex sympathetic dystrophy 117–18
  regional complex pain
    syndrome 117–18
  rotational deformity 105
  swelling 95
  tendon infection 116
  volar aspect *98*
hand fractures 103–10
  distal phalanx 108, *109*
  metacarpal 103–5, *106*
  phalangeal 103–4, 105, 106, *107*
  proximal phalanx *107*
  'terminal' phalanx 110
  'tuft' fracture 110
hand injuries 95–118
  digital nerves 100, *103*
  dorsal digital nerve 100, *103*
  examination 96–103
  extensor tendons 99–100
  flexor tendons, superficial/
    profundus 99–100, *99*
  fractures, *see* hand fractures
  infants/pre-school children 96–7
  interphalangeal joint
    dislocation 106–8
  median nerve 101, *101*
  nerves 100–1, *101–2*, 114–15
  older children 97–8
  palmar digital nerve 100, *103*
  radial nerve 100, *102*
  swelling 95
  tendon 99–100, 114–15, 116
  terminology 97, *98*
  ulnar nerve 100, 101, *101*

hand injuries (*cont.*)
  volar plate 108, *109*
  wound exploration 102–3
  see also fingers
head, blanket wrap for short
    procedures 194, *194*, 195
headache 31, 35
head injuries 30
  assessment 31–3
  discharge instructions 35
  examination 32–3
  management 33–5
  mechanism of 31
  minor **9**, 30, 31–2
  non-accidental 30, 31, 33, 34
  symptoms 31–2
Health Visitors 186
  role in prevention of accidents 4, 17
heat illness 154–5
heel
  Achilles bursitis 143
  Achilles tendinitis 143
  Achilles tendon 143
  calcaneal bursitis 143
  calcaneum fracture 142, *143*
  plantar fasciitis 143
  retrocalcaneal bursitis 143
  Sever's disease 126, 143
Heimlich manoeuvre 169, *170*
hepatitis 157, 158
hip
  avulsion fractures around 126, *126–7*
  'irritable hip' 120, 121
  limping children 119
  pain 123
HIV infection 157, 158
human bites 157–8
humerus
  glenohumeral dislocation 71
  humeral shaft fracture 74–5, *74*
  proximal humerus fracture 73, *73*
  radiographic studies **66**
  spiral fracture *74*, 185
  supracondylar humeral
    fractures 77–9, *79*, *80*
hypersalivation 15
hyphaema 38, 43
hypotension 160, 161
hypothermia 150, 155

ibuprofen **9**, 11, *13*
  contraindications *13*
ice packs 11, 27, 28, 56, 159
idiopathic chondrolysis 119
infection risk 20
inflammatory bowel disease 182
injury
  non-accidental, *see* non-accidental
    injury
  prevention of, *see* prevention of
    accidents/injury
  see also specific injury sites
Injury Minimisation Project for Schools
    (IMPS) 3
insect bites 159
'irritable hip' 120, 121
ischaemia 79

jellyfish stings 160
Jelonet 151
Jobson Horne's probe 195–6
juvenile idiopathic arthritis 119

Kaltostat 111
ketamine 15
  guidelines 15
'kissing technique' 195
Klein's line 123, *124*
knee
  effusion 130
  extensor mechanism 131
  injuries 128–35
  ligament injury 130–1
  'locked' 129–30
  Osgood-Schlatter's disease 126,
    134–5, *135*, 143
  Ottawa knee rules 131
  pain 119, 121, 122, 123
  radiographic studies **66**

Langer's lines 19–20, *19*, *20*, 23, 199
laryngospasm 15
lateral condyle injury 81–3, *82*
latex allergy 160
leaflets on accident prevention 4
legal issues 211
  child's capacity to consent 212–13
  clinical documentation 213
  confidentiality 214–15

consent 211
documentation and reports 213–14
General Medical Council guide 211
parental responsibility 211, 212
telephone enquiries 214
legislation, accident prevention 4–5
lichen sclerosus et atrophicus 182
lidocaine 12, 36, 72, 167, **200**, 204, 205, 206, 209
lightning 154
lignocaine, *see* lidocaine
limping 119–25
age of child and 119
trauma and 123
lip
lacerations 41
swelling 160
lipohaemarthrosis 131, *132*
'locked' knee 129–30
log-roll examination 53, *53, 54*
lower limb 119–45
radiographic studies 66
see also femur; fibula; patella; tibia
lumbar spine
fractures 46
log-roll examination 53, *53, 54*

magnetic resonance imaging (MRI) 46
mallet fingers 115
mallet splints 115
mandible, fractures 44, *45*
manipulation under general anaesthetic (MUA) 67, 68, 79
medial epicondyle injury 80–1, *82*
medication
dosage 6, 7
intranasal analgesia 11–12, **12**
oral 11
memory, poor 35
Mepitel 111, 151
metacarpal block 205, *206*
metaphyseal corner fractures 60, *62, 63*
metatarsal injuries 144–5, *144*
metronidazole 158
midazolam 15
mistakes 215
Montegia injury 87, *89*
morphine 110

intravenous **9**
contraindications *13*
oral 11
mouth, swelling 160
mydriatic eye drops 37

nails, *see* finger nails
naloxone 14
nasal injuries 40
epistaxis 40
National Health Service (NHS), complaints procedure 215
National Institute for Health and Clinical Excellence (NICE), guidelines 14, 34, 52, 184
National Poisons Information Service 152, 159
nausea 160
neck
clinically clearing 52–3
injuries 46–57
radial fractures 83–5
reluctance of patient to move 52–3
sprains 56
needle phobia 17
needlestick injuries 26
neglect 3, 184
neighbour (buddy) strapping 103, 106, 145, 193, *193*
nerve blocks 14, 204–10
auricular 166, 205–6, *207*
digital 111, 116, 145, 204–5, *205*
femoral **9**, 206–7
foot 208–9, *209–10*
metacarpal 205, *206*
'three in one' **9**, 206–7, 208, *208*
NICE guidelines 34
nitrous oxide 12, 15, 72
non-accidental injury (NAI) 17, 53, 60, 63, 74, 183–7
concern about 187
genitalia 178
information sources 186
pointers to 184–5
record keeping 186–7
specific injuries 185
see also deliberate self-harm
non-steroidal anti-inflammatory drugs 11, 143

nose
    examination 190
    foreign bodies 167, 195
nosebleeds 40
numbness 46

olecranon fractures 83, *84*
open fractures 67–8
open reduction with internal fixation
    (ORIF) 67, 68, 79
opiates
    intranasal 11, 150
    intravenous 11, 14, 15
oral injuries 41–2
    penetrating intra-oral 42
Oramorph 11
ortopantogram (OPG) 45, *45*
Osgood-Schlatter's disease of the
    knee 126, 134–5, *135*, 143
ossification centres, elbow 75, **75**, *76*
Ottawa ankle rules 138–9, *139*
Ottawa knee rules 131

pain
    assessment 6, 7–9, **8**
    management, *see* pain management
    treatment, *see* pain treatment
pain management 6–15
    psychological strategies **9**, 10
    strategies for **9**
pain treatment 9–15
    acute pain *13*
    aspects of 6–7
    medication 6, 7, 11–14
    non-medication 11
    procedural sedation 14–15
panda eyes 33
papilloedema 33
paracetamol **9**, 11, *13*
parents
    parental responsibility 211, 212
    role in prevention of accidents 4
paronychia 29, 116
Pasteurella multocida 158
patella
    congenital bipartite 133
    dislocation 133, 134
    fractures 132–3, *133*
    sleeve fracture 132, 133

peanut allergy 160
pelvis, radiographic studies **66**
penicillin 158
    allergy 158
penis
    blunt injury 181
    strangulation injury 181
    zip injuries 180–1
peripheral vasodilation 160
Perthes' disease (avascular necrosis of
    the femoral head) 119, 123–5, *125*
phalanges, *see under* hand fractures
photophobia 37, 38
physiotherapy 141
physis 60
pinna 39
plantar wounds of the foot 26
plaster casts 68
plaster of Paris (POP) 68
platelet count 27, 40
Play Specialists 10
pneumonia 171
pre-school children, injuries 17
prevention of accidents/injury 3–5, 17
    children's own role 4
    education in 3
    enforcement/legislation 4–5
    engineering 4
    health visitors' role 4
    parents' and carers' role 4
    teachers' role 3
prevention of injury 3–5
propofol 14, 15
proprioception (balance), loss of 140
proxymetacaine 37
Pseudomonas aeruginosa 26
psoriasis 182
psychological strategies in pain
    management **9**, 10
puncture wounds 18, 20, 26

rabies 157
radial head/neck fractures 83–5, *85*
radiocapitellar line 87, *89*
radiographic studies
    requests for **66**
    see also X-rays
radius
    distal radius fracture 90–1, *90*, *91*

Galeazzi injury 90
mid-shaft fractures *61*, 87, *88*
mid-shaft greenstick fractures *88*
radial neck greenstick fractures 83, *85*
torus fracture 91, *91*
rectum, foreign bodies 177
reflex sympathetic dystrophy 117–18
regional complex pain syndrome 117–18
reports, formal 213–14
respiratory depression 14
retrocalcaneal bursitis 143
RICE (rest, ice, compression, elevation) 28
Royal Society for Prevention of Accidents, information from 4

'saddle nose' deformity 40
safeguarding 183
Salter-Harris fracture classification 58, 60, *61*, 83, 115, 138
scalds 146, 185
scalp lacerations 36
scaphoid *92*
fractures 92–3, *93*, *94*
radial and ulnar deviation *94*
radiographic studies **66**
School Nurse 186
SCIWORA (spinal cord injury without radiographic abnormality) 46, 57
scoop (bivalve) stretcher 50–1, *50*
scrotum, injuries 181–2
secondary intention wound healing 23
self-harm, *see* deliberate self-harm; non-accidental injury
septic arthritis 119, 120–1
v. transient synovitis 121
Sever's disease of the heel 126, 143
sevoflurane 169
shaken baby syndrome 33
shoulder, radiographic studies **66**
shoulder dislocation 71–2, *71*
anterior 71, *71*
glenohumeral 71
posterior 71
slow external rotation 72
shoulder injuries 69–70
silver sulphadiazine 150
Sinding-Larsen-Johansson syndrome 134–5

skin abscesses 29
skull
base of skull fractures 33
fractures 31, *34*, 185
X-rays and computed tomography 33–4
sleeve fracture 132, 133
slings
broad arm 190, *191*
'collar and cuff' 190, *193*
high arm 190, *192*
slipped upper femoral epiphysis (SUFE) 119, 121–3, *122*, *124*
snake bites 158–9
social deprivation 3
soft tissue injuries 16
speaking, difficulty in 160
spinal boards 50, *50*
spinal cord injury without radiographic abnormality (SCIWORA) 46, 57
spinal immobilization 47, *47*, *48*, 51
necessary initially 51
reasons for/against 51
spinal injuries 46
multiple levels 54
spine
fractures and dislocations 56–7
radiographic studies 66, **66**
X-rays 54
see also lumbar spine; thoracic spine
splinter forceps 164
splinters 164
splints 19, 25
'cricket pad splint' 132, 134
mallet splints 115
Zimmer splints 115
sprains 27–8
ankle 140–1
neck and back 56
stab wounds 18
staphylococci 151, 152
steristrips, *see* adhesive strips
stings 159–60
strapping, neighbour (buddy) 103, 106, 145, 193, *193*
streptococcal infection 182
streptococci 151, 152
stretchers, scoop (bivalve) stretcher 50–1, *50*

stridor 160
sunburn 146, 155
supracondylar humeral fractures 77–9, *79*, *80*
sutures 23, 201–4, *202–3*
  consent for 211
  removal 25
swallowed foreign bodies 173–5, *174*
  management *176*
swallowing, difficulty in 160
sweating 160
swelling, hand 95
synovitis, *see* transient synovitis

talar shift 139, 141
teachers, role in prevention of accidents 3
teeth
  avulsion 42
  wobbly/chipped 43
telephone enquiries 214
tendinitis, Achilles 143
testes, injuries 181–2
tetanus immunization 17, 147
  allergy to 160
tetanus immunoglobulin 157
thigh pain 121, 122, 123
thoracic spine
  fractures 46
  log-roll examination 53, *53*, *54*
threadworms 182
'three in one' nerve blocks **9**, 206–7, 208, *208*
throat
  examination *189*, 190
  foreign bodies 167–8
thumb, telescoping 92, *93*
tibia
  avulsion fractures 129
  fractures *131*, 136–8, *136–7*
  radiographic studies **66**
  spiral fracture 185
Tilleaux fracture 138
Tilley's forceps 195
tingling 46
tiredness 35
tissue glue 23–4, 198–9, *199–200*
'toddler's fracture' 58, 63, 136–8, *137*
toenails 145

toes, injuries 145
tongue
  lacerations 42
  swelling 160
torticollis 51, 52, 56
torus ('buckle') fractures 58, *59*
  distal radius 91, *91*
tourniquets 205
toxic shock syndrome 151, 152
transient synovitis 119, 120
  vs septic arthritis 121
transitional fractures 138
trauma, limping and 123
trephining fingernails 197–8
  paper clip technique 198
triplane fracture 138
tympanic membrane injuries 39–40

ulna
  distal ulna fracture 90, *90*, 91
  Galeazzi injury 87, 90
  mid-shaft fractures *61*, 87, *88*
  mid-shaft greenstick fractures *88*
  Monteggia injury 87, *89*
upper arm injuries 73–5
  humeral shaft fractures 74–5, *74*
  proximal humerus fractures 73, *73*
upper limb
  fractures 69
  injuries 69–94
  radiographic studies 66
  see also forearm; hand; radius; shoulder; ulna; wrist
urticaria 160

vacuum mattresses 47, *49*, 51
vagina, foreign bodies 177
Vaseline 150
vertebra
  anterior wedging 57
  unifacet dislocation 51, 56
Vipera berus 158
vision, blurred 35
vomiting 31, 35
vulvovaginitis 182

wasp stings 159
wax in ear 166
wheezing 160, 161, 171

wounds 16
  adhesive strips 23–4, 198–9
  aftercare 24–5
  anaesthesia 21, 22
  bandages 24
  cleaning 21–2
  closure techniques 23–4
  complications 25
  concurrent illness 17
  dehiscence 25
  depth 18
  description 18
  dressings 24
  edges 21
  examination 18
  exploration 22
  healing, factors involved in 19–21
  history 16–17
  immobilization 25
  infection risk 20–1
  irrigation 21–2, 198
  management 198–204
  management principles 21–4
  mechanism of injury 16–17
  needlestick injuries 26

  plantar wounds of the foot 26
  puncture wounds 18, 20, 26
  repair principles 22–4
  secondary intention healing 23
  site 18, 19
  size 18
  splintage 19, 25
  sutures 23, 25
  time elapsed since injury 17
  tissue glue 23–4, 198–9,
    199–200
wrist 90–3, 94
  deliberate self-harm (DSH) 117
  distal radius fracture 90–1, 90, 91
  radiographic studies **66**
  scaphoid fracture 92–3, 93, 94

X-rays
  fractures and dislocations 65
  interpretation 65–6
  neck and back injuries 54, 55
  skull (SXR) 33–4

Zimmer splints 115
zygoma, fractures 44, 44